20,000 STEPS
AROUND
THE WORLD

STUART BUTLER & MARY CAPERTON MORTON

20,000 STEPS AROUND THE WORLD

GREAT HIKES, WALKS, ROUTES & RAMBLES

UNIVERSE

First published in English in the United States of America in 2023 by
Universe Publishing
A division of Rizzoli International Publications, Inc.
300 Park Avenue South
New York, NY 10010
www.rizzoliusa.com

ISBN: 978-0-8478-7352-4
Library of Congress Catalog Control Number: 2023933741

2023 2024 2025 2026 / 10 9 8 7 6 5 4 3 2 1

Printed in Malaysia

Visit us online:
Facebook.com/RizzoliNewYork
Twitter: @Rizzoli_Books
Instagram.com/RizzoliBooks
Pinterest.com/RizzoliBooks
Youtube.com/user/RizzoliNY
Issuu.com/Rizzoli

Conceived, designed, and produced by
The Bright Press, an imprint of the Quarto Group
1 Triptych Place
London SE1 9SH
United Kingdom
www.quarto.com

Publisher: James Evans
Editorial Director: Isheeta Mustafi
Managing Editor: Jacqui Sayers
Senior Editor: Joanna Bentley
Art Director: James Lawrence
Project Editor: Sara Harper
Design and Illustration: Tony Seddon
Picture Research: Kathleen Steeden
Cover Concept: Studio Noel

Cover photos Front: Shutterstock/kasakphoto.
Back, clockwise from top, all Shutterstock: tolobalaguer.com, Tilpunov Mikhail, iwciagr, Oomka.

RIGHT Hiking along the GR11 on the Spanish side of the Pyrenees.

Contents

DIFFICULTY RATINGS

Easy: Walks on clear trails with fairly gentle inclines. No real orientation experience or special equipment required. Max. walk time of 4-5 hrs per day. Easy day walks are always family-friendly.

Moderate: For walkers with some prior experience, basic navigation skills, and hiking equipment (hiking boots, hiking backpack, and walking poles). Trails not always obvious. Some steep inclines. Max. walk time of 6-7 hrs per day. Some walks require self-sufficiency.

Hard: Experienced hikers only. Good navigational skills, know how to use a compass and map. Trails can be partially off-piste. Some very steep inclines. Can involve numerous long walking days if a multi-day trek. Need to be self-sufficient.

'WALK HERE NEXT' SYMBOLS

Each featured trail in this book includes suggestions for similar walks to try next, linked by themes such as terrain, region, wildlife, or sights. The symbols below are used alongside each, color-coded according to continent, to give you an idea of what to expect.

- **Mountains / High terrain**
- **Forest / Woodland**
- **Rivers / Lakes**
- **Coastal / Ocean**
- **Overnight camping**
- **Navigation skills required**
- **Marked trail**

Introduction

Walking brings you close to the land—and the people and animals who live there—in a way that rushing by in a vehicle never can. It brings moments of peace that are otherwise increasingly hard to find in a world that never seems to pause. It brings a sense of adventure and personal challenge. And walking rewards with unforgettable views earned the hard way. After a quarter of a century of writing hiking guidebooks, as well as more traditional travel guidebooks to countries around the world, I can say without hesitation that for me there's no more satisfying way of exploring the world than on foot.

How to use this book

The purpose of this book is to inspire. Whether your idea of a good hike is a pleasing riverside ramble with the family or a daring multiday traverse of a high-altitude Himalayan pass, you'll find something here to match your interest and skill level.

The following pages focus on fifty main hikes, from short day hikes to multiweek treks. They cover all four corners of the world and every kind of landscape: coastlines and rivers, canyons and caves, deserts and salt flats, forests and jungles, mountains, glaciers, waterfalls, and volcanoes. Each of these hikes was chosen because it offers something unique—from scenic wonders to cultural, historical, or natural world interest. They are widely considered to be classic trails that should be on the radar of everyone interested in hiking.

RIGHT Hikers on the French side of the Tour du Mont Blanc.

But this book does not provide a step-by-step route guide. Instead, it aims to inspire dreams for your next great hiking adventure. Each featured hike is described in a way that gives you a feel for the trail and what makes the route so special. Alongside these descriptions you'll find information and stories on the history of the area, the flora and fauna that may be encountered, and the background into unmissable regional food delicacies, and local customs and legends. There's also a brief overview of the actual route, which will give you an idea of how hard the hike is going to be and whether it's suitable for you, as well as a map with highlights marked on it, and a photo gallery.

Divided into six sections, the book groups the main hikes by continent. Following each hike are ideas for other trails that offer a similar experience, but not necessarily in the same country or even in the same part of the world. These supplementary hikes feature handy symbols indicating what type of terrain is present, whether camping is permitted, and if the route is signposted too.

Discover the world's top treks

If you were to ask me what my personal favorite trails are, then the answer would probably depend on my mood that day. Padding breathlessly toward a soaring Himalayan peak is hard to beat. Walking cautiously past herds of gazelle and wildebeest on the grasslands of East Africa is an experience that will remain with me forever. Or perhaps I would simply choose to stroll through the rich flower meadows of the Pyrenees—the mountains I see every day from my home, and a mountain range of such diversity that I know I will never tire of it.

So whether you already have your favorite hiking trail or are still searching for it, don't waste any more time. Lace up your hiking boots, turn the page, and let this book take you on a journey along the world's best hiking trails.

Stuart Butler

LEFT Hiking the GR10 along the French side of the Pyrenees.

West Coast Trail

Hike in the footsteps of shipwreck survivors along Vancouver Island's rugged coastline.

LOCATION
Pacific Rim National Park Reserve, Vancouver Island, British Columbia, Canada

DURATION
5–7 days

DIFFICULTY
Hard

DISTANCE
47 miles (75 km)

MAP
National Geographic Trails Illustrated Vancouver Island Map #3128

START/END
Port Renfrew/Bamfield

TRAIL MARKING
Signs

LEFT The West Coast Trail is well marked and maintained, but not recommended for novice backpackers.

The West Coast Trail follows the southwestern edge of Vancouver Island, through part of Pacific Rim National Park Reserve. Long before it was a national park, this region was inhabited by the Pacheedaht, Ditidaht, Huu-ay-aht, and Nuu-chah-nulth peoples. The island's temperate rain forest is lush with vegetation and rich in marine life, making this area an important resource for seasonal hunting, gathering, and trade.

The Graveyard of the Pacific

In the 1800s, this coastline became known as the Graveyard of the Pacific. More than five hundred ships ran aground or sank here, with hundreds of lives lost to the freezing, crashing waves. After the wreck of the SS *Valencia* off Cape Beale in 1906, and the tragic deaths of over a hundred passengers, the Canadian government built a lighthouse at Pachena Point and established the Dominion Lifesaving Trail to give shipwreck survivors access to an emergency telegraph line and a series of lifesaving shelters, spaced at 5-mile (8 km) intervals along the coast.

In 1973, the trail was renamed the West Coast Trail and became part of the national park. Today the route passes over rocky beaches, beside tide pools, and through rain forest, as well as several Indigenous reserves. Frequent rains make the terrain muddy and slippery, and the route requires climbing or descending dozens of wooden ladders.

The Route

The West Coast Trail runs between Port Renfrew and Bamfield and can be hiked in either direction, but most people hike north to south, to save the especially rugged sections for the end of the hike and to climb down most of the ladders. Overnight permits are available from May to September with July and August typically being the driest months, but keep in mind that rainy weather can drown out a trip any time of the year.

The trail is known for being wet, muddy, and slippery, as it crosses through mossy forests, bogs, and countless creeks. Some water crossings have bridges, and some have suspended cable cars, while others may require wading. In many places, you have the choice to stay high in the forest or descend to the beach on parallel trails. Both choices have their own challenges, as the forest is often mucky, but the rocky beaches are slow going with some sections impassable at high tide. Be sure to bring a tide table and a map, issued by Parks Canada.

1 OLD GROWTH RAIN FOREST AND RAIN

Vancouver Island boasts one of the lushest temperate rain forests on Earth. The moss-covered trees and ferny undergrowth make for a dramatically green setting against the deep blue of the Pacific Ocean. Rain forests require a lot of rain, and this is one of the rainiest regions in North America. Some places on Vancouver Island see over 150 inches (3,810 mm) of precipitation a year. Most of this occurs in the fall, winter, and spring months, with July and August being a hiker's best bet for a clear-weather trip.

BAMFIELD

West Coast trailhead

Pacific Rim National Park Reserve

2

Nitinat Narrows

5

NORTH PACIFIC OCEAN

Carmanah Lighthouse

5

SHIPWRECKS

With hundreds of ships wrecked on the rocks offshore, you're bound to come across some maritime history on your hike. Parks Canada provides info about where to look for wreckage, like rusting hulls and metal and glass debris, just offshore or scattered along the rocky beaches. Remnants of the SS *Valencia* can be seen 11 miles (18 km) south of the northern trailhead. Please be respectful of this and all other shipwrecks and leave any artifacts that you find in place.

LADDERS

The West Coast Trail may run along the coast, but that doesn't mean it's flat. The trail gains and loses over 5,000 feet (1,524 m) of elevation along its route. More than three dozen ladders, some three stories high, help hikers ascend and descend the rugged terrain. If you hike north to south, you'll descend most of the ladders, an arguably scarier but physically easier feat than climbing up them with a loaded backpack.

WILDLIFE

Vancouver Island is rich in wildlife that thrives in the dense, temperate rain forest. Hikers should be aware that black bears, cougars, and wolves live here, although you'd be very lucky to spot any of these elusive predators. Be sure to use the provided bear boxes in camps to keep black bears from associating people with food. Offshore, you might spot the dorsal fins of orcas and spouts of gray whales, while seals and sea lions are often seen resting on the beaches. Never approach or disturb wildlife, including seal pups.

BEACH SNACKS

To hike the West Coast Trail, you'll need to be entirely self-supported for your weeklong trek, but there are two opportunities to buy hot food along the route. At Nitinat Narrows (mile 20/km 32) you'll find a crab shack that only takes cash, and at Carmanah Lighthouse (mile 27/km 11) is a burger joint that accepts credit cards. But don't bet on these meals as their hours vary.

Cowichan Lake

Nitinat Lake

Carmanah Walbran
Provincial Park

PORT RENFREW

5 mi.
5 km

Walk here next

Long walks on the beach sound romantic, but hiking through deep sand isn't always appealing. Fortunately, not all coastlines are sandy beaches. Here are a few places to take lengthy walks over headlands and past tide pools, where the views are expansive and the sea life is plentiful.

Go with the flow

NORTH COAST ROUTE

Tides are king on this 37-mile (60 km) route along the west coast of Olympic National Park, Washington State, USA. During high tides, waves will cover the route, blocking your way and potentially trapping you between the rocks and the ocean. You'll need to bring a tide chart and plan your days around the tides. Also be sure to pack all your food in a bear canister, as bears and birds alike are quite clever about stealing human food.

Follow in the footsteps of giants

CAUSEWAY COAST TRAIL

The 31-mile (50 km) Causeway Coast Trail runs along the tops of the rugged cliffs of Ireland's northern coast between the tourist towns of Ballycastle and Portstewart. The route passes several world-famous attractions, including the Giant's Causeway, the Carrick-a-Rede Rope Bridge, the Old Bushmills Distillery, and the ruins of Dunluce and Dunseverick castles. This trek is easily broken up into a series of day hikes thanks to public transportation and the many small towns and hamlets along the way, where you'll be able to buy meals and find rooms.

Waterfalls and wildlife

OTTER TRAIL

The coastline of South Africa has it all: white-sand beaches, rocky headlands, teeming tide pools, and incredible waterfalls, not to mention abundant wildlife such as seals, dolphins, monkeys, and the route's namesake, the Cape clawless otter. Most people tackle this 28-mile (45 km) trek in five days, staying in a series of simple huts along the way. Be sure to pack a tide chart and beware of dangerous river crossings.

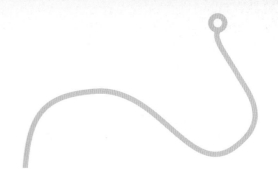

Skyline Trail

LOCATION
Jasper National Park,
Alberta, Canada

DURATION
3–4 days

DIFFICULTY
Moderate

DISTANCE
27 miles (44 km)

MAP
National Geographic Trails
Illustrated Jasper National
Park #902, #903

START/END
Maligne Lake/Signal Mountain

TRAIL MARKING
Signs

Explore the Canadian Rockies on one of the highest trails in the range.

Once upon a time, grizzly bears roamed across much of western North America, from the high plains to the Pacific Coast. But by the mid-1900s, most of the population of *Ursus arctos horribilis* had been wiped out by hunting, trapping, and poisoning. Today the great bear is making a recovery but is generally still confined to the northern Rocky Mountains in Wyoming, Montana, Canada, and Alaska.

Hiking in bear country, where humans are not at the top of the food chain, is a humbling experience that will heighten all your senses. Jasper National Park in Alberta, Canada, is home to around two hundred grizzly bears (and several hundred black bears). Grizzly bears only live in the wildest places, and this hike is famous for being one of the highest, most scenic routes in the Canadian Rockies. Most of the route is above the tree line, providing panoramic views of the surrounding peaks and glaciers, as well as any bears that may be ambling along the ridgeline.

LEFT The Skyline Trail, here with Mount Edith Cavell in the background, is one of the highest in the Canadian Rockies.

The Route

This 27-mile (44 km) hike is usually tackled over two to four days, moving between the six designated campsites along the route. The trail can be hiked in either direction, but most people choose to start at the higher trailhead in the south, Maligne Lake, and hike north to Signal Mountain to lessen the overall elevation gain. The well-maintained, well-graded trail makes for relatively easy hiking, where you can keep your eyes on the scenery and not on your feet. But the altitude can be a factor, as the trail tops out at 8,200 feet (2,500 m) at the Notch. Snow can also linger on the trail into July, with snowstorms possible any month of the year.

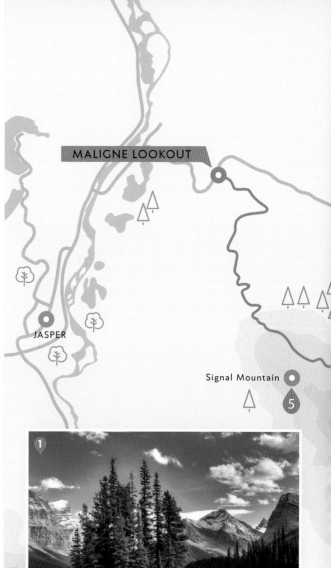

MALIGNE LOOKOUT

JASPER

Signal Mountain

5

1 MALIGNE LAKE

The Skyline Trail begins at Maligne Lake, a long and skinny car-accessible alpine lake 27 miles (44 km) south of the town of Jasper. Several high peaks and three glaciers—Maligne, Charlton-Unwin, and Coronet—are visible from the lake, which is famous for canoeing, kayaking, and fly-fishing. Spirit Island is a small islet on the lake that is one of the most photographed spots in the park.

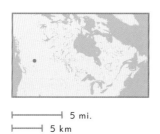

├───────┤ 5 mi.
├───────┤ 5 km

② BEAR ETIQUETTE

The first few miles are in the trees, where you may have a higher chance of running into a bear. The most important tactic for hiking in bear country is to make noise. Bears generally don't want anything to do with people, and if you let them know you're around by yelling or singing, they usually make themselves scarce. Parks Canada also recommends hiking with bear spray on your hip, where it can be quickly deployed to avert an attack. Bear spray is concentrated red pepper oil that shoots up to 30 feet (9 m) and is designed to put a cloud of noxious gas between you and the bear.

③ SKYLINE TRAIL CAMPSITES

There are six designated campsites—from south to north: Evelyn Creek, Little Shovel, Snowbowl, Curator, Tekarra, and Signal—along the Skyline Trail, each with an outhouse, running water (bring a filter), and food storage boxes for storing food and all scented items. When camping in bear country, you should be vigilant with anything that might smell edible to a bear. Keep a clean camp to minimize odors, and always store all scented items, including toiletries, in a food storage box.

④ THE NOTCH

The highest point of the Skyline Trail is located 13.5 miles (22 km) from Maligne Lake, at the Notch. This 8,200-foot (2,500 m) pass is one of three high mountain passes on the Skyline Trail. Snow can linger in the Notch until late July. If there is still snow, consider packing traction devices and trekking poles to aid in crossing this section.

⑤ SIGNAL MOUNTAIN FIRE LOOKOUT

A short distance from Signal camp, the last campsite on the Skyline Trail if you're traveling from south to north, you'll find the Signal Mountain Fire Lookout. The 270-degree views from this spot of the town of Jasper, the Athabasca River, and the Icefields Parkway are worth the side trip.

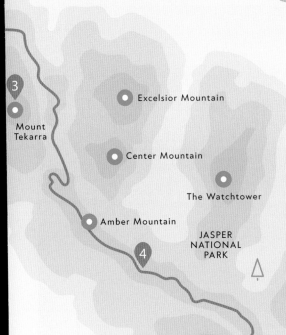

Medicine Lake

Excelsior Mountain

Mount Tekarra

Center Mountain

The Watchtower

Amber Mountain

JASPER NATIONAL PARK

Curator Mountain

Snowbowl

Little Shovel

Evelyn Creek

Trowel Peak

MALIGNE LAKE

Walk here next

There are only a few places left in the world where you can hike in brown bear territory. With proper bear etiquette, food storage precautions, and constant vigilance of your surroundings, these trips are sure to be some of the most memorable hikes of your life.

Traverse the toothy Tetons

TETONS CREST TRAIL

The Tetons in Wyoming, USA, are one of the world's most iconic mountain ranges, their jagged granite teeth rising straight out of the sage green valley of Jackson Hole with no perfunctory foothills. The 40-mile (64 km) Teton Crest Trail offers the best views of the range short of scaling the 13,775-foot (4,200 m) canine, the Grand Teton. Be vigilant: grizzly bears, black bears, and moose all migrate between this park and Yellowstone National Park to the north.

Say ciao to Italian brown bears and wolves
IORIO REFUGE LOOP

Abruzzo, Lazio, and Molise National Park in central Italy is home to around fifty Marsican brown bears, Italy's highly endangered version of the Eurasian brown bear, a relative of the North American grizzly. The park also protects more than seven hundred Italian wolves. One of the best places in the park to view both species is on the Iorio Refuge Loop, a 6.6-mile (10.6 km) loop from Pescasseroli that runs past two backcountry refuges and over the summit of Mount Ceraso. Marsican brown bears are known for being one of the more docile large bear species, but they should still never be approached. Parks generally advise keeping 100 yards (91 m) away from any large predator.

A gentle stroll through serious bear country
FIVE LAKES LOOP

You might think that an island is an improbable place for a large predator to survive into modern times, but the island of Hokkaido, the northernmost island of Japan, remains home to thousands of brown bears. As many as ten thousand Ezo brown bears are found in Hokkaido, and the incidents of bear attacks on humans here are some of the highest in the world. If you're brave enough to explore this territory on foot, head out on the 2-mile-long (3.2 km) Five Lakes Loop. During peak bear activity from May to July you must hike with a guide. The rest of the year, Shiretoko National Park officials recommend hiking in groups, making noise, and carrying bear spray to avoid close encounters with the bruins.

Sliding Sands Loop

LOCATION
Haleakalā Crater, Hawaii, USA

DURATION
6 hours

DIFFICULTY
Moderate

DISTANCE
11.5 miles (18 km)

MAP
National Geographic Trails Illustrated Haleakalā National Park #227

START/END
Visitor Center, Haleakalā Highway/Halemau'u trailhead

TRAIL MARKING
Signboards

LEFT An aerial view of the Haleakalā Crater at the summit shows how the interplay of light and shadow creates astonishing colors in the volcanic landscape.

Hike across a volcanic crater that makes you feel as if you're on a different planet.

Everything about the Haleakalā Crater arouses wonder. At 10,023 feet (3,055 m), the summit (known as Pu'u 'Ula'ula, or Red Hill), is the third-highest peak on the Hawaiian Islands, and from this point you can gaze down across a vast, weather-scorched crater some 7 miles (11.2 km) across and 2,625 feet (800 m) deep. The mountain as a whole makes up around three-quarters of the island of Maui and is home to some highly unusual and critically endangered life-forms. The play of light and shadow over this barren volcanic landscape produces an ever-changing array of colors and spotlights unexpected moments of green fertility in the desolate terrain. It's no wonder that those who take on the challenge of the hike down into the crater and across its rock- and sand-covered floor imagine the experience must be like being on the surface of Mars.

House of the Sun

Haleakalā means "house of the Sun," and the name came about because the ancient Hawaiians considered the crater floor to be the home of the grandmother of the demigod of the island of Maui, who captured the sun and forced it to slow its traverse of the sky. This led to a lengthening of the day and an increase in heat, which helped to turn Hawaii from a cold, dark place with short days into the kind of tropical paradise that, eons into the future, would become one of the world's favorite honeymoon destinations.

The Route

This is one of those routes where the hiking is a total pleasure. The path is generally wide, simple to follow, and easy underfoot. Most of the descents and ascents are gentle and the signage excellent. Compared to most hiking trails, the standard Sliding Sands Trail runs the wrong way around: hikers start at the highest point (the visitor center on the Haleakalā Highway), descend slowly down into the crater, and then ease their way back up along the same route. For a complete traverse of the crater, follow the Sliding Sands Trail from the visitor center on the Haleakalā Highway until you meet the Halemau'u Trail, which will lead you back out of the crater along a slightly more strenuous route, finishing up at the Halemau'u trailhead parking area. No shuttle buses operate within the park, so you either need to have left a second car here or do as most people do and hitchhike back to the visitor center (even the national park authorities recommend this approach). The influence of the warm surrounding ocean means that cloud cover rolls in early on an almost daily basis, so set out as soon after dawn as you can to ensure fine weather.

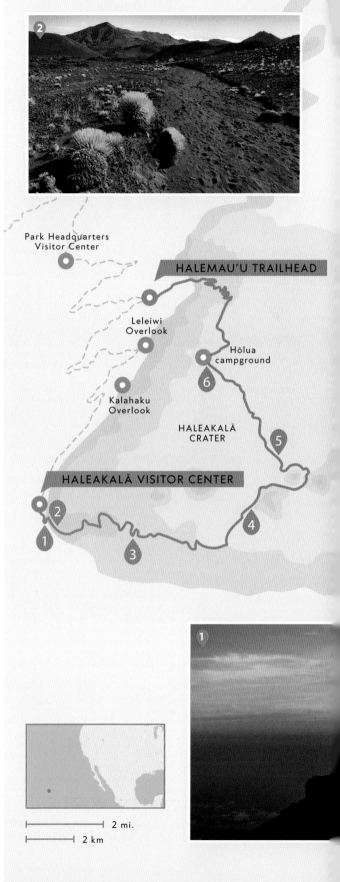

1 ALIENS

Technically there aren't any aliens to be seen on this hike (well, not normally anyway), but that doesn't mean people aren't searching for them here. The clear skies above Haleakalā make it one of the world's best stargazing destinations. The summit is home to an important astrophysical complex and crowned in giant telescopes. For a slightly less high-tech perspective, if you're here at night, then it's well worth bringing a pair of binoculars (or better still a telescope) and scanning the star-flecked night skies for signs of life.

Park Headquarters Visitor Center

HALEMAU'U TRAILHEAD

Leleiwi Overlook

Hōlua campground

Kalahaku Overlook

HALEAKALĀ CRATER

HALEAKALĀ VISITOR CENTER

2 mi.
2 km

numbers are controlled by the park authorities, and you must reserve a spot in advance through the national park website.

LIGHT CHANGING

For many hikers one of the most memorable elements of this trail is the otherworldly manner in which just the slightest shift in light and shadow reveals a whole new palette of colors. Brown becomes glowing red, dunes have a yellow sear, and the shadow of clouds turns bold colors to somber ones.

HŌLUA CABIN AND CAMPSITE

With the whole hike being only around six hours long (excluding stops), the huge majority of people do this in a day. But the Hōlua cabin, deep within the bowels of the crater, is a small hikers' hut with a campground. Staying here not only allows you to wish upon a star as you gaze up at the vivid night skies, but it's also likely to bring a real air of solitude because so few others get to stay here. You must reserve camping or bed spots in advance on the park website.

6 RED FERNS AND NĒNĒS

For the most part the crater floor and walls are a rock and sand desert with only the most minimal of plant life visible, but as you start the climb back up out of the crater on the Halemau'u Trail, the landscape suddenly becomes more fertile and plants more common. One of the most eye-catching of the plants is the red fern, which spends most of its existence in autumnal orange-red. Listen out also for the call of the nēnē, or Hawaiian goose. Mottled gray, black, and yellow, this is one of the world's rarest geese but can be found in quite some abundance in this park.

2 SILVERSWORDS

Are there really sword-wielding knights in armor inside a volcanic crater? Well, not quite. The Haleakalā silversword is a critically endangered succulent plant covered in fine silver hairs that help protect it from the extreme climate. It is found nowhere else in the world but around this crater. Silverswords can live for up to ninety years but only flower once. Their numbers declined rapidly during the twentieth century thanks to human and livestock disturbance, but today they are highly protected and can be seen fairly easily along various parts of the trail. A word of warning: stick to the trail at all times as the plants are easily damaged by people.

3 THE SUN

From the 10,023-foot (3,055 m) summit of Haleakalā, the views of the rising and setting sun are without equal. Be up here for sunrise and there's a moment when the star-spangled night sky fades away in the growing light of dawn and the sun, gently rising up above the coastal clouds, sends a spark of glowing orange-red light across the vast crater. But you need to plan for this inspiring sight: sunrise visitor

Walk here next

Hawaii offers mountains to climb, tropical beaches and rain forest, and awe-inspiring views. Here are some of the best hikes that showcase the islands' natural beauty and jaw-dropping scenery with a side order of local legend.

Tropical paradise—if you play it safe

THE KALALAU TRAIL

This is a hike into paradise! The 22-mile (35 km) return hike along the cliffs of Kauai offers memorable views of hidden tropical beaches, a surging Pacific Ocean, and deep, forested valleys. Did we say a hike into paradise? Well, it can also be a hike into hell. *Outside* magazine famously labeled it one of the world's most dangerous hikes due to the risk of rockfall and the dangers from swimming in the sea (it's hard to resist, but don't do it!). Most people take two days to hike this trail. Permits are required.

A view of the underworld

KA'ENA POINT

A walk to the spot where Hawaiian tradition says the souls of the dead go in order to leap off the cliffs and down into the underworld might not sound like the makings of a happy jaunt. But this short and easy 3.5-mile (5 km) stroll to the northwestern tip of the island of O'ahu reveals dramatic coastal scenery, a beautiful but dangerous beach, and the chance to see some of the endangered Hawaiian monk seals who enjoy this place as much as the spirits of the dead.

Hike to Hawaii's highest peak

MAUNA KEA

Go to Hawaii and end up standing proudly in the snow atop the biggest mountain in the world. Yes, believe it or not, Mauna Kea rises 33,000 feet (10,058 m) off the floor of the Pacific Ocean, which some people say makes it the highest mountain in the world. And while anyone standing on the summit of Everest is unlikely to agree, there's no arguing with the fact that Mauna Kea is the biggest mountain in Hawaii and can even get a coating of snow. This 12.5-mile (20 km) trek makes for a long and demanding day out.

Half Dome

LOCATION
Yosemite National Park,
California, USA

DURATION
12 hours

DIFFICULTY
Hard

DISTANCE
15 miles (24 km)

MAP
National Geographic Trails
Illustrated Yosemite #206

START/END
Happy Isles trailhead

TRAIL MARKING
Signs

Gecko your way up steel cables to Yosemite's iconic summit.

In a park famous for silvery gray granite, Half Dome stands out for its unique curved shape, which presides over Yosemite Valley. Half Dome was never a whole dome, though it may have been about 20 percent bigger before glacial action sheared off its northwest face, leaving a 2,000-foot-high (610 m) vertical wall.

In the 1870s the smooth-faced dome was described as "perfectly inaccessible" by the California Geological Survey. But it was climbed just five years later by summiteer George G. Anderson using a series of iron eyebolts he drilled into the sloping northeast face. The northwest face remained one of the last unclimbed big walls in Yosemite until 1957, when three climbers spent five days inching their way up the wall, before they were able to blaze a route to the summit. The Northwest Route is now one of Yosemite's most famous climbs, with the majority of climbers taking two days to reach the summit.

A Class Above

Today hundreds of hikers ascend Half Dome every day between late May and early October via steel cable handrails installed near Anderson's original route. Half Dome's cable route is considered a class 3 climb, meaning that you'll need to use your hands to maintain balance. Many hikers wear gloves to protect their hands and enhance their grip on the metal cables. If you step outside of the cables, the slope is characterized as class 5 terrain, where ropes are necessary safety equipment.

LEFT Climbers ascend Yosemite's granite Half Dome via steel cable handrails.

The Route

You don't need to be an experienced rock climber to reach the summit of Half Dome via the cable route, but you'll need to be a fit hiker and comfortable with heights and exposure. The trail begins at Happy Isles and gains over 4,800 feet (1,463 m) of elevation in about 8 miles (13 km) to the summit. You'll need to win the permit lottery for this very popular hike. Most people do it as a long day hike, but there are also options for overnights and longer multiday trips.

① DECISION POINT

Yosemite is also famous for waterfalls cascading over granite ledges, often dropping hundreds of feet into Yosemite Valley. A mile and a half (3 km) into the Half Dome hike you'll cross over the Merced River on a footbridge. Here you'll reach a signed junction with the choice of staying dry on a section of the John Muir Trail (JMT), or taking the Mist Trail, which is shorter but steeper and wetter, as you'll be in the spray zone from 317-foot-high (97 m) Vernal Fall and 594-foot (181 m) Nevada Fall. Most people hike up the Mist Trail and down the JMT.

② LITTLE YOSEMITE VALLEY

After you reach the top of Nevada Fall, you'll enter Little Yosemite Valley, dramatically flanked by 2,000-foot-high (610 m) glacier-carved granite walls and drained by the Merced River. Hikers who want to break the trek up into multiple days will find a campground here, about 4 miles (6.5 km) from the trailhead and 3.5 miles (5.5 km) from the summit of Half Dome. To stay here you'll need an overnight permit in addition to your Half Dome permit.

③ SPRING WATER

Around 5.3 miles (8.5 km) into the hike you'll pass a small spring that flows out of the ground to the left of the trail, just after a sharp left-handed switchback. If you bring a water filter, you can fill up your water bottles here and drink a couple of pints before continuing up the switchbacks to the cables. Dehydration saps energy and strikes quickly at altitude.

④ THE SUB DOME

For many hikers, the sub dome, just before the cables, is the hardest part of the hike, as it gains around 400 feet (122 m) of elevation up a series of steep steps. Here the views begin to open up, but the uneven steps cut into granite mean you'll also need to watch your feet. This is also where you'll likely get your permit checked by a park ranger. Hikers without permits risk steep fines.

⑤ THE CABLES

The final 400 feet (122 m) of the ascent up Half Dome runs through parallel steel cables held at waist height by metal poles. Clipping into the cables isn't recommended, as you would have to clip and unclip constantly to bypass the poles. With hundreds of hikers tackling the cable route each day, you're likely to be in a conga line up the narrow route, which is also shared with people coming back down from the summit. Be patient with fellow hikers and try to let faster hikers pass when it's safe to do so. Many people find gloves helpful. Every few years, somebody slips and falls to their death from the cables, often when the rock is wet. Lightning is also a threat so be ready to cancel your trek or turn back if storms are forecast.

⑥ SUMMIT

On the summit of Half Dome, you'll be rewarded for your efforts with some of the best views in Yosemite. The top is flat and open, often with several ravens flying around, looking for crumbs (don't feed wildlife). To the west lies Yosemite Valley and El Capitan, to the northeast, Tenaya Canyon. On the southwest and northwest sides, you may even be surprised by rock climbers topping out on Snake Dike, the Northwest Route, or one of the other technical climbs up Half Dome.

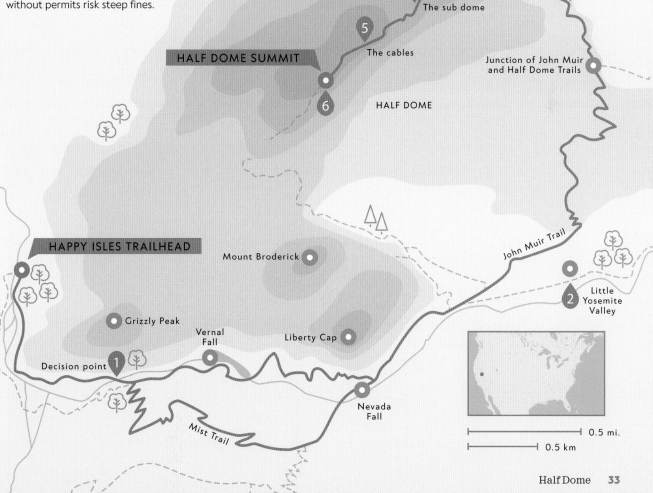

HALF DOME SUMMIT

The sub dome ④

The cables ⑤

Junction of John Muir and Half Dome Trails

HALF DOME ⑥

③

HAPPY ISLES TRAILHEAD

Mount Broderick

John Muir Trail

Little Yosemite Valley ②

Grizzly Peak

Vernal Fall

Liberty Cap

Decision point ①

Nevada Fall

Mist Trail

0.5 mi.

0.5 km

Walk here next

There's something special about hiking on rocks that were born deep underground. After you've summited Half Dome, here are a few more ideas for treks through granite wonderlands.

Yosemite's most scenic route
JOHN MUIR TRAIL

For some lucky long-distance hikers, Half Dome is the first stop on a two- to three-week trek on the John Muir Trail in California, USA, which runs for 211 miles (340 km) over the crest of the Sierra mountains from Yosemite Valley to the top of Mount Whitney, the highest point in the Lower 48 states. Mile for mile, this is widely considered one of the most scenic and challenging multiweek treks in the world.

Walk on the wild side
CIRQUE OF THE TOWERS

Yosemite might be the most famous granite wonderland in the United States, but it's also quite busy and backcountry permits can be hard to get. For a wilder experience, look to Wyoming's vast and remote Wind River Range. Home to grizzly bears and wolves, the three-day trek to visit the ring of 12,000-foot-high (3,658 m) granite peaks, called the Cirque of the Towers, requires no permits.

Scramble up Shenandoah's famously bald summit

OLD RAG MOUNTAIN

Topping out at 3,291 feet (1,003 m), Old Rag Mountain in Virginia, USA, is one of Shenandoah's few bald summits, topped by massive crystalline granite boulders. Part hike, part scramble, the route up Old Rag follows a series of blue arrows pointing the way through the granite maze. After you top out on the boulder-strewn summit, you can follow the Saddle Trail to Weakley Hollow Fire Road to make a 10-mile (16 km) loop back to your car.

Scenic sunsets in the golden hour

HEAVENLY PEAK

China's Huangshan Mountains, meaning Yellow Mountains, are named for the Yellow Emperor. In fact, the towering walls, peaks, and spires here are silvery gray granite, reminiscent of Yosemite. This easy to moderate 3.7-mile (6 km) trek hits several of the park's high points, including stunning overlooks of Alchemy Peak, Lotus Peak, and Celestial Capital Peak.

Grand Canyon Rim to Rim

LOCATION
Grand Canyon National Park, Arizona, USA

DURATION
2–4 days

DIFFICULTY
Hard

DISTANCE
24 miles (38.6 km)

MAP
National Geographic Trails Illustrated Grand Canyon, North and South Rims #261

START/END
North Kaibab trailhead on North Rim/Bright Angel trailhead on South Rim

TRAIL MARKING
Signs

Hike across billions of years of geological time exposed by the Colorado River.

The Grand Canyon isn't the oldest, widest, or deepest canyon in the world, but it is indeed the grandest, boasting a colorful and complex geological layer cake that exposes some of the world's oldest rocks. Surprisingly, the Grand Canyon itself is a relatively young feature of the landscape; the Colorado River only began carving this incredible gash around six million years ago, but the rocks it has revealed at the bottom of the canyon are 1.84 billion years old.

As it cut downward into the high desert landscape, the Colorado River uncovered more than forty distinct geological layers between the rims and where the river now runs, 6,000 feet (1,829 m) below the rims. Most of these layers are colorful sandstones, limestones, and shales, which sit atop the glittering basement of metamorphic rocks that line the river in the deepest parts of the canyon.

The views from the North and South Rims of the canyon are stupendous, but the best way to experience the majesty of the Grand Canyon is to hike across it, from the North Rim to the South Rim. As you descend into the canyon, every downward step will take you back sixty thousand years of geological time. This is a grueling hike, both physically and logistically, for which you'll need to prepare for months ahead of time. But it's well worth the effort.

LEFT View from the South Rim at sunset in Grand Canyon National Park.

The Route

The most efficient route across the Grand Canyon begins on the North Rim, descends 6,000 feet (1,829 m) of elevation down the North Kaibab Trail for 14.3 miles (23 km) to the Colorado River at the famous Phantom Ranch, and then ascends 4,500 feet (1,372 m) to the South Rim on the Bright Angel Trail in 9.6 miles (15.5 km). This route can be done in a day by elite athletes—the current record for a Rim to Rim crossing is under three hours!—but most people will want to take two to four days to cross. With so much to look at and so much elevation lost and gained, this hike is better savored, not rushed.

1 THE NORTH RIM

The North Rim of the Grand Canyon is higher and remoter than the South Rim. Because it sits at an elevation of 8,300 feet (2,530 m), the North Rim gets a lot more snow in the winter, and all roads and facilities close each year from mid-October to mid-May. This means that to do a Rim to Rim hike, you'll need to plan to go in late spring or early fall. Summers are brutally hot in the canyon, with no shade and little water, and long hikes are not recommended in June, July, or August. Another option is to hike Rim to Rim to Rim, starting and ending on the South Rim, a 47-mile (76 km) trek that can be done from September to late May.

2 WINTER HIKING

Winter is often the best time for a Grand Canyon trek, as the Rims can be chilly and snowy, but temperatures rise as you descend into the canyon. On a sunny midwinter day, it can be T-shirt weather down by the Colorado River. However, you should always bring extra layers, ice traction devices for your shoes, and trekking poles, as ice tends to get packed down by boots and mule hooves at the tops of the most popular trails like Bright Angel and South Kaibab.

3 ROARING SPRINGS

The North Rim of the Grand Canyon is much wetter than the South Rim, due to the canyon's north-sloping hydrology that funnels water toward the North Rim. In fact, all of the water for the South Rim's hotels, visitor centers, and facilities is piped from the north side across the river and up to the south side. Around 5 miles (8 km) into your Rim to Rim trek you'll pass the main source at Roaring Springs, where you should top off your water bottles. Treated tap water is available here (and a few other locations in the canyon) during the warmer months, but you should always carry a water filter in case the taps are shut off and you need to fill up from creeks.

Colorado River

1 mi.

1 km

6

Havasupai Gardens

BRIGHT ANGEL TRAILHEAD

Grand Canyon Village

COCONINO OVERLOOK

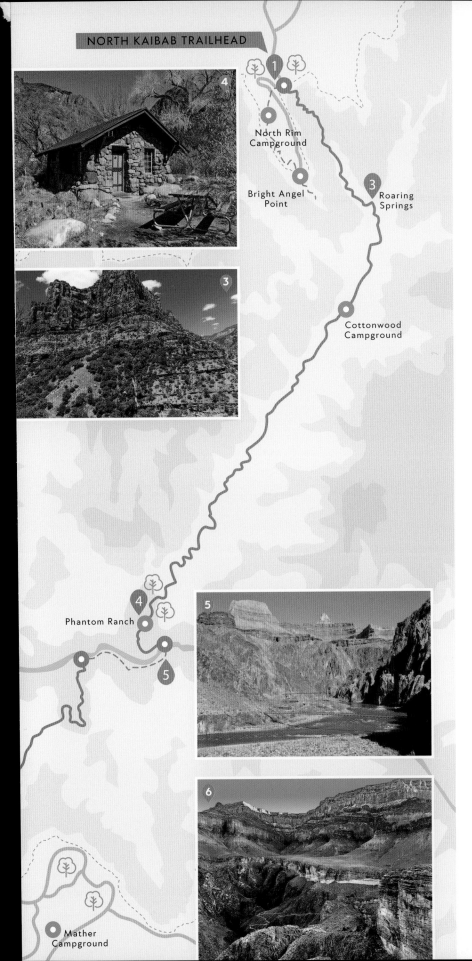

① North Rim Campground

Bright Angel Point

③ Roaring Springs

Cottonwood Campground

Phantom Ranch ④

⑤

⑥

Mather Campground

④ PHANTOM RANCH

At the confluence of Bright Angel Creek and the Colorado River lies Phantom Ranch, a collection of cabins that opened for guests in 1922. With year-round crystal-clear creek water and shady cottonwood trees, people have been living in this idyllic spot for thousands of years. The foundations of several pit houses and a ceremonial *kiva* dating to 1050 CE can be seen down by the river. Getting a permit to stay in a cabin is extremely difficult, but permits for the Bright Angel Campground are easier to come by.

⑤ CROSSING THE MIGHTY COLORADO

At Phantom Ranch the fast-moving Colorado River is over 300 feet (91 m) wide. To get to the South Rim, you'll have to cross the Colorado River on one of two suspension bridges, the only two crossings of the Colorado River in the park. The upstream 440-foot-long (134 m) Black Bridge is built for stock and you might get to see a string of mules crossing the river on their way to the ranch or back up to the rim. The downstream 500-foot-long (152 m) Silver Bridge is narrower and built for foot traffic. You don't have to choose; it's easy to make a loop so you can enjoy the views from both bridges.

⑥ HAVASUPAI GARDENS

From Phantom Ranch, the most gradual route up to the South Rim is via the Bright Angel Trail through Havasupai Gardens, named for the Havasupai people who lived here before it became a national park (now they live in the Supai Reservation in Havasu Canyon). Most people will plan to camp at Havasupai Gardens to break the hike out of the canyon into two days. During warm weather, treated tap water is available at the campground and at two rest houses on the way out of the canyon.

Grand Canyon Rim to Rim   39

Walk here next

Canyon hiking is a special challenge, where you lose lots of elevation at the beginning of the trip, often resulting in very sore legs and feet, and then have to gain it all back at the end. As the ubiquitous signs in the Grand Canyon constantly remind hikers, down is optional, up is mandatory!

Hike in North America's deepest canyon
HELLS CANYON

After hiking Rim to Rim in the Grand Canyon, tackle the deepest canyon in North America: Hells Canyon, on the border between Oregon and Idaho, USA. The Rim to River Loop is a 56-mile (90 km) loop that begins and ends at the Freezeout trailhead and makes a loop on the high Temperance Creek, Oregon Snake River, and Saddle Creek trails, gaining and losing around 6,000 feet (1,829 m) of elevation. Hells Canyon doesn't have as many distinct geological layers as the Grand Canyon, but the views of the nearly 8,000-foot-deep (2,438 m) canyon cut by the Snake River are incredible.

From peaks to depths
COTAHUASI CANYON

Reaching depths over 11,000 feet (3,353 m), Peru's Cotahuasi Canyon near Arequipa is more than twice as deep as the Grand Canyon. This landscape of extremes is topped by the mountains flanking the canyon, which reach elevations of 20,000 feet (6,096 m). Most hikes into the canyon leave from the village of Cotahuasi, north of Arequipa. Several suspension bridges run over the Cotahuasi River, connecting trails on either side of the canyon.

Explore the world's deepest canyon
YARLUNG TSANGPO
GRAND CANYON

It makes sense that the planet's deepest canyon runs out of its highest mountains: the Himalayas. As it descends off the Tibetan Plateau, the Yarlung Tsangpo River cuts a precipitous gorge 19,714 feet (6,009 m) deep into the Earth, called the Yarlung Tsangpo Grand Canyon. Access to this still largely unexplored gorge is limited, but several hanging bridges make a four-day trek possible between Pailong Village and Drachu Camp.

North Country Trail

LOCATION
Pictured Rocks National Lakeshore, Michigan, USA

DURATION
4 days

DIFFICULTY
Moderate

DISTANCE
42 miles (68 km)

MAP
MichiganTrailMaps.com

START/END
Grand Marais/Munising

TRAIL MARKING
Signs, blazes

LEFT Ominous skies and fall colors frame waves crashing against Chapel Rock on the route between Grand Marais and Munising, considered to be the most beautiful section of the trail.

Cross cliffs and sand dunes on the scenic southern shoreline of Lake Superior.

Stretching for over 4,800 miles (7,725 km), the North Country Trail (NCT) is the longest of the eleven National Scenic Trails in the United States, passing through eight states from New England to the Midwest between Vermont and North Dakota. This 42-mile (68 km) section of the NCT hugs the southern shoreline of Lake Superior between Grand Marais and Munising, in Michigan's remote and scenic Upper Peninsula. Between the dramatic cliffs, Grand Sable sand dunes, countless waterfalls, and ever-present views across the largest of the Great Lakes, this is often touted as the most picturesque section of the entire North Country Trail.

Pictured Rocks National Lakeshore is named for the colorful sandstone cliffs that tower 200 feet (61 m) high over Lake Superior. The rocks that make up the Technicolor cliffs are over five hundred million years old, dating back to the Cambrian period, when the earliest complex life-forms were just starting to emerge. The streaks that adorn many of the cliff faces are produced by mineral-rich groundwater leaching out of the rock face, leaving stripes of red iron, black manganese, green and blue copper, and yellow limonite. During winter storms, pounding waves impact the cliffs, carving them into caves, arches, and castle-like turret formations.

The Route

Most people hike this route from east to west, beginning in Grand Marais and ending in Munising. Plan to park your car at Munising Falls Visitor Center at the end of the hike and ride the park shuttle back to the start at Grand Sable Visitor Center. Permits are required for overnight hikes, and it's possible to reserve some of the backcountry sites. Campsites are spaced between 5 and 10 miles (8–16 km) apart, each with an outhouse and bear boxes to store food and scented items. Parts of this route can also be skied or snowshoed in winter, but be prepared for frigid temperatures and freak storms.

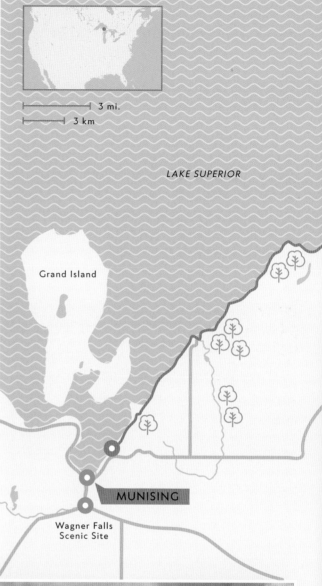

LAKE SUPERIOR

Grand Island

MUNISING

Wagner Falls
Scenic Site

① GRAND SABLE DUNES

Soon after setting off from the Grand Sable Visitor Center, you'll encounter the Grand Sable Dunes, a 5-mile-long (8 km) expanse of sand perched high above the lake. The sand has been washed ashore over millennia by wave action and then blown upslope by north prevailing winds, piling in dunes up to 275 feet (84 m) high. The dunes sit atop a glacial moraine, a pile of rocks left behind by glaciers during the last ice age.

GRAND MARAIS

Au Sable Light

③

Pictured Rocks
National Lakeshore

② LIGHTHOUSES AND SHIPWRECKS

Twelve miles (19 km) west of Grand Sable, you'll pass the Au Sable Light, a lighthouse built in 1874 to help guide ships safely past Au Sable Point. Today the light is still in operation, but now it's run on solar power, with a steady white beam that shines bright for 17 miles (27 km) across Lake Superior. The lighthouse couldn't save every ship, and there are many shipwrecks just offshore. Debris from these wrecks, such as rusted metal and broken glass, often washes ashore so keep an eye out for artifacts as you hike, but always leave everything where you found it.

③ BEAVER BASIN WILDERNESS

This series of crystal blue lakes, some surrounded by stark white sands, is Lake Superior's little slice of the Caribbean. In 2009, this area was designated as the Beaver Basin Wilderness, a protected area within the National Lakeshore. There are six backcountry campsites within this 13-mile-long (21 km) section, as well as a car-accessible campground on the shore of Little Beaver Lake.

④ BIRDWATCHING

It's important to pack lightly for a backpacking trip as carrying extra weight is hard on the body and the psyche. But you might consider bringing a good pair of binoculars on this trek, as the Great Lakes are an international flyway for hundreds of migrating bird species, not to mention the endless entertainment to be had watching the ships and tour boats cruising around Lake Superior.

⑤ BLACKFLIES

Birds aren't the only flying creatures in the Great Lakes region. At certain times of the year, blackflies, gnats, and mosquitoes can be legion. It's best to avoid this area in early summer when the biting flies are particularly bad. Throughout the summer months, you'll want to dress in loose, light layers and bring a head net and your preferred form of bug spray. Fall is often the best time to hike, after the first frosts have killed off the worst of the insects and the autumn colors add even more interest to the landscape.

Walk here next

With bright blue basins reflecting the sky, lakeshore trails are some of the world's most scenic hikes, usually offering great campsites, plentiful freshwater, abundant wildlife and birdwatching opportunities, and nonstop views. Here are a few more ideas for trekking around some of the world's most beautiful lakes.

Loop around the largest alpine lake

TAHOE RIM TRAIL

This 170-mile (274 km) loop traces the shoreline of Lake Tahoe, the largest alpine lake in North America. Lake Tahoe is famous for its deep blue hue, enhanced by its extreme depths, down to 1,645 feet (501 m). With the backdrop of the often snowcapped Sierra mountains and the fun resupply towns along the way, this trail has all the ingredients for a spectacular two-week backpacking trip.

Step out in Siberia
GREAT BAIKAL TRAIL

Russia's Lake Baikal is the largest freshwater lake in the world. Eventually, the Great Baikal Trail will run all the way around its 1,300-mile (2,092 km) circumference, but for now, only a few sections have been completed. One of the most accessible is the 14-mile (23 km) stretch on the southwest shore of the lake between the villages of Listvyanka and Bolshiye Koty. Hike this as an out-and-back overnight trek, or hitch a ride on a ferry to make it a long one-way day hike.

Marvel at a migration hot spot
LAKE ICHKEUL

Millions of migrating birds, including ducks, storks, and flamingos, make this lake in northern Tunisia, near the Mediterranean Sea, a stopover on their twice-annual seasonal migrations. Be sure to pack your binoculars on the 33-mile (53 km) loop trail that encircles the lake, as this may be one of the world's best birdwatching backpacking trips.

The Bubbles

LOCATION
Acadia National Park, Maine, USA

DURATION
2 hours

DIFFICULTY
Easy

DISTANCE
1.5 miles (2.5 km)

MAP
National Geographic Trails Illustrated Acadia National Park #212

START/END
Bubbles Divide trailhead/ Park Loop Road

TRAIL MARKING
Signs

Visit remnants of the last ice age in Acadia National Park.

Acadia National Park has been a long time in the making, with a geological history more than five hundred million years old. The national park protects about half of Mount Desert Island, the largest of thousands of islands off the coast of Maine. Much of this two-lobed island is formed from Cadillac Mountain granite, a 420-million-year-old pink-hued rock that erodes very slowly. But during the last ice age, this granite met its match in the form of massive ice sheets over 1 mile (1.6 km) thick.

During the Pleistocene, between two and three million years ago, a series of ice sheets descended south from the Arctic, covering what is now Canada and the northern United States in ice. As these ice sheets flowed and then retreated across what is now Maine, they deeply eroded the Cadillac Mountain granite, rounding off mountaintops, deepening valleys, and scooping out the Somes Sound, a body of water that nearly cuts Mount Desert Island in half. Evidence of this extreme glaciation can be seen throughout the park in the form of U-shaped valleys, glacial striations—deep grooves worn into rock by moving ice— piles of rocky glacial debris called moraines, and giant boulders called glacial erratics.

LEFT Sunrise at Eagle Lake overlooking the Bubbles in Acadia National Park.

The Route

This classic Acadia hike visits one of the park's most famous glacial erratics: the Bubble, which was carried from miles away by glacial ice, then dropped onto a cliff's edge overlooking Jordan Pond and the eastern lobe of Mount Desert Island. The hike offers a window into Acadia's glacial past, as well as astounding views over the park and the North Atlantic Ocean. Beginning at the Bubble Divide parking area, the trail climbs about 500 feet (152.4 m) of elevation onto a ridge that links two rounded mountains called the North and South Bubbles via short spur trails. The Bubble—the glacial erratic—sits on a cliff edge on the side of South Bubble. For a longer hike, you can also descend a trail to the west to hike the 3-mile (5 km) loop around Jordan Pond.

1 THE BUBBLE

The Bubble is a rounded boulder, about the size of a minivan. While boulders sometimes erode out of ridgetops, this one is different. If you look closely at the boulder and at the bedrock it sits upon, you'll notice they are two different kinds of granite. The bedrock is pinkish Cadillac Mountain granite, and the boulder is grayish Lucerne granite. Lucerne granite isn't found on Mount Desert Island; it comes from about 30 miles (48 km) away to the northwest, near Lucerne, Maine. This boulder was carried by ice and dropped when the ice became too thin to support its weight; it may look precariously balanced on the edge of a cliff, but the 100-ton (90.7 tonnes) rock has likely been sitting in this location for at least eleven thousand years.

North Bubble

1/10 mi.

100 m

Jordan Pond

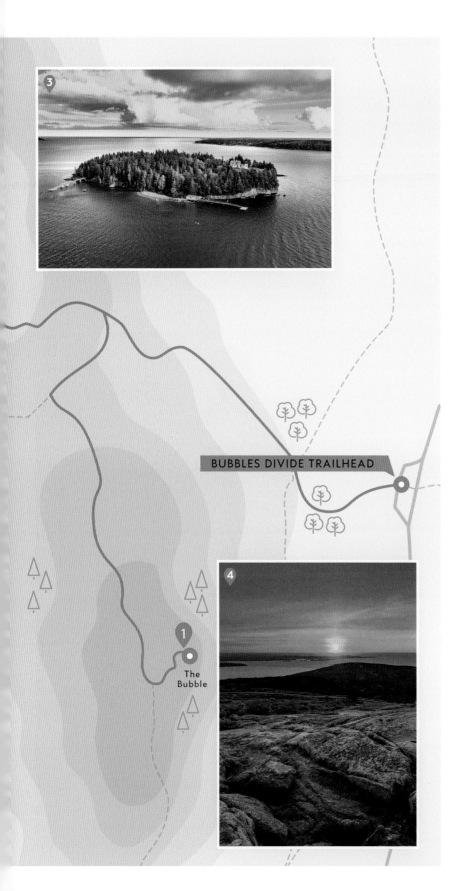

JORDAN POND

Looking west from the Bubbles, you'll see Jordan Pond. This small lake sits in a U-shaped valley scooped out by a passing glacier. U-shaped valleys are one of the hallmarks of postglacial terrain, as the ice spreads out and gouges a path as it moves slowly downhill under the force of gravity. Streams and rivers tend to carve V-shaped valleys as they move through their narrow channels. The edges of Jordan Pond are walled in by piles of rocks known as moraines. This glacial debris gets pushed to the edge of the glacier as it moves, creating piles that reveal the extent of long-lost glaciers.

FOUR THOUSAND ISLANDS

From the top of North and South Bubble, you'll be rewarded with astonishing views of Maine's convoluted coastline. Mile for mile, counting all the inlets and peninsulas, Maine has more coastline than California! Maine also boasts more than 4,500 named islands. To the south, you'll see the Cranberry Isles, a grouping of five inhabited islands named Great Cranberry, Little Cranberry, Sutton, Baker, and Bear Islands as well as Little Duck and Great Duck Islands.

CADILLAC MOUNTAIN

East of the Bubbles looms Cadillac Mountain at 1,530 feet (466 m), the highest point in the park. A road runs to the top of the mountain, as do several trails. Legend has it that since Cadillac is the highest, easternmost mountain on the east coast of North America, sunlight hits the summit before anywhere else each morning. This is only true part of the year but driving or hiking to the top of Cadillac Mountain for the first rays of sunrise is one of the park's long-standing traditions.

Walk here next

The last ice age came to a close around eleven thousand years ago, but the ghosts of glaciers past have left their mark on landscapes all over the world. Glacial erratics are some of the most compelling glacial landforms, as it's often possible to trace the source of the rock and calculate how far it was carried by the ice before coming to its final resting place.

Follow the edge of a long gone ice sheet

ICE AGE TRAIL

To get an idea of the incredible extent of the last glaciation in some parts of North America, set out on the Ice Age Trail. This 1,200-mile (1,931 km) hike follows the edge of an ice sheet that once stretched across Wisconsin, USA. The former edge of the ice is marked by a terminal moraine of rocks that piled up at the brink of the glaciers that once dipped well south of the Great Lakes. Along the way you'll pass dozens of glacial erratics and other glacial landforms including moraines, kettle holes, and glacial striations.

See northern Europe's largest boulder

EHALKIVI

Estonia is famous for its glacial erratics: sixty-two boulders over 100 feet (30 m) in diameter are found throughout the country, carried to their resting places by glaciers during the last ice age in Europe. The Ehalkivi boulder, also known as the Sunset Glow Boulder, is on a 5-mile (8 km) hike along the Gulf of Finland from the city of Kunda and is the largest glacial erratic in northern Europe, with a mass of approximately 2,756 tons (2,500 tonnes).

Mosey past moss-covered boulders

FOREST LOOP TRAIL

This easy 1.1-mile (1.8 km) loop in Glacier Bay National Park, Alaska, USA, runs through a lush forest studded with moss-covered glacial erratics, car-sized boulders that were dropped by glaciers during repeated advances and retreats of ice over the last few thousand years. The trail starts at the Bartlett Cove campground and wraps around part of Bartlett Cove, one of many inlets in the Alexander Archipelago, a grouping of 1,100 islands that make up part of the Inside Passage: the sea route along the Pacific Northwest coast.

Shenandoah National Park

Experience family-friendly outings in the Blue Ridge Mountains.

LOCATION
Shenandoah National Park, Virginia, USA

DURATION
1 day

DIFFICULTY
Easy

DISTANCE
Varies

MAP
National Geographic Trails Illustrated Shenandoah National Park #228

START/END
Skyline Drive

TRAIL MARKING
Signs, blazes painted on trees and rocks, painted arrows

Perched on the crest of the majestic Blue Ridge Mountains in western Virginia, and bisected by the incredibly scenic Skyline Drive, this is a famously family-friendly park, with dozens of accessible overlooks within a short walk of the road. From the overlooks on the west side of the road, you'll enjoy panoramic views along the backbone of the Blue Ridge Mountains with the pastoral Shenandoah Valley stretched out below.

On the eastern side of Skyline Drive you'll find densely forested creeks that often tumble over granite waterfalls, as well as Old Rag Mountain, one of the most famous mountain summits on the East Coast. The 2,190-mile-long (3,542 km) Appalachian Trail also runs for 101 miles (163 km) from north to south through the narrow park, frequently crisscrossing Skyline Drive, so it's easy to customize a hike of any length in this national park. Many of the high points along Skyline Drive are topped with lichen-encrusted granite boulders, the last holdouts of the highly eroded Appalachian Mountains, one of the world's oldest mountain ranges. Because North America, Africa, and Europe were connected at that time into a supercontinent, segments of the Appalachian mountain range can also be found on all three continents.

If you have multiple days to spend in the park, plan on driving the entire Skyline Drive, but be aware it's a dizzying, winding road with a 35 mph (56 kmh) speed limit, and frequent deer and black bear crossings. It's best to break the drive up into multiple days, with frequent stops to settle the stomach and take in the views.

LEFT The view from Hawksbill Mountain in Shenandoah National Park.

The Route

Most hikes in Shenandoah begin from the many trailheads, parking areas, and overlooks along Skyline Drive. The Hawksbill, Dark Hollow Falls, and Bearfence hikes all clock in between 1 and 1.5 miles (1.6–2.4 km), so with some planning, it's possible to hit all three trails in one day. The three hikes fall in order as you drive from north to south, entering at the Thornton Gap entrance station, midway on Skyline Drive.

1 HAWKSBILL MOUNTAIN

Plan to tackle Hawksbill first (or last, if you want to catch the sunset), as you'll want fresh legs to gain the 670 feet (204 m) up to the top of Hawksbill Mountain. At 4,042 feet (1,232 m), Hawksbill is the highest mountain in Shenandoah and the 360-degree views from the top are stellar, especially at sunset. Just before the summit you'll pass the Byrd's Nest 2 shelter, a day-use picnic area that's an excellent example of the three-sided shelters scattered along the length of the Appalachian Trail. A little farther up, on the summit, you'll find a stone viewing platform.

2 DARK HOLLOW FALLS

Dark Hollow Falls is a prime example of the trails on the eastern side of Skyline Drive, many of which follow creek drainages and feature waterfalls. This 1.5-mile (2.4 km) out-and-back hike to two overlooks of Dark Hollow is short and sweet but if you have a little more time, you can make a 4-mile (6.5 km) loop and visit Rose River Falls as well. Both falls spill over mossy, granite ledges and are particularly beautiful in the fall, when the oak and maple leaves take on their autumnal hues.

Park boundary

SHENANDOAH NATIONAL PARK

Skyline Drive

Bearfence Mountain

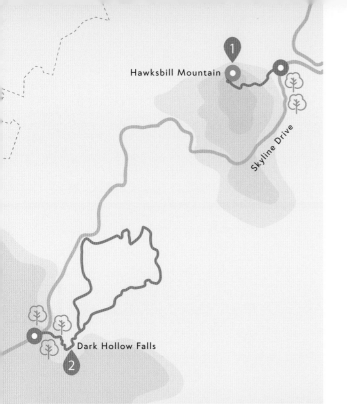

Hawksbill Mountain

Skyline Drive

Dark Hollow Falls

1 mi.

1 km

BEARFENCE MOUNTAIN

If your kids are old enough to be trusted with a scramble, the route up Bearfence Mountain is exhilarating and tops out at another 360-degree viewpoint. The 1-mile (1.6 km) hike follows a rocky ridge that requires some careful hand and foot placements, especially just below the summit, where there is some exposure. Avoid this hike during or after storms and be sure everybody is wearing hiking shoes with good treads.

BLACK BEARS

As many as a thousand black bears may live within and roam through Shenandoah National Park's 300 square miles (770 sq km). With that many bears, your chances of crossing paths with one on a road or trail are relatively high. But don't fret! Black bears are normally very shy and avoid interacting with people. Make noise as you hike and they'll likely run away from you. It's very important to keep bears from habituating to human food; never leave food unattended, and always make use of the bear-safe garbage bins provided by the park.

Walk here next

The Appalachian Trail, or AT, runs for 2,180 miles (3,508 km) from Springer Mountain in Georgia to Mount Katahdin in Maine. But in geological terms, the Appalachian mountain chain doesn't end in Maine—and neither does the trail. The International AT continues north into Canada and then across the Atlantic Ocean into Europe and Northern Africa.

Toast the end of the AT
MOUNT KATAHDIN

If you don't have five months to devote to hiking the whole AT, skip to the grand finale on Mount Katahdin in Maine, USA. This 11-mile (17.7 km) out-and-back hike follows the final few miles of the Appalachian Trail via the Hunt Trail to the summit of Mount Katahdin, where you'll find the iconic brown wooden sign that marks the end of the AT. If you go in September, you'll have a good chance of witnessing a few thru-hikers finish their trek. If you really want to make somebody's day, bring champagne to share on the summit!

Step back in a time loop
HARPERS FERRY

The historic town of Harpers Ferry, West Virginia, USA, marks roughly the halfway point of the AT. Situated at the strategic confluence of the Potomac and Shenandoah Rivers, Harpers Ferry played an important role in the Civil War (1861–65). Today the town operates as a tourist attraction, with reenactors in period dress. Get a taste of Civil War–era life, and Appalachian Trail life, on the 1.8-mile (3 km) Appalachian Trail Harpers Ferry loop that runs through the town and along the Shenandoah River to the confluence with the Potomac.

Reach the geological end of the AT

INTERNATIONAL AT

The US segment of the AT may end on top of Mount Katahdin, but the International AT keeps going north through eastern Canada into Newfoundland, following the Appalachian mountain chain to its geological end in North America at the northern tip of Newfoundland, at Belle Isle. Hiking the 1,900-mile-long (3,058 km) IAT requires careful planning, as you'll need to catch ferries between New Brunswick, Prince Edward Island, Nova Scotia, and Newfoundland.

Continue the AT on the West Highland Way

INTERNATIONAL AT

The Appalachians were uplifted by continental collisions during the formation of the supercontinent Pangaea, around 250 million years ago, long before the opening of the Atlantic Ocean. Thus, the IAT continues across the Atlantic in Greenland, Iceland, and Scotland, where the West Highland Way trail has been designated as part of the IAT.

Walk the African AT

INTERNATIONAL AT

Remnants of the Appalachian Mountains are also found in Morocco, where they are known as the Atlas Mountains. In recognition of this geological connection, a section of the IAT runs between Marrakech and to the ancient walled city of Taroudant, with plans to extend the trail farther, along the crest of the Atlas Mountains from the Mediterranean Sea to the Sahara Desert.

Alum Cave Trail

Visit geological formations in the most popular park in the United States.

The Great Smoky Mountains are the largest protected area in the eastern United States, encompassing an area of over 800 square miles (2,072 sq km) of eastern hardwood forest that straddles parts of North Carolina and Tennessee. The name comes from the Indigenous word for this region: *shaconage*, which means "place of the blue smoke." But the Smokies aren't actually smoky, they're foggy. The fog is produced by the region's vast forests, which exhale oxygen and volatile organic compounds during photosynthesis, giving off a whitish-blue vapor that often hangs over the range.

The Great Smoky Mountains National Park is the most visited park in the United States, but with over 850 miles (1,368 km) of hiking trails, most running along densely forested creek bottoms or along rocky ridge tops, there's room for everybody. This hike to the Alum Cave Bluff offers the best of both worlds, as well as some distinctive rock formations, with an option to take a longer hike to one of the highest points in the park.

LEFT Stone steps passing through Arch Rock, a natural arch formation that the Alum Cave Trail passes through.

The Route

The route to the Alum Cave bluffs follows Alum Cave Creek upstream through a shady old-growth forest of stately hemlocks and graceful yellow birches as it cascades over mossy rocks and small waterfalls. In early summer, rhododendrons bloom along the trail, adding bright pink hues to the palette. In about 1.3 miles (2 km), you'll reach Arch Rock, a unique formation you'll burrow through to reach the bluffs above and the aptly named Inspiration Point.

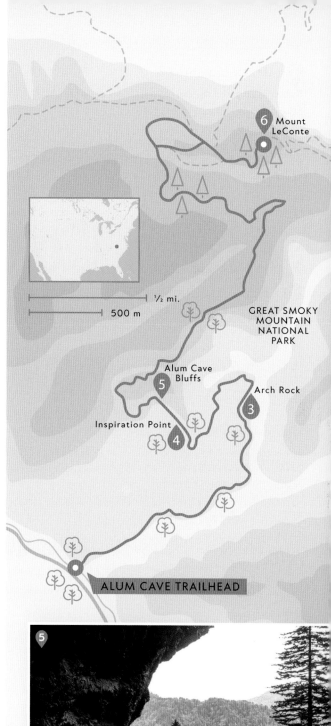

1 EASTERN OLD GROWTH

This national park was established in 1934, before eastern logging operations got around to clear-cutting the region. Today, nearly 95 percent of the Great Smoky Mountains National Park is forested, with around a third of the woods being old-growth forest that predates European settlement, one of the largest surviving blocks of deciduous, temperate old-growth forest in North America.

2 A BIODIVERSITY HOT SPOT

The ancient hardwood forests of the Smokies support an astonishing array of life-forms, from plants to amphibians to mammals. Over nineteen thousand species have been documented in the park, including over one hundred species of trees, two hundred species of birds, fifty species of fish, and forty-three species of amphibians. The park is also home to around 1,500 black bears and several hundred elk, which were reintroduced in 2001 after being hunted to extinction. Elk are most often seen in the Cataloochee Valley, in the southeastern section of the park.

3 ARCH ROCK

After 1.3 miles (2 km) of hiking you'll come to Arch Rock, a large natural arch formation. You'll get an excellent view of this arch as the trail passes right through it, up a flight of stone steps protected by a steel cable handrail drilled into the rock. The arch is made up of jagged slabs of Anakeesta slate, a sedimentary rock found throughout the park in layers up to 4,500 feet (1,372 m) thick. The arch opening formed over geological timescales when water found its way into cracks and froze, breaking apart the rock until it formed the wide opening the trail passes through today.

4 INSPIRATION POINT

Beyond Arch Rock the trail leaves the company of the Alum Cave Creek to follow the smaller creek called Styx Branch. Soon you'll reach Inspiration Point, an outcropping of rocks at an elevation of 4,700 feet (1,433 m) with excellent views. On a clear day you'll be rewarded with views of the surrounding mountains, including Myrtle Point to the northeast, Little Duck Hawk Ridge to the west, and the Eye of the Needle, a window eroded into the rocky ridgeline of Little Duck Hawk Ridge. Keep an eye out for the inspiration for the nickname Little Duck Hawk: peregrine falcons—the fastest flying animal on Earth—are often seen in this area.

5 ALUM CAVE BLUFFS

About 2.3 miles (3.7 km) into the hike, you'll reach the Alum Cave Bluffs, an 80-foot-high (24.3 m), 500-foot-long (152.4 m) geological formation made up of soft orange clay minerals. Despite the name, Alum Cave isn't actually a cave; it's a giant alcove that has been scooped into the flank of Peregrine Peak by erosion and by miners. During the Civil War, these bluffs were mined for potassium nitrate, a mineral also known as saltpeter, one of the main ingredients in gunpowder. Alum was also mined here, another mineral that is used in a variety of applications from dyes to medications. Mining activity ceased after the Civil War, and the area is now protected within the national park. In winter, huge icicles form on the edge of the cave. They are beautiful but dangerous: be careful not to walk underneath!

6 MOUNT LECONTE

Many people turn around at the Alum Cave Bluffs but those looking for a longer hike can continue onto Mount LeConte. LeConte is one of the Smokies' major summits; at 6,593 feet (2,010 m) in elevation, it's the third-highest peak in the park. From the trailhead it's 5.5 miles (8.9 km) to the top, up 2,763 feet (842 m) of elevation. But with some planning, you can make this an overnight hike by making reservations at the LeConte Lodge. This rustic retreat predates the founding of the national park and is the only backcountry lodge accommodation in the park. No roads run to the lodge, and all food and supplies are brought in by llamas.

Walk here next

Arches can form in many types of rock, in many kinds of settings. From the iconic sandstone arches of Arches National Park, to the massive spans of eastern Europe, to sea caves and lava arches carved by wave action, here are a few more places you can see these improbable rock formations.

Spectacular sandstone arches

DOUBLE ARCH

Arches National Park in southeastern Utah, USA, has the world's greatest concentration of arches, with more than two thousand spans found throughout the 199-square-mile (515.5 sq km) park. Most of these arches are formed in Entrada Sandstone, which erodes into long, narrow fins. This easy 0.6-mile (1 km) walk takes you right underneath Double Arch, a twin span of two joined arches that's the highest arch formation in the park.

Marvel at Europe's largest natural sandstone span

THE PREBISCH GATE

If the Prebisch Gate in the Czech Republic looks familiar, it may be because it was featured in the 2005 movie *The Chronicles of Narnia: The Lion, the Witch, and the Wardrobe*. The 6-mile (9.6 km) out-and-back trek to the gate is worth the effort to see the 86-foot-wide (26.2 m) span, the largest natural stone arch in Europe. Don't expect to be able to walk across the span like the characters in the movie, however. The actors were CGI'd onto the sandstone span, which is not open for climbing.

Witness wave action on a dramatic coastline walk

HŌLEI SEA ARCH

This easy 1.5-mile-long (2.4 km) out-and-back trail on the southeast coast of the Big Island, Hawaii, USA, begins at the end of the Chain of Craters Road, which was overrun by lava in 1969. Along this dramatic, constantly evolving coastline, the lava flows from Kīlauea to the Pacific Ocean, often rapidly cooling into fantastic shapes and clouds of steam. The trail runs to an overlook of the Hōlei Sea Arch, a 90-foot-high (27.4 m) span of lava that has been eroded into an arch by wave action.

Candameña Canyon

LOCATION
Basaseachic Falls National Park, Mexico

DURATION
2 days

DIFFICULTY
Moderate

DISTANCE
10.8 miles (18 km)

MAP
National Geographic Trails Illustrated Mexico #3108

START/END
Basaseachic Falls viewpoint parking lot

TRAIL MARKING
Signs, cairns

LEFT The dramatic single-drop Basaseachic Falls in Candameña Canyon.

Stand in the refreshing spray of Mexico's two highest waterfalls.

The Sierra Madre Occidental mountains of northwestern Mexico form part of the "backbone" of the Americas, also known as the American Cordillera, a chain of mountain ranges that runs through North, Central, and South America. These mountains are perhaps most famous for their steep and rugged canyon systems, especially the six rivers that drain the western side of the subrange Sierra Tarahumara mountains, known as the Copper Canyons.

The Copper Canyons rival the Grand Canyon in depth, scope, and scenery, but they cut down through fewer geological layers, exposing only tens of millions of years of geological history in contrast with the Grand Canyon's billions of years. The canyon walls are primarily volcanic rock, sourced from explosive ash flows and mudflows and then cut by six major rivers that merge into one, the Rio Fuerte, which flows into the Sea of Cortez.

Many of the Copper Canyons' trails are strenuous due to the nature of this precipitous canyon system. But the overnight hike down Candameña Canyon—a major side canyon in the Copper Canyon system—to the two highest waterfalls in Mexico is one of the more accessible routes in the area. Going with a local guide is recommended but not required. The hike begins at Basaseachic Falls, a 853-foot-high (260 m) single-drop waterfall that is the second-highest falls in Mexico, and continues down the canyon past Piedra Volada, meaning "Flying Stone Falls," Mexico's highest waterfall at 1,494 feet (455 m).

The Route

This hike starts at the top of Mexico's second-highest waterfall and runs downstream through the towering walls of Candameña Canyon, passing Piedra Volada, Mexico's highest waterfall, and Peña del Gigante, the country's highest vertical rock wall. Some people can complete this out-and-back hike in one day, but you'll enjoy it more as an overnight, as there is much to see and the route requires some scrambling around giant boulders in the bottom of the canyon.

① TOP OF THE FALLS

From the parking area, the path to the top of the falls is easy and well maintained, but the viewpoint is a bit of a tease: from here you can only see the top of the waterfall as it cascades over the edge of the cliff. The impressive volume of water that flows over Basaseachic Falls is the result of two rivers, the Duraznos and Basaseachic Rivers, which feed into the falls to form the Candameña River.

② OVERLOOK JUNCTION

After leaving the overlook at the top of the falls, follow the signs to the base of the falls. Soon you'll pass a junction with the San Lorenzo Overlook Trail. This trail runs out to three overlooks of the face of the waterfall and the canyons on the opposite canyon rim. The vantage point is spectacular, but you'll be far from the falls and the hike is strenuous, gaining over 2,000 feet (610 m) of elevation, so it's best to leave this hike for another day.

③ BASE OF THE FALLS

The trail to the base of Basaseachic Falls is steep but well maintained, quickly losing 850 feet (259 m) of elevation. At the bottom, you can scramble across rocks to the base of the waterfall and feel the spray booming down from one of the highest waterfalls in North America.

④ FLYING STONE FALLS

Located 4.2 miles (6.8 km) downriver from Basaseachic Falls, and reachable only on foot, Piedra Volada, or Flying Stone Falls, is the highest waterfall in Mexico, but it only flows part of the year, during the rainy season from midsummer to early fall. The rest of the year the falls dry up, making the much higher volume Basaseachic the highest year-round falls in Mexico.

⑤ PEÑA DEL GIGANTE

You'll be hiking through Candameña Canyon, a major side canyon of the Copper Canyon system, which reaches depths of 5,775 feet (1,760 m). Along the way you'll pass under Peña del Gigante, at 2,290 feet (697 m) the highest vertical rock wall in Mexico. This wall was climbed for the first time in 1998 and is now considered one of Mexico's premier rock-climbing localities. Plan to camp near the wall and return the way you came the next day.

⑥ THE RARÁMURI

The steep and rugged Copper Canyons have produced some of the world's fastest ultramarathon runners: the Rarámuri. Rarámuri means "those who run fast." Not only do they run fast, they run fast for long distances, with ceremonial races stretching over 200 miles (322 km). In recent years, Rarámuri runners have climbed to the tops of race podiums all over the world, often wearing their traditional dress and sandals.

⑦ OAKS AND COUGARS

The Copper Canyons are a high desert environment but are rich in flora and fauna, most notably the pine-oak forests that provide perfect cover for the canyon's thriving population of mountain lions. At least ninety-two species of conifers and seventy-six species of oaks are found within the densely forested canyons. The healthy population of deer provide ample food for large cats—rarely seen by humans but ubiquitous throughout the canyons.

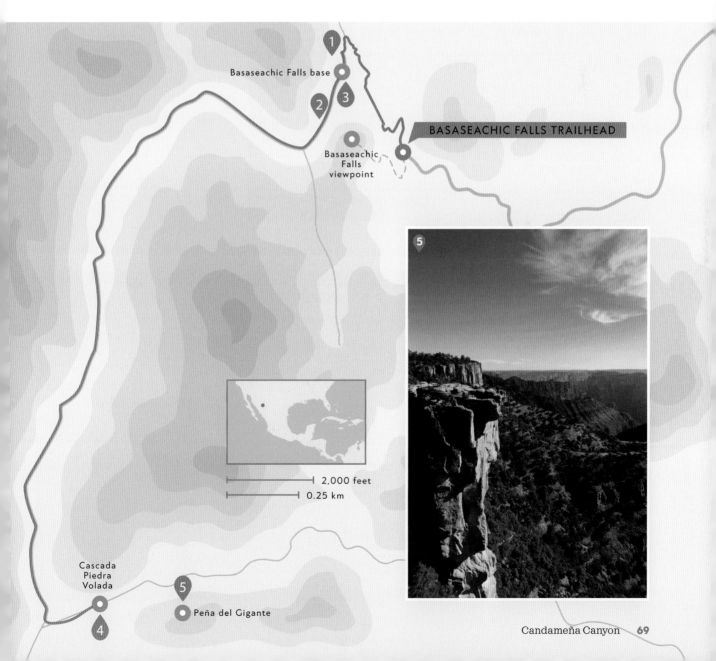

Basaseachic Falls base

BASASEACHIC FALLS TRAILHEAD

Basaseachic Falls viewpoint

2,000 feet
0.25 km

Cascada Piedra Volada

Peña del Gigante

Walk here next

Of all the waterfalls in the world, no two are alike, and each is constantly changing from moment to moment and season to season. No wonder waterfall hikes are often people's favorite kind of hikes.

Take it easy on the lower loop trail

YOSEMITE FALLS

Divided into three sections, the Upper, Middle Cascades, and Lower Falls, which collectively drop 2,425 feet (739 m) over the edge of sheer granite walls, Yosemite Falls in California, USA, is one of the most iconic waterfalls in the world. The 1.2-mile (1.9 km) loop trail to the base of lower Yosemite Falls is easy, while the 7.6-mile (12.2 km) round-trip hike to the Upper Falls is strenuous but offers unparalleled views of the falls and Yosemite Valley every step of the way.

Hike to turquoise waters

HAVASU FALLS, ARIZONA

Tucked deep in a side canyon of the western Grand Canyon, Arizona, USA, the bright turquoise-blue Havasu Falls is a place of legend, which has been protected by the Havasupai people for many generations. The hike to Havasu Falls is 10 miles (16 km) from the rim of the canyon, and to visit you'll need permission from the tribe and an overnight reservation at the tribal campground or lodge in Supai Village.

Trek past temple ruins

ANTELOPE FALLS

The rugged rain forests of Belize are home to some incredible waterfalls. Mayflower Bocawina National Park has several famous falls to visit, but the 2.2-mile (3.5 km) round-trip hike to Antelope Falls may be the most rewarding. The trail begins from the park's visitor center and soon passes by the Maintzunun Mayan temple ruins, an unexcavated mound that dates to 800 CE. The trail then climbs about 500 feet (152.5 m) of elevation in just over a mile (1.6 km) to reach the falls. Just below the top, a short spur trail leads out to a spectacular viewpoint of the Caribbean Sea. At the end of the trail you'll find a deep, strikingly blue-green swimming pool surrounded by rocky ledges. Antelope Falls drops over 1,000 feet (305 m) in a series of falls, making this one of the tallest waterfalls in Belize.

Experience the power of Mosi-oa-Tunya

VICTORIA FALLS

Over a mile (1.6 km) wide from bank to bank, Victoria Falls, also known as *Mosi-oa-Tunya* or "The Smoke that Thunders," is the world's largest waterfall, on the border between Zimbabwe and Zambia. The sheer power of this waterfall in Zimbabwe is best appreciated from below; a 1.5-mile (2.4 km) out-and-back trail descends into the Zambezi River gorge below the falls, ending at an overlook of a violent stretch of rapids called the Boiling Pot.

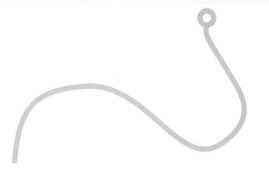

Volcán Parícutin

LOCATION
Pico de Tancítaro National
Park, Michoacán, Mexico

DURATION
7 hours

DIFFICULTY
Moderate

DISTANCE
12.5 miles (20 km)

MAP
Available at Centro Turistico,
Angahuan, Mexico

START/END
Centro Turistico, Angahuan,
Mexico

TRAIL MARKING
Signs, blazes, rock cairns

Trek across the aftermath of a catastrophic volcanic eruption.

On February 20, 1943, a farmer named Dionisio Pulido was burning brush in his cornfield in Michoacán, Mexico, when the ground near him swelled upward and cracked open, creating a hissing, sulfur-smelling fissure about 7 feet (2.1 m) across. Pulido had witnessed the birth of a volcano. Within hours, the fissure expanded into a crater and by that night, flames shooting hundreds of feet into the air were visible from the nearby village.

The volcano, called Parícutin after one of the towns it destroyed, would quickly grow into a 9,187-foot-high (2,000 m) cinder cone that would erupt for the next nine years, damaging an area of 90 square miles (230 sq km), destroying two towns, and displacing hundreds of people. Scientists flocked to the volcano to study the entire life cycle of a volcano in real time. After four distinct eruptive phases, the volcano quieted by 1952 and is now considered extinct.

Parícutin is the youngest of over 1,400 volcanic vents in the Trans-Mexican Volcanic Belt, a 560-mile-wide (901 km) swath that runs west to east across central Mexico. Some of these volcanoes are scoria cones, like Parícutin, while others take the form of shield volcanoes, tuff rings, maars (shallow craters), and lava domes. The region is crowned by the Sierra Nevada mountain range, which includes Pico de Orizaba, an 18,491-foot (5,626 m) stratovolcano that is Mexico's highest mountain.

LEFT The steep-sided volcanic cone of Parícutin, now considered extinct.

The Route

The hike up and around Parícutin begins on the outskirts of the village of Angahuan, which was heavily impacted by the 1940s eruptions but not destroyed. Most people elect to go with a local guide on foot or on horseback, as the route through the lava field is not well marked. GPS is very helpful in finding and staying on the route and helping you to avoid stumbling across the lava. It's possible to do this hike as an out-and-back up the north side of the cinder cone to the summit or as a loop, dropping down the west side of the volcano and following a marked route northwest through the lava fields back to a dirt road that runs from the neighboring town Santa Ana Zirosto back to Angahuan.

1 AGAVE AND AVOCADOS

This region of Mexico, about 200 miles (322 km) west of Mexico City, is highly agricultural, as volcanic ash produces very fertile soil and is known for growing agave and avocados. On the approach from Angahuan, you'll pass by spiky fields of agave, used to make tequila, mezcal, and sweeteners, and groves of avocado trees. Resist the urge to pick any of the avocados on the trail and instead buy them from the stands selling local foods and souvenirs you'll pass by along the route.

2 SCORIA CONE

Parícutin is a type of volcano called a cinder cone or scoria cone, the most common type of volcano in Mexico. Scoria cones are typically steep-sided cones formed from loose fragments of volcanic rocks and ash that erupt explosively from a central vent. Parícutin's summit crater is around 660 feet (183 m) across and still occasionally emits steam and smoke as water seeping through the volcano encounters hot pockets in the rocks.

3 SAN JUAN PARANGARICUTIRO CHURCH RUINS

One of the most striking survivors of the Parícutin eruptions is the San Juan Parangaricutiro Church, a white church

Santa Ana Zirosto

that sits half-buried in hardened, black lava. The church is the only remaining building from the town of San Juan Parangaricutiro, which was once the seat of this municipality but was destroyed by Parícutin. The church is a well-known pilgrimage site, and the old altar is often adorned with candles, flowers, and religious offerings.

4 A NATURAL WONDER

With its near-mythical origin story and decades of scientific study, Parícutin is considered one of the world's Seven Natural Wonders, along with the Grand Canyon, Victoria Falls, Rio de Janeiro Harbor, Great Barrier Reef, Mount Everest, and the northern lights.

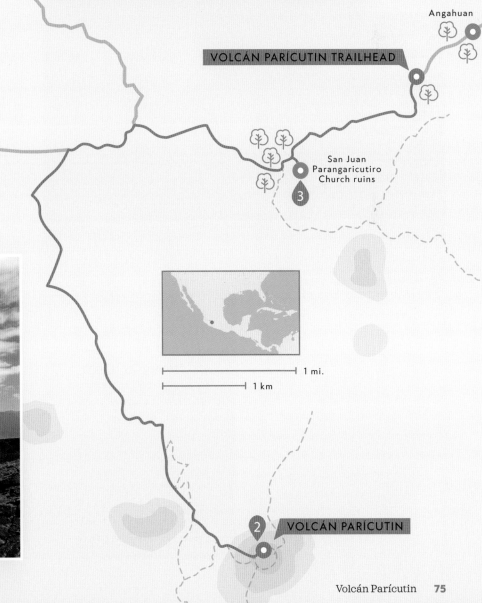

Angahuan

VOLCÁN PARÍCUTIN TRAILHEAD

San Juan
Parangaricutiro
Church ruins

3

1 mi.

1 km

VOLCÁN PARÍCUTIN

2

Walk here next

Volcanic landscapes are some of the most dynamic landscapes in the world. An eruption can dramatically change the terrain around a volcano and many long-term scientific studies have tracked how the ecology of an area recovers after a major event. Witness the devastation and regrowth yourself on these treks in relatively recent volcanic landscapes.

Hike across a solidified lava lake
KĪLAUEA VOLCANO

You can't walk across the main vent of Kīlauea on the Big Island in Hawaii, USA, because it's often erupting, and it's also sacred ground for the Hawaiian people, but the nearby Kilauea Iki (meaning "little Kilauea") Trail runs across a still warm but solidified lava lake. The easy 3.2-mile (5.1 km) loop trail begins on the crater rim and descends through rain forest to the steaming crater floor.

Loop across black sand
MOUNT ETNA

Pay a visit to Europe's most notorious volcano on this 4-mile (6.5 km) loop atop Mount Etna, on the island of Sicily, Italy. The loop starts from the La Montagnola cable car terminal and runs across black volcanic sand around the Barbagallo Craters, bowl-shaped depressions on the southern flank of Mount Etna. Etna is almost continuously erupting, so check conditions before setting out.

A grueling hike around a smoking crater rim

MOUNT SAINT HELENS

The May 18, 1980, eruption of Mount Saint Helens in Washington State is the largest and most destructive eruption to date on US soil. Hundreds of square miles of terrain were impacted by the explosive eruption, which blew an enormous crater into the north side of the mountain, creating a lateral blast zone to the north as well as setting off dozens of devastating mudflows called lahars. This hike up Mount Saint Helens via the Ptarmigan Trail is a strenuous 8.2-mile (13.2 km) round trip that ends on the still-smoking crater rim.

Ice climb on an ice cap

KATLA VOLCANO

Even though Katla is one of Iceland's largest and most active volcanoes, it's not easy to see because it's hidden under the island's fourth largest ice cap, Mýrdalsjökull. With proper equipment, it's possible to hike on a tongue of the ice cap called the Sólheimajökull. If you don't have glacier travel experience, plan to hire an ice climbing guide for an adventurous expedition onto the ice.

La Ciudad Perdida

LOCATION
Sierra Nevada de Santa Marta, Colombia

DURATION
4 days

DIFFICULTY
Moderate

DISTANCE
27.5 miles (44 km)

MAP
National Geographic Trails Illustrated Colombia Map #3400

START/END
Machete Pelao

TRAIL MARKING
Signs

LEFT Teyuna, the mountaintop ruined "lost city" in the Colombian jungle.

Rediscover the lost city of Teyuna on a four-day jungle trek.

The Colombian jungle keeps many secrets, but none so enchanting as this lost stone city, shrouded for centuries under lush vegetation near the country's northern coast. Ciudad Perdida, Spanish for "lost city," was rediscovered in 1972 by looters who removed untold treasures from the site before it was investigated by archaeologists in 1976. Today the city is guarded by a 27.5-mile (44 km) round-trip trek and a flight of 1,350 stone steps that lead to terraces and circular plazas linked by paved paths, all wrought from native rock.

The Lost City was built by the Tairona people around 800 CE, about 650 years before the Incas built Machu Picchu. They called it Teyuna, and in its heyday, it supported as many as eight thousand people. Located on the Buritaca River, along one of the main routes connecting the north coast to the mountainous interior, the Lost City is thought to have been a center of trade and commerce until European colonizers devastated the New World's Indigenous communities.

Partly protected by its location, Teyuna may have held out against the Spanish for a hundred years, much longer than most other communities. Few tribes survived the Spanish conquest intact, but some still live in modern-day Colombia. The Kogi people are the modern descendants of the Tairona people and maintain their traditional way of life in the jungle around the Lost City; they are often seen along the trails and in the city itself. To the Kogi, Teyuna was never lost, and they are still intimately involved with its preservation.

The Route

The hike to the Lost City begins in Machete Pelao, also known as El Mamey, a small outpost two and a half hours by vehicle away from the closest city, Santa Marta. To visit, you must go with a guide who will ensure that the trail, the site, and the locals are all respected and also that you don't get lost in the dense jungle. Most people can make the out-and-back hike to the Lost City in four days, but there are also five- and six-day tour options, which allow for a slower approach and more time at the site. The trail tends to be steep and muddy, with numerous creek and river crossings, so good footwear and trekking poles are recommended.

THE JUNGLE

For the first days of your trek, the jungle is the star of the show. You'll be trekking through the Sierra Nevada de Santa Marta mountains, a coastal range that's separate from the Andes. Colombia lies just north of the equator, and the plentiful rain and lack of cold weather means it's always growing season in this lush jungle. Colombia's rain forests are famous for their high biodiversity of both flora and fauna, and the towering canopy, abundant vines, and ample epiphytes—plants that grow on top of other plants—make a rain forest feast for all the senses.

THE RIVER

The trail to the Lost City follows the Buritaca River, one of thirty-six rivers that drain the Sierra Nevada de Santa Marta mountains. At times you'll be hiking in the river, a welcome respite from the often hot and humid weather. Unfortunately, lots of water means mosquitoes. Be sure to bring bug spray and a head net!

Parque Nacional
Natural Tayrona

3 CAMPS

Along the route to the Lost City, you'll camp in designated campsites. Most tour companies offer porter services, where people or mules carry most of your food and equipment, so you can hike with just a day pack. They'll also provide three meals a day, although you may want to bring extra snacks. Overnight accommodations are in dirt-floor huts in bunk beds or hammocks, with a mosquito net to keep off all kinds of insects and lizards.

4 THE VILLAGES

Four different tribes still live in the rain forest along the Buritaca River, and you are likely to encounter these peaceful people on your trek, as the trail passes by several villages. Keep an eye out for palm leaf-roofed huts, livestock, and agricultural fields sprouting crops such as sugar and coffee. The most visible inhabitants, the Kogi, traditionally wear all-white tunics, in homespun cotton and wool, and carry a bag across their shoulders, which contains both practical and sacred personal items.

5 THE GRAND ENTRANCE

After two full days of hiking, you'll awake early on the third day to begin the final climb up to the Lost City. The entrance is straight out of *Indiana Jones*, with a seemingly endless flight of stone stairs ascending through the jungle to the site. Although some of these stairs have been rebuilt since the city was rediscovered, the stone pavers are all original. As you climb the stairs, take your mind off the burn in your calves by imagining all the feet—bare, sandaled, and sneakered—that have come before you.

6 TEYUNA

After days of trekking the dense rain forest, the views across the Lost City are astonishing, especially when you consider that only a fraction of the city has been uncovered from the rain forest. The mountainside site is covered with terraces and circular plazas, linked by stone steps and paved walkways. Even after hundreds of years of erosion, the advanced technology and engineering that went into constructing this city is impressive, and it's possible to imagine what life may have been like here for the Tairona.

TRAILHEAD

TEYUNA

2 mi.

2 km

Walk here next

People have adapted to living in all kinds of environments for thousands of years by building shelters. Homes made from rock tend to stand the test of time for longer than those of wood or thatch. Here are a few places where you can hike to visit innovative ancient dwellings that have survived in place for hundreds of years.

Petroglyphs, pictographs, and ruins galore
GRAND GULCH

Between two thousand and seven hundred years ago, this network of deep sandstone canyons in what is now Bears Ears National Monument, in southeast Utah, USA, was a neighborhood, home to hundreds of people who grew crops on the fertile riverbanks. But as drought conditions worsened, food became scarce, and people began building defensible cliff dwellings high up on the canyon walls. The 20-mile (32 km) point-to-point hike down Bullet Canyon to Grand Gulch and out Kane Gulch is one of the Southwest's richest backpacking trips, with ruins, pictographs, and artifacts found around nearly every bend of the canyon. Water can be scarce in this canyon system so careful planning is advised.

Trek past troglodytic caves

ZEMI VALLEY LOOP

Caves were some of the earliest dwellings for ancient people to take shelter from the elements. In what is now Göreme National Park, in central Turkey, people figured out how to make their own caves by scooping out rooms in soft volcanic tuff. This white rock, formed from solidified ash, is easily carved, and over time people hollowed out a vast network of rooms and tunnels through the tuff, creating a subterranean city that extends eight stories underground. The national park offers many trails, including an easy 2-mile (3.2 km) loop through an archaeological museum.

Stroll around a vast temple site

ANGKOR WAT

Angkor Wat means "city of temples," and indeed this sprawling 400-acre (160 ha) complex in Cambodia is the largest religious monument in the world. Exploring the entire Angkor Wat complex on foot on the 11.3-mile (18.2 km) Small Circuit trail takes at least an entire day. Built during the twelfth century, originally as a Hindu temple, the site gradually evolved into a Buddhist temple by the end of that century. The site is entirely built from millions of sandstone blocks, using more rock than all the Great Pyramids of Egypt combined.

Inca Trail

Follow the Incas' paved trails to the ancient city of Machu Picchu.

LOCATION
Peruvian Andes

DURATION
4 days

DIFFICULTY
Moderate

DISTANCE
25 miles (40 km)

MAP
National Geographic Trails
Illustrated Peru Map #3404

START/END
Ollantaytambo/Sun Gate,
Machu Picchu

TRAIL MARKING
Signs

Perched on a mountain high in the Peruvian Andes sits Machu Picchu, a sprawling walled citadel of perfectly fitted, polished stones that was once a ceremonial center of the Incan Empire. It's possible to take a train to Machu Picchu, but the experience of approaching on foot to arrive at the Sun Gate at dawn is one of the most glorious and rewarding hiking experiences on Earth.

The Inca Trail is just one small, incredibly scenic section of the Incan road system, a sprawling network of 25,000 miles (40,233 km) of roads built to connect communities throughout the Andes. Before the Spanish conquest, twelve million people lived under the Incan Empire, which encompassed over 770,000 square miles (about 2 million sq km) of territory from the Andes to the Pacific coast of South America. This empire was connected by two parallel north to south running roads on the eastern side of the Andes and along the coast, with numerous branches and passes across the mountains.

This road system rivaled that of the Roman Empire, requiring advanced technology to build paved sections, flights of stairs, drainage systems, retaining walls, and bridges. To this day, much of the Inca Trail—the famous section between Ollantaytambo and the Sun Gate—is still paved with precisely fitted stones of volcanic diorite.

LEFT Ruins of Machu Picchu, an ancient Incan citadel perched high in the Andes.

The Route

There are many routes that run to Machu Picchu but none that welcome cars. To reach Machu Picchu you can either buy a train ticket to Aguas Calientes and then take a thirty-minute bus ride up the mountain or sign up for one of several multiday hikes to the ancient city. To mitigate overuse impacts to the ancient trail, the Peruvian government requires that all hikers go with a licensed guide, and permits are limited to five hundred hikers a day, including guides and porters. The classic Machu Picchu trek, covered here, takes four days to cover 25 miles (40 km), starting near Ollantaytambo and ending at the Sun Gate.

1 CUSCO

Before embarking on the Inca Trail, most hikers elect to spend a few days acclimatizing in Cusco, a beautiful historic city near the trail in southeastern Peru at 11,200 feet (3,414 m) of elevation. The Inca Trail never dips below 8,000 feet (2,438 m), topping out on the ominously named 13,776-foot (4,199 m) Dead Woman's Pass. By spending time at altitude in Cusco first, you will help your body prepare for hiking at such a high elevation.

2 ARCHAEOLOGY

Machu Picchu is the largest and most famous ruin along the Inca Trail, but the route passes many other archaeological sites. Some of these are small outposts, built to house messengers as they traveled the Inca Trail, while others are much larger villages. Perhaps the most uniquely beautiful of these is Wiñay Wayna, a steep hillside of agricultural terraces connected by long stone staircases. The terraces are linked by stone irrigation troughs that still run with water, keeping the fields lush and green.

PORTERS

To hike the Inca Trail, you must go with a licensed tour guide. Most of these guide services also offer porter services, where people carry most of your camping gear, meals, and kitchen equipment, so that you can hike with a day pack. Pack animals are not allowed on most of the trail due to the erosion they cause to the path. Most companies also provide and cook three meals a day, but you should plan on bringing your own snacks. When choosing a guide service, be sure to check that they pay and treat their guides and porters fairly and provide them with modern backpacks and equipment.

 SUN GATE AND MACHU PICCHU

After three days of trekking, plan to wake up before dawn on the fourth day to hike the final mile to the Sun Gate for sunrise. Also known as Inti Punku, in honor of the Incan sun god, this was the original entry gate into Machu Picchu. The Sun Gate is located on a ridge overlooking Machu Picchu, positioned such that the sun aligns with the Sun Gate on the summer solstice.

 MACHU PICCHU

From the Sun Gate you'll hike down into Machu Picchu, marveling at the intricate stonework and innovative layout of the city. Machu Picchu is thought to have been the royal estate for the Incan ruler Pachacuti Inca Yupanqui. Radiocarbon dating suggests that the site was occupied from 1420 to 1530, housing a population of around seven hundred people. There are over two hundred stone buildings, including temples, ritualistic altars, storage buildings, and houses.

 HUAYNA PICCHU

If you have any life left in your legs, plan to hike to the top of Huayna Picchu, the mountain that looms over Machu Picchu. The hike up Huayna Picchu (8,835 feet; 2,693 m) takes about an hour, ascending finely cut stone steps built by the Incas. At the summit you'll be rewarded with a spectacular view of the city, 850 feet (259 m) below, as well as the opportunity to explore several temples and terraces at the top.

Huyana Picchu

MACHU PICCHU

Sun Gate

Wiñay Wayna

Cerro Runcuracay

PISCACUCHO

Cusco→

Dead Woman's Pass

2 mi.
2 km

Walk here next

The Inca Trail to Machu Picchu is one of the most popular hikes you can have for very good reasons. To lessen damage to the trail, the Peruvian government limits the number of permits and requires that hikers go with a licensed guide. If permits are full or you'd rather visit Incan ruins on your own, here are several other quieter options for independent hikers.

The Inca Trail for independent explorers

SALKANTAY TREK

If you'd like the experience of hiking Incan roads past ancient ruins but don't want to go with a guide, consider the Salkantay trek. This 43-mile (69 km) hike runs between Mollepata and Hidroelectrica, where you can catch a train to Aguas Calientes, the gateway town to Machu Picchu. The four- to six-day trek can be done with a guided group or on your own. The route passes by clusters of Incan buildings and outposts, as well as through several villages, where you can pay for overnight accommodations and meals, or you can camp on the trail.

Hot springs and a high pass

LARES TREK

The Lares trek is a shorter alternative to the Inca Trail that explores the Sacred Valley of the Incas (Urubamba Valley) and begins and ends in small towns with hot springs. The 33-mile (53 km) hike begins in Lares and heads to Huacahuasi, a traditional Andean weaving village, for the night, before tackling the 14,600-foot (4,450 m) Ipsaycocha Pass, the highest point of the hike. On day three you pass through several more villages before reaching Ollantaytambo, where you'll catch a train to Aguas Calientes and a bus from there to Machu Picchu.

Discover a less famous lost city

CHOQUEQUIRAO HIKE

Choquequirao is another lost Incan city, located about 30 miles (48 km) southwest of Machu Picchu in the Vilcabamba mountain range, near the Apurímac River. The site is only about 40 percent excavated, and it's more overgrown than Machu Picchu, but many of the buildings are well preserved, and many people prefer the site's rougher state to the groomed appearance of its more famous sister site. Choquequirao can only be reached by a 28-mile (45 km) round-trip hike from San Pedro de Cachora. Currently no guides are required to visit the site.

Vergel Canyon Trail

LOCATION
Torotoro Canyon, Bolivia

DURATION
2.5 hours

DIFFICULTY
Easy

DISTANCE
4.5 miles (7.3 km)

MAP
National Geographic Trails
Illustrated Bolivia Map #3406

START/END
Torotoro

TRAIL MARKING
Signs

Dodge dinosaur footprints on the edge of Torotoro Canyon.

Kids and adults alike will delight in this unique trek, where the trail runs alongside the fossilized footsteps of dinosaurs. Today Torotoro National Park sits on the edge of the town of the same name, near the middle of Bolivia. This region on the eastern slope of the Andes mountain range is a semiarid environment, deeply dissected by canyons and riddled with caves. But eighty million years ago, during the Cretaceous period, this area of Bolivia was much wetter. The wetlands attracted many species of dinosaurs, who left countless footprints in the mud. Over geological timescales, the mud was turned into rock, preserving thousands of dinosaur footprints in stone.

So far, more than 3,500 footprints from at least eight species of dinosaurs have been identified in Torotoro National Park. The park is not as well known for dinosaur bones, but fossilized footprints and trackways are also highly valuable to paleontologists, who can glean a lot of information about dinosaur behavior and ecology from tracks.

Torotoro became a national park in 1989, but people have been visiting the canyon for a long time. The Batea Q'ocha pictographs are precolonial rock paintings found along the river that depict geometric patterns and animals in red pigments. Outside of Torotoro are the ruins of Llamachaki, a multilevel complex with fortified walls and a watchtower that likely served as a pre-Spanish military outpost.

LEFT The colorful canyon walls in Torotoro National Park.

The Route

The Vergel Canyon Trail is a 4.5-mile (7.3 km) lollipop loop that begins on the northern edge of the town of Torotoro and follows the rim of Vergel Canyon to a notch where you can descend a series of steps 800 feet (244 m) down into the canyon. In contrast with the arid canyon rim, the river bottom is a lush, mossy paradise. The hike ends at a refreshing swimming pool at the base of a gushing spring-fed waterfall, where you can take a dip before climbing the stairs back up to the rim and completing the loop.

1 SYNCLINE VALLEY

As you hike along the canyon rim, you'll be looking across a wide valley edged with crumpled rock formations. Here the Earth's crust has been folded and eroded into a colorful tapestry of geologic layers. Some of the most striking features are the numerous arched hogbacks, triangular toothlike hills that line the valley. Called k'asas, the hogbacks are considered sacred by the local Quechua people.

② DINOSAUR DANCE FLOOR

The landscape is beautiful, but as you hike, don't forget to look down at the rocks under your feet. Many kinds of dinosaurs are represented in the footprints of Torotoro. Huge plant-eating sauropods left 2-foot-wide (0.6 m) saucerlike prints, while carnivorous bipedal theropods are represented by three-toed birdlike tracks: fitting as these types of dinosaurs would eventually evolve into modern-day birds. The footprints of Torotoro are eighty-six million years old and are quite delicate; don't step in them or pour water into them (a common but potentially destructive method of highlighting hard-to-see tracks for photos).

③ TOROTORO CANYON CONDORS

The Torotoro Canyon is nearly 1,000 feet (305 m) deep, cut down through many geological layers of sandstone, limestone, and shale by the Torotoro River. Andean condors make their nests on the steep canyon walls. With wingspans over 10 feet (3 m) from tip to tip, Andean condors are the largest birds of prey in the world. Once found throughout the Andes, the massive birds' population was decimated by habitat loss and poisoning from lead bullets in carcasses, its main source of food. But thanks to captive breeding and hunter education programs, they are making a comeback.

④ HUMAJALANTA CAVERNS

Bolivia's largest cave, Humajalanta Caverns, is also in Torotoro National Park. The cave was carved out by the Umajalanta stream, which flows into a thick layer of soluble limestone that underlies the park. To date, nearly 3 miles (5 km) of passages have been explored in Humajalanta Caverns, which contains impressive flowstone formations. Cave tours are available, but Humajalanta is not for the claustrophobic as many sections involve tight, muddy squeezes. A population of vampire bats also calls the cave home, although they don't usually pose a threat to people.

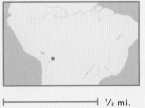

|—————————| ½ mi.
|———| 0.5 km

Walk here next

From the microscopic to the colossal, fossils are some of nature's most precious treasures. Hidden among rock layers spanning nearly four billion years of geological time, fossils tell us about how life evolved, from algal mats to dinosaurs, to great apes to the first humans. Here are a few locations you can visit to search for evidence of the Earth's evolutionary history.

Visit the cradle of humanity
STERKFONTEIN CAVES

Make a pilgrimage to where we all began: South Africa's Cradle of Humankind is home to the greatest collection of early hominid fossils, dating back 3.5 million years ago, when the first bipedal apes emerged from the trees onto the African plains. The Sterkfontein Caves are a series of limestone caves that have produced many exciting fossils, including over 1,500 *Homo naledi* fossils found in one cave chamber. The park offers daily tours of the caves.

Hike to the world's most famous Cambrian quarry

BURGESS SHALE

The Burgess Shale fossils in Yoho National Park, Canada, are famous for being the earliest known complex life-forms, dating back 505 million years to the Cambrian era, when new species were evolving at such a furious rate that paleontologists refer to this time period as the Cambrian explosion. To visit the famous Walcott Quarry, still rich in fossils, you must go with a guide from Parks Canada and hike 13.5 miles (22 km) point-to-point to a city-block-sized quarry on a ridge between Wapta Mountain and Mount Field in the Canadian Rockies. At the quarry you'll be able to sift through the shale layers for trilobites and Wiwaxia fossils, but don't pocket any! The Burgess Shale fossils are protected as scientists are still learning about how life evolved from these specimens.

Stroll past famous Mesozoic fossil sites

JURASSIC COAST

The Atlantic Ocean has done a lot of the work to expose fossils along England's Jurassic Coast, where over 185 million years of geological history is found in rocks spanning the Triassic, Jurassic, and Cretaceous periods. Storms regularly trigger new erosion along these cliffs, occasionally unearthing entire skeletons of ichthyosaurs, pterosaurs, and plesiosaurs dating to the Mesozoic era, when dinosaurs ruled the Earth. Smaller fossils of seashells, sea urchins, and belemnites are also found, along with chunks of pyrite, also known as fool's gold. The most prolific layers tend to be found between Lyme Regis and Charmouth, and the entire coastline can be walked as part of the South West Coast Path, a 630-mile-long (1,014 km) footpath that runs from Somerset to Dorset.

Caminho da Gruta do Janelão

LOCATION
Cavernas do Peruaçu
National Park, Brazil

DURATION
4 hours

DIFFICULTY
Easy

DISTANCE
3 miles (4.8 km)

MAP
National Geographic Trails
Illustrated Brazil Map #3401

START/END
Cavernas do Peruaçu National
Park Visitor Center

TRAIL MARKING
Signs/guides

Marvel at one of Brazil's grandest show caves.

Large areas of Brazil are underlain by limestone, a type of sedimentary rock that's readily eroded by slightly acidic water. Water flowing through underground aquifers often creates massive cave systems in limestone regions all over the world, including along the Peruaçu River in south central Brazil, where Cavernas do Peruaçu National Park boasts more than 180 caves and grottoes.

Since the national park was established in 1999, eight show caves have been opened to the public. The largest and most famous of these is the 3-mile-long (4.8 km) Caverna Janelão or Janel Cave, the ceilings of which soar nearly 600 feet (183 m) high, making this one of the largest cave chambers in the world. Janel Cave is known for its extensive flowstone formations, where mineral-rich groundwater dripping through the cave's roof slowly creates unique rock formations like stalactites, which hang from the ceiling, and stalagmites, which form on the cave floor. Flowstone formations are often given evocative names that reflect their shapes, such as cave curtains or cave bacon.

Janel Cave is more than just an underground rocky chamber; a series of circular skylights eroded through the ceiling of the cave allows enough light to reach into its depths to grow subterranean miniature forests of canopy trees, vines, and flowering plants. The Peruaçu River also runs through the cave, creating a lush riverine underground Eden unlike anywhere else in the world.

LEFT Janel Cave, with its subterranean river and underground forest.

The Route

To enter any of the park's caves, visitors must sign up for one of six cave tours with a park service guide. The six tours offer caving trips of varying lengths and difficulties, but no caving experience is necessary for any of them. Helmets are provided for all visitors. The walking tour of Janel Cave is a 3-mile-long (4.8 km) loop that takes around four hours to complete, allowing for lots of time to study the cave's many unique features. Steps and railings help visitors navigate the cave, and there is no crawling or squeezing required in these vast underground chambers.

 Lapa do Carlucio

 Lapa do Caboclo

Lapa do Indio

 Lapa dos Desenhos

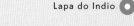 **GRUTA DO JANELÃO**

GRAND ENTRANCE

The entrance to Janel Cave is a yawning portal 328 feet (100 m) high, and from there the cave gets even grander. The trail through the cave runs alongside the Peruaçu River and crosses it twice via well-placed stepping stones. Here the river is slow and shallow as it flows through its deep underground canyon, enclosed by high limestone walls. In some sections, the roof of the cave has collapsed completely, while in others, the river is topped by limestone bridges and skylights.

BIG WINDOWS

The name Janelão means "big window" in Portuguese, in honor of Janel Cave's sinkhole openings that allow light to pierce deep into the cave. The most famous of these openings is the Clarabóia do Coração, meaning "heart skylight." Seeds from the nearby forest find their way into the openings, settling on the cave floor. Some rainwater can enter the cave through the openings, but the interior environment of the cave is quite arid, so plants must be adapted to growing in dry conditions. Despite the challenges of growing underground, dozens of species of plants have been recorded in Janel Cave, a rare example of an underground forest.

ANCIENT UNDERGROUND ART

Cavernas do Peruaçu National Park may be a relatively new park, but people have been visiting Janel Cave for thousands of years. The walls of the cave are adorned with red, black, and ocher pictographs that date back as far as ten thousand years; the dry nature of this cave system helps preserve these panels, which are some of the oldest in the Americas. The panels are mainly abstract geometric paintings that may represent calendars or seasonal hunting records. The most famous of these panels in Janel Cave is called Sítio Ateliê Janelão.

STUNNING STALACTITE

The planet's largest stalactite, called the Perna da Bailarina, or Ballerina's Leg, is also found in Janel Cave. Measuring 91 feet (27.7 m) long, this pinnacle hangs from the cave's ceiling, formed over eons from mineral-rich water dripping slowly through the cave's roof. For comparison, the famous *Christ the Redeemer* sculpture above Rio de Janeiro is 98 feet (30 m) high with arms stretching 92 feet (28 m) wide, just long enough to cradle the Ballerina's Leg.

 Lapa do Rezar

Walk here next

After you see Janel Cave, you may be ready to graduate onto more intensive cave tours. Brazil is rich in caves due to its predominantly limestone underpinnings. Here are a few options if you're willing to strap on a headlamp, a harness, or even scuba gear to visit some of the country's underground treasures.

See cave flowers

TORRINHA CAVERN

Located just outside of Chapada Diamantina National Park, Gruta da Torrinha is considered Brazil's most beautiful cave. That honor is mostly due to its abundance of speleothems: flowstone rock formations built by drips of mineral-rich water over thousands of years. This cave also contains one of the world's largest known aragonite flowers: a spiky, fist-sized cluster of calcium carbonate crystals that resembles a blooming flower, growing deep underground. There are three different cave tour options in Torrinha, the longest being a 2.5-mile (4 km), three-hour-long subterranean trek.

Explore a deep blue pool

POÇO AZUL

This underground pool, in Chapada Diamantina National Park, is also called the Blue Well and is known for its deep blue hues. It's also famous for fossils: over four thousand fossils from forty-five species of animals, many now extinct, including giant sloths, saber-toothed cats, and mastodons, have been recovered by scuba-diving paleontologists from the bottom of the pool. It's an easy quarter-mile walk down to the water, but to explore further you'll need to don scuba gear. If that's not enough mileage for you, Chapada Diamantina National Park has over 185 miles (298 km) of hiking trails.

Valle de la Luna

LOCATION
Atacama Desert, Los Flamencos National Reserve, Chile

DURATION
1 day

DIFFICULTY
Easy

DISTANCE
2 miles (3.2 km)

MAP
National Geographic Trails Illustrated Chile Map #3400

START/END
San Pedro de Atacama

TRAIL MARKING
Signs

LEFT The Valle de la Luna in the Atacama Desert with snowcapped peaks of the Andes in the background.

Visit the surfaces of both the moon and Mars in the world's driest desert.

Tucked in the rain shadow on the western side of the Andes mountain range, the Atacama Desert is the driest place in the world. In fact, the most arid region of the Atacama is wedged between two mountain chains, the Andes and the Chilean Coast range, creating a two-sided rain shadow that blocks moisture from both the Pacific and Atlantic Oceans.

The Atacama has been very dry—the average rainfall is less than half an inch per year, with some areas not receiving any moisture in several decades of monitoring—for a very long time, since at least the middle Miocene, around fifteen million years ago. All that time as a severely dry desert has resulted in some distinctive rock formations and soil types, which are so otherworldly that the Atacama has been used as a movie stand-in for other planets and a testing ground for multiple Mars landers.

Whereas some regions of the Atacama are likened to Mars, the Valle de la Luna is more reminiscent of the moon. Formed in the Salt Mountain Range, where the Atacama Desert meets the edge of the Andes, the Valley of the Moon is a geological spectacle created by millions of years of plate tectonic movements and aeolian wind erosion. Here an ancient salt lake bed has been folded and sculpted into a unique landscape of ridges, mounds, and hollows, all covered with a crystalline layer of white salt.

The Route

The Atacama Desert supports many highly evolved plants and animals that are specially adapted to live in such a dry place. But it is not especially conducive to hosting humans. Long treks here are difficult and potentially dangerous, so the region is best appreciated by taking a series of short hikes to visit specific rock formations and vistas. This series of jaunts in the Valley of the Moon are all in the Los Flamencos National Reserve, just outside of San Pedro de Atacama in northern Chile. You'll want to rent a four-wheel drive vehicle to drive around the park or join a tour group.

 FLAMINGOS AND FRIENDS

The Los Flamencos National Reserve is named for the flocks of flamingos that occasionally descend on the region in wetter years when the surrounding salt flats collect water, providing migratory birds with seasonal nesting grounds. Three species of flamingos, the Andean, Chilean, and James's flamingos, can be observed here, sitting on nests they build from mud into mounds about a foot high. Other commonly seen animals include hawks, condors, and rheas (South American ostriches), as well as vicuñas (a South American camelid), foxes, and viscachas, a type of large rabbitlike rodent.

```
|——————————| 2 mi.
|——————————| 2 km
```

② TULOR RUINS

This archaeological site, located outside of San Pedro de Atacama, is a testament to the tenacity of humans to live in even the most marginal places, as well as the inexorable erosion of extreme aridity. The Tulor ruins are a massive former village complex covering nearly 60,000 sq ft (5,574 sq m) of desert. Radiocarbon dating places the origins of the settlement between 380 BCE and 200 CE. Drilled wells into the site have revealed a pattern of gradually increasing aridity until the site was abandoned around 1,800 years ago. The desert is reclaiming the circular walls made of mud and clay, and this is classified as a highly endangered archaeological site by the World Monuments Watch List.

③ DESERT BLOOMS

You might think that a hyperarid environment would be inhospitable to life, but in fact a rich tapestry of flora and fauna live in the Atacama. Cacti, succulents, and even flowering plants thrive here. Seeds can lay dormant for decades until the slightest rainfall triggers massive floral blooms. The most famous blooms occur in wetter El Niño years between September and November in the coastal valleys and Chilean Coast Range. In 2022, the Chilean government announced the creation of the Flowering Desert National Park to protect the blooming areas of the Atacama and support the region's unique biodiversity of over two hundred species of flowering plants.

SAN PEDRO DE ATACAMA

Mars Valley

The Three Marias

VALLEY OF THE MOON

Mirador Achaches

④ Duna Mayor

② Tulor ruins

④ DUNA MAYOR, MIRADOR ACHACHES, AND THE THREE MARIAS

This desert has many unique landforms worth exploring. Three of the most photographic features are all located a short walk from the road through the park. Duna Mayor is a tall sand dune created by the prevailing winds. Mirador Achaches is an overlook of a dramatic eroded basin. The Three Marias are three standing rock formations in a line that some say represent a woman kneeling, praying, and rejoicing. Sunrise and sunset are generally the best time for photographing the colorful rock formations and landscape, and if you're brave enough to stay after dark, you'll be treated to an incredible view of the southern night sky.

Walk here next

South America is most famous for its rain forests, mountains, and beaches, but a few deserts are found scattered throughout the continent, including the world's driest desert. Here are a few treks into starkly beautiful arid landscapes.

Summit a volcano for superb desert views

CERRO TOCO

Gain an arresting vantage of the world's driest desert from atop Cerro Toco, an 18,387-foot (5,604 m) volcano that towers over the Atacama Desert in Chile. Located near San Pedro de Atacama, the 2.5-mile (4 km) round-trip hike starts high and gets higher, gaining 1,000 feet (305 m) of elevation on the way to its summit. Altitude sickness can be a real danger on this trek, so take time to acclimatize, hike slowly, and drink lots of water. From the top the views over the desert are legendary, especially in winter when the snowcapped peaks add a new dimension to the desert landscape.

Trek between two oases

DUNES TREK

One of the most unique landscapes in South America is found on the northwest coast of Brazil, in Lençóis Maranhenses National Park, where a sea of sand dunes meets the Atlantic Ocean. During the rainy season, from January to May, rainwater collects in vivid blue pools in the low point between the bright white dunes. You can cross these dunes in a three-day, 26-mile (42 km) point-to-point trek that links two oases: Oásis Baixa Grande and Oásis Queimada dos Britos. The trek starts in Atins, on the Preguiças River, and ends in Betânia.

Explore the salt flats

SALAR DE UYUNI

The salt flats of Bolivia are one of the most surreal scenes on the globe, with stark white horizons reaching as far as the eye can see. The Salar de Uyuni is the world's largest salt flat, covering more than 4,000 square miles (10,360 sq km), created by a prehistoric lake that evaporated long ago leaving behind polygonal patterns of crusted salt. Hikers can explore the flats from Uyuni. There are no marked trails, and it's surprisingly easy to get disoriented in this flat, featureless landscape, so be sure to take a map and compass along with your GPS.

Fitz Roy Trek

LOCATION
Argentine Andes

DURATION
8–9 hours

DIFFICULTY
Hard

DISTANCE
12.7 miles (20 km)

MAP
National Geographic Trails
Illustrated Chile Map #3400

START/END
El Chaltén

TRAIL MARKING
Signs

Get up close and personal with the planet's most iconic granite skyline.

Mount Fitz Roy may be one of the most recognizable skylines in the world, as it adorns the Patagonia clothing company label. The founder of the company, Yvon Chouinard, was one of the first people to climb to the top of the highest toothy peak in 1968.

To this day, Fitz Roy is one of the most coveted summits in mountaineering, with new records still being set. In February 2014, a new route was blazed by American rock climbers Tommy Caldwell and Alex Honnold across the summits of Fitz Roy and its satellite peaks, called the Fitz Traverse. In September 2022, American mountaineer Colin Haley became the first person to ascend the classic Supercanaleta Route solo in winter.

The Fitz Roy is the crown jewel of Argentina's Los Glaciares National Park, which borders Chile's Torres del Paine National Park. The parks protect a huge swath of the Southern Patagonian Ice Field, the largest ice cap in the southern hemisphere outside of Antarctica. This ice cap flows out of the Andes and feeds into forty-seven major glaciers, thirteen of which flow into the Pacific Ocean, creating numerous icebergs, with the rest feeding into strikingly clear alpine lakes.

LEFT The jagged snow-covered granite peaks of Mount Fitz Roy in Patagonia.

The Route

The summit of Fitz Roy is a technical feat best left to experienced mountaineers, but hikers can get close to the granite spires on a 12.7-mile (20.4 km), round-trip day hike, starting on the northwest edge of El Chaltén and ending at the lake at the base of the peaks, Laguna de los Tres, or Lake of the Three. The hike can be done in a day or as an overnight. The route gains more than 3,300 feet (1,006 m) of elevation on the way to Laguna de los Tres, with the steepest part of the trail coming in the last mile. Trekking poles are a must, and ice traction devices can help on this section, especially if there is snow or ice lingering on the trail.

1 EL CHALTÉN

The trailhead for this hike is found at the end of San Martin Avenue, on the edge of El Chaltén, a small mountain village known for being Argentina's trekking capital. The picturesque village, at the edge of the Southern Patagonian Ice Cap, on the banks of the Rio de las Vueltas, only has around 350 year-round residents, but populations can swell during the busy hiking season from October to March. Weather can be unpredictable here, but the best weather window usually occurs in January and February, at the height of the southern hemisphere's summer. As you ascend from El Chaltén, be sure to look backward a few times at the views over the town and the Las Vueltas River valley.

② LAGUNA CAPRI

Los Glaciares National Park is famous for its abundance of stunningly blue alpine lakes, including Lake Capri. You'll reach the lake only 2.5 miles (4 km) from the start of the hike, making it a good stop for rest or even an overnight campsite. There is a tenting area on the northeast side of the lake, with perfect picture-postcard views of Fitz Roy across the aquamarine water.

③ RIVER PLAINS

Before beginning the big climb up to the final lake, you'll pass a flat section of trail that crosses two river outlets from Lake Sucia. You'll also find two more campsites here, Poincenot and Rio Blanco, where you can break the hike up into an overnight. Poincenot is the most popular campsite in the park, whereas Rio Blanco is intended as a base camp for rock climbers. All of these campsites offer basic tent pads and pit toilets. This is a good place to rest and stretch before tackling the final mile and a half (2.4 km) to the Lake of the Three.

④ LAGUNA DE LOS TRES

After gaining 1,500 feet (457 m) of elevation in the last mile and a half of trail, the footpath ends at the edge of the terminal moraine of the De los Tres Glacier. This mass of ice has advanced and retreated many times over the past few thousand years, creating a pile of rocks that marks the point of the farthest advance. From here you'll have extraordinary views of the lake, the glacier, and the soaring granite walls of Mount Fitz Roy and its six flanking peaks.

⑤ THE FITZ TRAVERSE

As you admire the precipitous ridgeline, try to trace the route for the Fitz Traverse, which starts on the right side of the range and scales 13,000 feet (3,962 m) of rock, snow, and ice to summit all seven of the Fitz Roy summits—from south to north: Aguja Guillaumet, Aguja Mermoz, Cerro Fitz Roy, Aguja Poincenot, Aguja Rafael Juarez, Aguja Saint-Exupery, and Aguja de l'S—in a single push. In February 2021, Belgian climber Sean Villanueva completed the Fitz Traverse in reverse, dubbing it the Moonwalk Traverse.

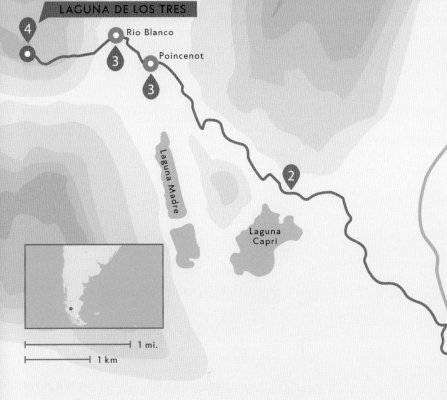

LAGUNA DE LOS TRES

Rio Blanco

Poincenot

Laguna Madre

Laguna Capri

EL CHALTÉN

1 mi.

1 km

Walk here next

Even if you're not a rock climber, there's something thrilling about standing at the base of a massive rock face and imagining what it would be like to leave terra firma and climb up into the vertical world. Here are a few hikes to visit famous climbing locations.

Lay eyes on top of the world

EVEREST BASE CAMP

You don't have to climb to the top of Mount Everest to set your eyes on the world's highest mountain, called Sagarmatha in Nepali and Chomolungma in Tibetan. The trek to Everest base camp is a Himalayan classic. The 80-mile (129 km) round-trip hike typically takes about twelve days: eight days to hike up 8,200 feet (2,499 m) of elevation to base camp at 17,598 feet (5,364) and four days to hike back down the beautiful Khumbu Valley.

An easy loop around a sacred sentinel

DEVILS TOWER

There are many tribal and geological legends about how this 867-foot-high (264 m) tower of black volcanic rock came to preside over Wyoming's Belle Fourche River in the USA. Many Indigenous tribes find its devilish name offensive, but efforts to officially change the name to Bear Lodge have not yet come to fruition. Pay your respects to Bear Lodge on an easy 1.3-mile (2 km) loop around the base of the tower, while keeping your eyes peeled for intrepid rock climbers following crack systems up the basalt blocks to reach the flat, grassy top of the tower.

Look up at the most famous North Face

EIGER TRAIL

Europe's most famous rock face is the north face of the Eiger, a 13,015-foot (3,967 m) mountain in the Bernese Alps. The last great rock problem in the Alps was finally climbed in 1938, but more than sixty people have died on the Eiger, and it continues to challenge rock climbers with its exposed and relentlessly steep face, which is often swept by avalanches and rockfall. A 3.7-mile-long (6 km) one-way trail runs along the base of the north side of the Eiger, providing hikers with incredible views of one of the world's most notorious climbing routes.

O Circuit Trek

LOCATION
Chilean Andes

DURATION
7–9 days

DIFFICULTY
Hard

DISTANCE
75 miles (120 km)

MAP
National Geographic Trails
Illustrated Chile Map #3402

START/END
Paine Grande

TRAIL MARKING
Signs

Take in a 360-degree view of the Paine Massif's surreal peaks.

For a few elite mountaineers, the granite spires of Chile's Torres del Paine National Park sing a siren song, beckoning them to climb to their summits. But hikers who want to keep their feet on the ground should plan on circling the peaks on foot on the park's spectacular O Circuit.

The 75-mile (120 km) O Circuit, a longer version of the park's famous W Circuit, circles the Torres del Paine massif, including the park's three iconic granite peaks: Torres d'Agostini, Torres Central, and Torres Monzino. These granite towers were sculpted by glaciers during the last ice age, when this region was completely covered by ice. The remnants of this glaciated landscape can still be seen in the Southern Patagonian Ice Field, the planet's second largest nonpolar ice field, which still covers the southern Patagonian Andes of both Chile and Argentina.

Torres del Paine is a place of extremes, including the weather, which can oscillate from snow to sunshine to torrential rain any time of the year. The only guarantee is the near-constant wind, which always blows from the west. But with the right gear and planning, the otherworldly landscape of Torres del Paine lives up to its reputation as one of the world's best backpacking destinations.

LEFT The three spectacular granite peaks of the Torres del Paine massif, sculpted by glaciers during the last ice age.

The Route

The O Circuit is a longer version of the W Circuit, a 43-mile (69 km) route that explores the south side of the massif, on a route that looks like a W on a map. The 75-mile (120 km) O Circuit includes the W Circuit but also circles counterclockwise around the north side of the peaks, providing 360-degree views of the striking granite spires. Starting from Paine Grande, on the southwest side of the massif, you'll trace the W Circuit first, delving deeper into the range up two valleys that make up the points of the W. You'll then proceed counterclockwise around the remoter and often more quiet back side of the mountains, before looping back to the start.

1 GLACIAL LAKES AND GUANACOS

The first part of the trail runs between the peaks of the Paine Massif on your left and the shore of Nordenskjöld Lake on your right, one of several glacially carved lakes you'll pass on this trek. The bright blue Paine River flows out of Nordenskjöld, dropping into a spectacular waterfall called Salto Grande, meaning "big jump." The western and southern sides of this lake are known for being one of the best places to spot guanacos, a South American relative of the llama.

2 FRANCES VALLEY AND ASCENSIA VALLEY

These two valleys, which make up the points of the W, follow drainages up into the lap of the Paine Massif. Some hikers elect to drop their gear at a campsite before heading up these out-and-back routes, but be mindful of critters getting into your food. Also be sure to bring plenty of layers and basic survival gear as the weather can turn in an instant in these mountains.

Camp Los Perros

John Garner Pass

Camp Paso

Camp Los Guardas

British Lookout

Cerro Paine Grande

Grey camp

Camp Italiano

Grey Lake

Torres viewpoint

French Lookout

Camp Los Cuernos

Lake Nordenskjöld

PAINE GRANDE

Lake Pehoé

3 mi.

3 km

③ NATIONAL PARK CAMPSITES

Backpackers must camp at designated sites or in reserved dorm beds in one of the park's backcountry *refugios* (shelters)—there is no wild camping allowed. The trickiest part of this hike is logistical: campsites must be reserved months ahead of time so you need to have a clear idea of your itinerary and daily mileage goals. If this seems like a daunting task, you can opt for a guided trek with a licensed guide, who will take care of reservations for you. The upside is that most campgrounds and *refugios* offer hot food, and with careful planning, you can embark on your trip carrying minimal food and cooking equipment.

④ MAGELLANIC SUBPOLAR FOREST

Torres del Paine is located in southern Patagonia, near the southern tip of the South American continent. The unique temperate forest found in the park and throughout this region is known as the Magellanic subpolar forest and is the southernmost forest on the planet, mostly composed of broadleaf trees, Antarctic mosses, and shrubby evergreens. The constant wind, always blowing from the west, often sculpts trees into flags, with all the branches clustered on the downstream side.

⑤ JOHN GARNER PASS AND GREY GLACIER

The literal high point of the O Circuit comes toward the end of the trek, with the trail climbing nearly 3,000 feet (914 m) of elevation to top out at 4,000 feet (1,219 m) above sea level on John Garner Pass. Named for the British mountaineer who helped blaze the O Circuit route in the 1970s, the pass overlooks the Grey Glacier and, on clear days, the South Patagonian Ice Field. Fed by the ice cap, the Grey Glacier feeds into Grey Lake, where it calves into countless icebergs that float across the lake's surface.

Walk here next

Glaciers are one of the most powerful erosive forces in nature. But they're also fragile and rapidly disappearing due to climate change. Here are a few places you can hike to see the planet's surviving glaciers in action.

Edge along the Continental Divide

THE HIGHLINE TRAIL

When Glacier National Park, Montana, USA, was established in 1910, the park had around eighty glaciers. Today less than twenty-five remain, but the ghosts of glaciers past can still be seen etched across the landscape. One of the best places to appreciate the postglacial landscape is on the Highline Trail, a narrow strip between the park's famous Going to the Sun Road and the Continental Divide. This hike is best done as a 12-mile (19 km) one-way hike, making use of the park's free public transportation.

Follow floating icebergs from lagoon to sea

JÖKULSÁRLÓN GLACIER LAGOON

In Iceland's Vatnajökull National Park, the Breiðamerkurjökull glacier used to reach the Atlantic Ocean but over the past century it has retreated 5 miles (8 km) from the coast, leaving a glacial lagoon in its wake. Jökulsárlón—meaning glacial river lagoon—is famous for its icebergs. Hike the 4.5-mile (7.2 km) out-and-back trail along the lagoon and Jökulsá River to see car-sized chunks of bright blue and milky white ice as they float across the lagoon, down the river to the ocean, often beaching along the shoreline of a black-sand beach.

Stroll within sight of glaciers

HOOKER VALLEY TRACK

Famous for being one of the best short hikes in New Zealand, the trail up Hooker Valley rewards day hikers with views of the Southern Alps, including New Zealand's highest point, Aoraki/Mount Cook (12,218 feet; 3,724 m), as well as the Hooker Glacier. The 6.7-mile (10.8 km) round-trip trail begins near Mount Cook Village and wraps around the shore of Mueller Lake, before following the Hooker River upstream to bright blue Hooker Lake, which is fed by the Hooker Glacier. Those with glacier travel gear and experience can go farther up the valley, overnighting at one of three huts along the glacier.

Laugavegurinn Trail

LOCATION
Iceland

DURATION
3–4 days

DIFFICULTY
Moderate

DISTANCE
34 miles (55 km)

MAP
Ferdakort: Þórsmörk–
Landmannalaugar, 1:100,000

START/END
Landmannalaugar/Þórsmörk

TRAIL MARKING
Yellow marker posts

Hike through a multicolored Arctic desert in the Land of Ice and Fire.

Iceland, the Land of Fire and Ice, is the world at its rawest. In this otherworldly landscape you can, quite literally, see the planet in a constant state of motion, destruction, and rebirth. Volcanoes (some with the power to shut down international air travel!), glaciers, hot springs, violent storms, snowfields, mountains, waterfalls, northern lights, and midnight sun all combine to create a scenic masterpiece unequaled anywhere else. And by far the best way to experience the monumental scale of Iceland's landscapes is on foot.

The three- or four-day Laugavegurinn Trail is Iceland's most popular hiking route, and for good reason. It is a walk straight through a lesson in volcanic action and plate tectonics. Over the course of this hike (and even more so if you add in the two-day extension to Skógar) you will walk through the whole array of Icelandic landscapes and get a hands-on understanding of the forces that created Iceland and shaped the world. Iceland sits on the battle lines of the Mid-Atlantic Ridge, an underwater mountain range that stretches down the entire length of the Atlantic Ocean. It's this ridge that separates—and continues to push apart—the North American and Eurasian plates. Magma bubbles up all along this battle line, and it was a great upwelling of the hot stuff that created Iceland and continues to shape it. And so, as you hike the beautiful geological chaos of the Laugavegurinn Trail, keep in mind that you are literally walking through our planet's creation.

LEFT The multicolored landscape seen along the Laugavegurinn Trail.

The Route

You can start this walk in either Landmannalaugar and walk to Þórsmörk, or the other way around: there's no real right or wrong way. Each of the four days is split into 7.5 to 9.5-mile (12–15 km) stages and, with no more than 1,640 feet (500 m) height gain on any of those days, this is a fairly relaxed walk. That is, if the weather plays ball, but up here in the subarctic that's far from guaranteed. At the end of each stage you'll find simple dorm accommodations in one of the hikers' huts. It's worth considering bringing camping gear, though, because this is a very popular trail and beds—which are expensive for what you get—book out way in advance. If you can, add on an extra two days, which would allow you to continue on to Skógar past at least twenty-three incredible waterfalls.

 COUNTING THE COLORS IN THE ROCKS

Who knew that rock could come in such a diverse array of colors? Yellows, greens, rust red, black, and snow-streak white: even brown looks beautiful here. With a palette of colors changing constantly, depending on the movement of light and shadow, when you stand atop a rounded summit to take in the view you could almost imagine that a rainbow had fallen violently to Earth and embedded itself into the Icelandic rock.

 HOT SPRINGS

On most multiday hikes you have to accept that you're not going to wash for the duration of the hike. But in Iceland things are a little different. Here, a hot spring is rarely far away and there are moments on the Laugavegurinn Trail where you will pass by small hot springs where you can splash about and wash off the sweat in volcanic heated water.

Jökultungur

3 JÖKULTUNGUR

From the summit of Jökultungur (2,940 feet; 896 m), marvel at the view out across not one, but three, different glaciers. Speaking of glaciers, Bláfjallakvísl is an icy cold river that runs straight out of the snout of a glacier and yes, you will have to wade across it.

4 LAVA, CANYONS, AND TEXTURE

It's not just the colors of the landscape that impress in Iceland, it's the texture of it as well. From the burned lava fields that mark the start of the trail, the canyons and ravines toward the end of the hike, or the scarred land formations that fill all horizons, you'll quickly be in awe of the raw powers that formed this landscape.

ÞÓRSMÖRK

5 WATERFALLS

Add on two extra days to end your hike in Skógar and the reward is a string of over twenty waterfalls along the way. Each is spectacular, but the most impressive (and yes, the busiest) is the 197-foot-high (60 m), 82-foot-wide (25 m) Skógafoss. It's such an impressive sight that it has virtually become the unofficial emblem of Iceland.

6 MIDNIGHT SUN

Hike this trail in summer—the only time when it's feasible to do so—and you'll never really have to worry about being far from your day's goal as night draws in, because for about six weeks during the hiking season the sun hardly sets and night, when it comes, is a mere twilight.

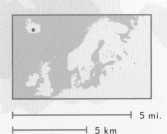

| | 5 mi. |
| | 5 km |

Skógafoss waterfall

Skógar

Walk here next

The frozen north of the planet offers some of the most spectacular wilderness walking in the world. The following hikes give guaranteed solitude but are still quite safe.

Take a summer hike across an ice cap

ARCTIC CIRCLE TRAIL

Most of the massive island of Greenland consists of a vast, uninhabited, and largely unexplored ice cap that covers 695,000 square miles (1.8 million sq km). To hike across a part of Greenland would seem to be the preserve of daring explorers, but that's only a part of the story. In summer there are parts of the island that are ice-free and the Arctic Circle Trail is a ten-day wilderness walk that allows hikers to experience the absolute silence of the Greenlandic landscape.

Hike through the world's largest forest

KARHUNKIERROS TRAIL

Forget the Amazon, the world's largest forest is actually the taiga forests, which run in a huge ribbon right around the subarctic regions of the world. For the most part this is difficult territory to explore, but running clean through northern Finland's Oulanka National Park is the Karhunkierros Trail, a 51-mile (82 km) hiking route that allows you to really get a feel for the wild taiga forests.

Trail through the tundra: one for adventurous hikers

KUNGSLEDEN

Sweden's Kungsleden, or King's Trail, is not one for the faint of heart. This month-long, 270-mile (440 km) hike is one of the great wilderness walks of Europe. With much of the route passing through only sparingly inhabited Arctic tundra, you'll likely see considerably more reindeer than other humans.

West Highland Way

Get a sweeping overview of the Highlands on Scotland's original long-distance trail.

The chances are you'll get wet; you'll almost certainly shiver with cold; and there's a very high possibility that there will be times when the rain and the cloud will enfold the land so completely that you won't be able to see much beyond the end of your hiking poles. But yet, despite or perhaps because of all this, there's something intrinsically romantic about hiking Scotland's West Highland Way.

Perhaps it's those moments when the sun does shine—whether it's light filtering through to the floor of a springtime woodland full of bluebells, or a break in storm clouds that allows a single strong beam to cast yellow light across weather-stained moorlands. Whatever it is, the movement of the light here is always unexpected and magical. Or maybe it's those moments when you couldn't be anywhere else but Scotland: with the moorlands aflame with purple heather, the shaggy haired Highland cattle staring at passing hikers, that time when you walk into a town and there in front of you is a man in a kilt, the welcome warmth of a bar, the bark of a red deer at dawn, the smell of whisky, or the full fried breakfast in an old-fashioned B and B. Together, all these things help to make the West Highland Way, Scotland's original long-distance trail, its most diverse and rewarding.

LEFT Loch Leven, Kinlochleven, and the West Highland Way during winter.

The Route

This epic path gets its tartan on in Milngavie, which is today a northern suburb of Glasgow. Tramping north across the heart of wilderness Scotland, the route takes in the full array of Scottish landscapes. Things start tamely enough with rural farming scenes aplenty; hikers then skim down the side of Loch Lomond before climbing stiffly into the powerful Highland wilds, over the ghostly Rannoch Moor, and then, having passed by beautiful Loch Leven and Glen Nevis, the trail ends in the likable town of Fort William, where a warm pub should be your first port of call.

Throughout, the trail is well marked and nicely divided into daily sections of 9 to 15 miles (14–24 km), with a choice of hostels, camping, or B and Bs at the end of each day. For the most part the trail keeps off the hilltops, which means that there's rarely more than 1,640-foot (500 m) elevation gain and loss per day and this helps to make this a good challenge for a first-time long-distance trail.

3 GLEN NEVIS

Created by the actions of ancient glaciers, this is Scotland at its most beautiful. The River Nevis runs excitedly down the glen as a series of small waterfalls and rapids cascading into deep rock pools. The whole setting seems designed for taking your time and enjoying the gentle amble down.

4 A DRAM OF WHISKY

Think of this as your reward for completing another long, hard, and possibly cold day on the trail. Enter the village pub and settle down by a roaring log fire to savor the dark, dignified, and oh-so-warming taste of a quality local whisky.

1 FALLS OF FALLOCH

A short detour off the main route between Inverarnan and Tyndrum will bring you to the Falloch Falls: a beautiful 33-foot-high (10 m) sheet of water that's the most impressive waterfall on the route. If you're lucky you might see kayakers plunging over the falls.

2 DEVIL'S STAIRCASE

Don't let the rather sinister name make you quake in your hiking boots. Clambering up the steep, zigzagging trail of this former eighteenth-century military road (named the Devil's Staircase by the soldiers who built it) to gaze out across Rannoch Moor and Glen Coe is a scenic highlight for most West Highland Way hikers.

5 BEN NEVIS

When you set out on the West Highland Way you had no intention of climbing Ben Nevis, but then, as you near the end of the trek, the UK's highest peak rises into view. At 4,411 feet (1,345 m), it's hardly Himalayan, but with a mere fourteen clear days a year on average at the summit and famously vicious weather, this is still no walk in the park. By now you'll be walk fit, and if the weather shines, then it would be hard to resist the lure of finishing the West Highland Way on the summit of Britain. Allow seven to nine hours to get to the summit and back down again.

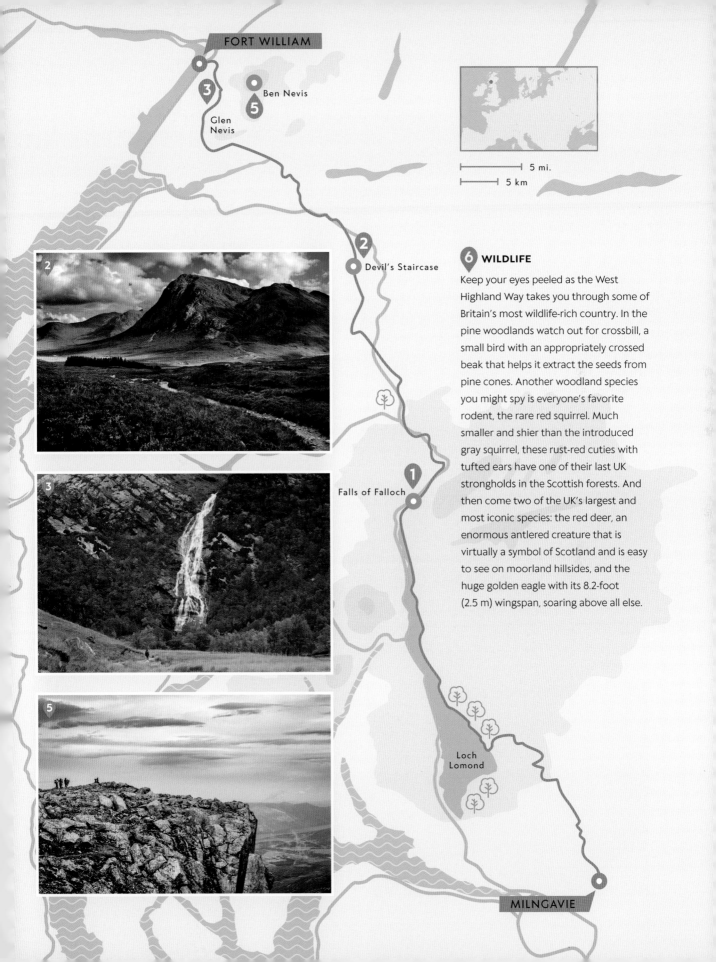

FORT WILLIAM

Ben Nevis

3 Glen Nevis

5

5 mi.

5 km

2 Devil's Staircase

6 **WILDLIFE**

Keep your eyes peeled as the West
Highland Way takes you through some of
Britain's most wildlife-rich country. In the
pine woodlands watch out for crossbill, a
small bird with an appropriately crossed
beak that helps it extract the seeds from
pine cones. Another woodland species
you might spy is everyone's favorite
rodent, the rare red squirrel. Much
smaller and shier than the introduced
gray squirrel, these rust-red cuties with
tufted ears have one of their last UK
strongholds in the Scottish forests. And
then come two of the UK's largest and
most iconic species: the red deer, an
enormous antlered creature that is
virtually a symbol of Scotland and is easy
to see on moorland hillsides, and the
huge golden eagle with its 8.2-foot
(2.5 m) wingspan, soaring above all else.

1 Falls of Falloch

Loch
Lomond

MILNGAVIE

Walk here next

Scotland is a truly addictive place to hike, and one long-distance Scottish trail is never enough. Once the last of the whisky is drained out of the West Highland Way, follow up with these routes.

March northward along an easy Highland route

THE GREAT GLEN WAY

Fort William might mark the end of the West Highland Way, but it's also the start of the Great Glen Way, and many people choose to continue the northward march on this 75-mile (121 km), six-day hike straight across Scotland to finish in Inverness. Along the way the path runs alongside multiple lochs including Loch Ness, where, if you look very carefully, you might spot a monster!

Trek past stormy seas and rugged mountains

THE SKYE TRAIL

For a coastal view of Scotland, what could be better than the Skye Trail, which traverses the Isle of Skye, an island of mythical beauty? But this incredible weeklong, 80-mile (128 km) hike is not one for first-time hikers, because it is unmarked and famously tough. You need navigational skills and a lot of self-reliance. However, the rewards are worth it, with endlessly changing views of angry seascapes and sweeping mountain vistas. There's nothing else like it in Scotland.

The Coast to Coast Trail

LOCATION
Northern England, UK

DURATION
15–18 days

DIFFICULTY
Moderate

DISTANCE
192 miles (308 km)

MAP
Ordnance Survey Explorer
Series (9 maps)

START/END
Saint Bees/Robin Hood's Bay

TRAIL MARKING
Varied (signs, cairns)

Wander in the footsteps of literary greats along this epic cross-country trail.

Walking England's epic Coast to Coast Trail is not just a journey through the best scenery northern England has to offer. And it's not just a seriously inspiring challenge that will provide tales of adventure for years to come. It's also a journey through English literary history. The hills and dales of this corner of the British Isles inspired the prose of nineteenth-century poet laureate William Wordsworth when he jotted down the eternal words, "I wandered lonely as a cloud." And if it weren't for the gentle charms of the Lake District—through which this trail wends—then perhaps Beatrix Potter would never have conjured up Peter Rabbit, Jemima Puddle-Duck, and all those other childhood favorites.

Meanwhile, farther east along the trail, it was the Yorkshire Dales that inspired the James Herriot books about life as a farm veterinarian, and even Bram Stoker found his vision for Dracula among the region's mist-hidden winter hilltops. But if there's one literary figure we can thank for the Coast to Coast Trail, it's Alfred Wainwright. Not officially a novelist or a poet, Wainwright was a keen hill walker and a prolific writer of hiking guidebooks. It was Wainwright's passion for the trails that lace through the Lake District and Yorkshire that led to him creating the Coast to Coast Trail and writing the very first guidebook to the route. In fact, so important was Wainwright to the trail that the Coast to Coast is often known as Wainwright's Coast to Coast Trail.

LEFT Looking down onto Grasmere from the Coast to Coast Trail.

The Route

As the name suggests, this trail spans the width of northern England. Although you can walk it in either direction, most people walk from west to east, the reason being that when the area's notoriously bad weather hits (and it almost certainly will, even in high summer), you will be walking with your back to the rain. For most people then, the walk begins from the russet sands and cliffs of Saint Bees, a small coastal village facing the Irish Sea. After a day or two of gentle meandering away from the coastal lowlands, you reach the Lake District. One of England's most beloved landscapes, this is scenically the most impressive part of the walk with the trail hauling up and down numerous mountain ridges, skipping along lake shores, and pausing in some of the most picturesque villages in the country. After several strenuous but rewarding days, the landscape suddenly changes as you enter the North York Moors National Park. Here the hills are rounded, and wind and drizzle streaks over haunted moorlands. Then, subtly, the land mellows, and the trail wends along valley floors checked with fields grazed by countless sheep and dotted with occasional villages. And then, before you know it, the land tilts downward and the North Sea tantalizes as you stride into the seaside village of Robin Hood's Bay.

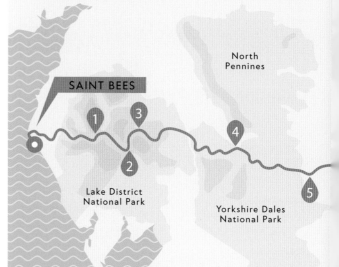

SAINT BEES

North Pennines

Lake District National Park

Yorkshire Dales National Park

Peak District

25 mi.

25 km

ROBIN HOOD'S BAY

North York Moors
National Park

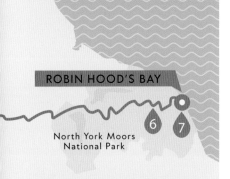

Patterdale trail offers the finest views and most variety, and this is especially the case if you take the alternative Saint Sunday Route, which takes you to a lofty vantage point (2,759 feet; 841 m) for views across half the Lake District.

4 NINE STANDARDS

The Nine Standards are great piles of stones standing like oversize walkers' cairns on the top of the bleak Pennines moorlands. We'd be lying if we called it a beautiful spot—and most days the weather is so bad you can't see much anyway —but it's certainly a desolate, cold, and mysterious place. Careful navigation is needed around here.

5 RICHMOND

Located almost exactly halfway along the Coast to Coast route, the thousand-year-old market town of Richmond is one of the urban highlights of northern England. The town centers on the ruins of its Norman castle, while the nearby Georgian Theatre Royal is the oldest (and certainly one of the most beautiful) working theaters in the British Isles.

6 LITTLEBECK WOOD

There's an unexpected final surprise close to the end of the walk. The 65-acre (26 ha) Littlebeck Wood is crowded with grand old oak trees, and in spring the forest floor turns a fairy blue as thousands of bluebells burst into flower.

7 ROBIN HOOD'S BAY

Tucked into a small coastal nook, Robin Hood's Bay couldn't be a nicer place to finish the Coast to Coast walk. On arrival, don't forget to sign the accomplishment book in the Wainwright's Bar at the Bay Hotel pub, then walk to the sea, dip your feet into the icy water, and treat yourself to an ice cream or fish and chips.

1 BORROWDALE VALLEY

Longthwaite, Rosthwaite, and Stonethwaite: with their slate roofed cottages and spring flowers in the gardens, a stout little church, and superb country pubs, these three tiny villages in the Lake District's Borrowdale Valley fulfill every English village cliché.

2 GRASMERE

Grasmere's most famous former resident, William Wordsworth, found the surrounding countryside so inspiring that he once described it as "the loveliest spot that man hath ever found." Visit Dove Cottage, Wordsworth's former home (now a museum), pay your respects at his grave next to the village church, and stop to buy a treat at the renowned Gingerbread Shop.

3 GRASMERE TO PATTERDALE VIA THE SAINT SUNDAY ROUTE

Deciding which is the best single stage of the Coast to Coast Trail is a surefire way of starting a debate, but our blistered feet reckon that the Grasmere to

Walk here next

Hiking in the United Kingdom is an enticing mix of barren moorland and soaring hills, idyllic villages and country pubs full of character. Sweep across the UK on one of these trails.

A fair path in the footsteps of Roman soldiers

HADRIAN'S WALL PATH

Following what's left of Hadrian's Wall, a defensive wall built by the Romans in 122 CE that marked the boundary between Roman Britannia (England) and unconquered Caledonia (Scotland), this 84-mile (135 km), six- to eight-day trek crosses the width of England in the form of one giant history lesson. With good facilities and fairly flat walking, this is an ideal first-timer multiday trek.

A riverside ramble

THAMES PATH

See London from a different perspective by strolling this 184-mile (296 km) trail from Kemble in Gloucestershire, close to the source of the River Thames, to Charlton in the southeast of the English capital. Taking some two weeks, the trail follows old towpaths for long stretches. Although the river, and the trail, slice right through the heart of London, the surprise for most is how much of the trail is out in quiet riverside country.

Bravehearts only: a marathon Highland trek

SCOTTISH NATIONAL TRAIL

Few people would doubt that the Scottish National Trail is the toughest trek in the UK and one of the toughest in Europe. Starting on the southeastern border of Scotland, the trail runs right up to the far northwest and on the way this 536-mile (864 km), forty-day marathon sweeps through the best of Scotland's magnificent mountain scenery.

Besseggen Ridge

Tiptoe along a knife-sharp ridge while hiking Norway's most famous trail.

LOCATION
Jotunheimen National
Park, Norway

DURATION
6–7 hours

DIFFICULTY
Moderate

DISTANCE
8.5 miles (14 km)

MAP
Jotunheimen Aust 1:50,000
Nordeca (Map 2503)

START/END
Memurubu/Gjendesheim

TRAIL MARKING
Red T waymarks

They say that Norse gods and giant trolls (or, as the Norwegians call them, *jötnar*) live in the rugged high country that makes up much of what is today central Norway. These huge mountain peaks, with summits weighed down under the crush of glaciers and snow, are exactly the kind of places where trolls and gods can safely hide away. So numerous are the trolls that when humans started exploring this wild region, and then created a national park here, they named it after the trolls.

Stuffed full of rivers, lakes, waterfalls, valleys, vast stretches of Arctic tundra, and the highest mountains in northern Europe, Jotunheimen National Park is Norway's showpiece protected area, which, in a country as endlessly beautiful as Norway, is quite a claim. And although trolls aren't sighted all that often anymore, rumors and stories do still circulate that there are certain magical parts of this mountain realm where strange beings are sometimes glimpsed.

The Besseggen Ridge, Norway's most popular mountain walk (with some sixty thousand people hiking it between June and mid-September, some might say that it's too popular) is certainly magical. As you creep carefully up the knife ridge of rock that leads to the hike's highest point (5,361 feet; 1,634 m), take a second to pause and look at the view around you. With a mysterious, dark lake just to your left and, far below you to the right, another even larger, turquoise-colored lake that stretches toward further ridges and rises, it's a view that seems to have been lifted straight out of a Norse myth.

LEFT Besseggen Ridge seen from the east with views over Lakes Gjende and Bessvatnet.

The Route

There are various approach routes to this trail. Most people leave their cars in the (pay) parking lot on the edge of Gjendesheim. A short boat ride will take you to the trailhead at the Norwegian Trekking Association (DNT) hut in Memurubu. The route then climbs hard uphill for longer than most people would like. Eventually though, the trail levels out a bit and the views open up as you move toward the ridge itself. At times, the climb up the ridge might require the use of hands and you'll need a bit of a head for heights. At the end of the 0.6-mile-long (1 km) ridge is the summit of Veslfjellnet (5,361 feet; 1,634 m), a rounded dome with super views. From here it's a long, winding, though not especially steep, downhill all the way back to Gjendesheim. You can also do this walk in reverse, but you run the risk of missing the last ferry back along the lake to the car.

 THE RIDGE WALK

The crux of the hike is the actual Besseggen Ridge, also known as the Strip. This sharp spine of rock, which climbs around 820 feet (250 m) to the rounded stone summit of Veslfjellnet (5,361 feet; 1,634 m), is around 0.6 miles (1 km) long and every step of it is a thrill as the land falls away hard on either side of you to the lakes far below. Although it looks daunting—and even dangerous— it's not quite as steep as it appears in photos, and even families do the ridge walk. That said, the ridge is very exposed to wind, and it would be risky to do it in wet or icy weather. Once safely up on the summit you can relax and take in astounding views over a huge swath of central Norway's most spectacular high country.

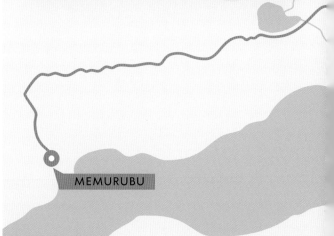

MEMURUBU

2 THE LAKES

Throughout central Norway it can seem as if lakes outnumber dry land, and the countryside passed on this walk is no exception. You will hike past a number of small lakes and pools, but it's the two biggest, the inky dark Bessvatnet, which is raised up on a high rock table, and huge Lake Gjende, a long finger of water the color of neon blue toothpaste, that are the real showstoppers.

3 FERRY RIDE

One of the unexpected highlights of this hike is the passenger ferry ride to the trailhead (or end, depending which way around you do this walk) along half the length of Lake Gjende. As you gently putter along the silk-smooth waters, look out for secluded farmhouses built at the base of steep cliffs rising hundreds of yards out of the lake waters.

4 DNT LODGES

There are two DNT hikers' lodges—Gjendesheim and Memurubu—at either end of the walk. Both are warm, cozy wooden buildings where hot drinks, snacks, and meals can be bought (and beds are available), making them ideal places to wrap your hands around a hot drink and celebrate your achievement.

5 MIDNIGHT SUN

In late June and early July, the sun this far north barely sets, and it never really gets properly dark. While we don't suggest climbing the ridge in the middle of the night (this could be dangerous), we do recommend the magical experience of sitting quietly on the shores of Lake Gjende watching the midnight twilight blues merge with the turquoise of the lake. Just remember to keep a watchful eye out for trolls!

LAKE BESSVATNET

Lake Gjende viewpoint

Besseggen Ridge

Veslfjellnet

GJENDESHEIM

LAKE GJENDE

1 mi.

1 km

Walk here next

When it comes to hikes with a tinge of vertigo, Norway has plenty to choose from. Fortunately, the stunning scenery is normally enough to stop you dwelling too much on the airy drop.

Tread on the troll's tongue

TROLLTUNGA HIKE

Standing on the tip of the Trolltunga ("troll's tongue") is like standing on a naturally formed diving board above the shiny blue waters, except that this "diving board" is a narrow rock outcrop hanging vertically 2,297 feet (700 m) above the waters of Lake Ringedalsvatnet. If you're brave enough to edge your way out onto it—and fatalities have occurred, so be careful—then the sensation of apparently being suspended in the air is something few other hikes can offer. The 14-mile (23 km), eight-hour round-trip hike begins from Skjeggedal.

Hike to a spectacular viewing point

PREIKESTOLEN

One of the signature images of Norway is that of brave souls standing on the sheer-sided shelf of rock known as Preikestolen (Pulpit Rock), a dizzying 1,982 feet (604 m) above the cool blue Lysefjord. The hike begins from the Preikestolen Mountain Lodge and is a gentle 3.7-mile (6 km) half-day return. Be warned that the combination of a short, easy route and stunning views mean this is a very popular hike. Try to avoid high summer.

Take a short, steep hike for panoramic views

SEGLA

Above the Arctic Circle, Senja Island is a jagged range of shark teeth rising up out of the frigid Arctic waters. At 2,096 feet (639 m), Segla, which means "sail," is the biggest of these. The 3.5-mile (5.5 km), steep half-day climb through stumpy dwarf forest and across Arctic bogs is the new "must do" day hike of Norway.

Camino de Santiago

LOCATION
Northern Spain

DURATION
30–35 days

DIFFICULTY
Moderate

DISTANCE
490 miles (790 km)

MAP
Village to Village Map Guide: Camino de Santiago Maps

START/END
Saint-Jean-de-Port/Santiago de Compostela

TRAIL MARKING
Blue with stylized yellow scallop shell

Walk with the ghosts of Camino past on this world-famous pilgrimage route.

During the ninth century, while staring up at the dark night sky, Pelayo, a Catholic hermit in northern Spain, saw one single star shining with unusual intensity. Intrigued, he followed the star, which led him to a forgotten tomb. Opening it up, Pelayo discovered the remains of none other than Saint James the Great (Santiago in Spanish). News of the discovery spread. The pope endorsed it, the first pilgrims came, and a small church was built atop the tomb. More pilgrims came, a town grew up around the church, the church became a cathedral, the town became a city, and ever more pilgrims came on foot from all four corners of Europe. The Camino de Santiago was born.

Fast-forward a thousand years and the Camino is more popular today than it has ever been. Pilgrims come from all over the world and just as before they come on foot, following the 490-mile (790 km) route from the French-Spanish border, across the hills, plains, and mountains of northern Spain. Pausing at stone chapels, sleeping in simple pilgrim rest houses, and eating in highway inns, each has come for their own personal reason, but each is drawn onward by a common goal.

This monthlong hike is the world's most popular pilgrimage route, but above that it's simply a wonderful excuse for a fabulous slow hike across the breadth of northern Spain.

LEFT Backpacking along the Camino de Santiago to the village of El Acebo.

The Route

The first thing you need to know about the Camino de Santiago is that it's not one particular route. There are many different caminos, which all start from different parts of Europe and point, arrowlike, at the city of Santiago de Compostela in northwest Spain. The principal route, the Camino Francés, runs from the small French Basque town of Saint-Jean-Pied-de-Port, goes over the Pyrenees, and then marches west across fields of wheat, past little stone villages, and alongside vineyards and olive groves to arrive at the green, rain-drenched hills of Galicia in the far west of Spain.

Each daily stage is around 15.5 miles (25 km) and for the most part is undulating rather than hard up and down. There are plentiful pilgrim-dedicated accommodations throughout, and the trail marking could not be any clearer and easier to follow. Most pilgrims head out in summer, which guarantees dry weather, but the heat will be intense. Opt for May to June or September to October if you can.

THE ATLANTIC

Cabo Fisterra

SANTIAGO DE COMPOSTELA

25 mi.
25 km

1 MEDIEVAL CHURCHES AND MONASTERIES

Whether it be the mighty cathedrals of Burgos or León, or one of a hundred small town churches or remote monastery complexes, one thing quickly becomes clear on the camino: the lines of passing pilgrims brought extraordinary wealth to otherwise out-of-the-way rural communities (although much of that wealth stayed in the hands of the church rather than the villagers). Almost every religious building along the way is a repository of religious treasures, art, and artifacts, and seeing them and learning the stories behind them is a real highlight.

2 SANTIAGO DE COMPOSTELA

It's a fitting culmination to an epic pilgrimage. The thousand-year-old cathedral of Santiago de Compostela awes with its grandeur, tradition, ceremony, and pomp. At its heart is the tomb of Santiago, and close by is an eight-hundred-year-old statue of the

BAY OF BISCAY

FRANCE

SAINT-JEAN-PIED-DE-PORT

THE PYRENEES

León

Burgos

SPAIN

saint that pilgrims must approach to kiss or embrace. It's a symbolic moment because it indicates that at that instant your pilgrimage is over.

③ THE PYRENEES

If you've started—as most people do—in Saint-Jean-Pied-de-Port in France, then one of the most challenging, and scenically impressive, sections of the camino comes up straightaway: the climb up, over, and back down the sublime Pyrenees. You'll go through thick, tangled beech forest, open highland pastures, over a low pass, and then drop down past the ancient monastery complex of Roncesvalles.

④ CAMARADERIE

Everyone walking the camino is doing it for their own personal reasons, but you are all united on a single mission: to get to the cathedral in Santiago de Compostela. You will meet a cross section of people from around the world. With some you will have no common language; others might be the kind of people you would never normally mingle with in your life back home. But here, westward bound on the back roads of Spain, you will become fast friends.

⑤ THE END OF THE WORLD

For some, reaching the cathedral of Santiago de Compostela can be a deflating moment. The adventure is over and a return to their old life is imminent. But it doesn't have to be that way. Continue walking west for another three to four days to reach the end of the known world: Cabo Fisterra (Cape Finisterre). This blustery headland has had spiritual significance since Neolithic times, and for many the cliffs here are the real spiritual end of the camino.

⑥ REFLECTION

Walking through peaceful countryside for hour after hour, day after day, produces a meditative state of mind and allows you to think clearly. Perhaps it's for this reason that so many people walk the Camino de Santiago when their life reaches a significant junction. And afterward many say that whatever was vexing them was cured on the camino.

Walk here next

You could say that all roads lead to Santiago de Compostela. Traditionally, the idea was to just step out of your house and start walking, and this means that there are many other caminos leading to the great cathedral of Santiago de Compostela. Try the following for a different camino perspective.

Follow the coastal route in northern Spain

CAMINO DEL NORTE

Running right along the north coast of Spain, the Camino del Norte is, arguably, the most beautiful of the different trails to Santiago. Most people begin in either the French Basque town of Bayonne or the Spanish Basque seaside resort of San Sebastián. It's then a solid month of hiking 514 miles (828 km) up and down coastal cliffs, along wave-splashed beaches, past hardy fishing villages, and through big coastal towns.

Hike via Portugal for coastal views and scenic countryside

CAMINO PORTUGUÉS

As the name suggests, the Camino Portugués kicks off in the Portuguese capital, Lisbon (although many people begin in Porto in the north of Portugal) and bends inland to pass the important Catholic pilgrimage center of Fátima before hitting the coast in Porto and then wending through southern Galicia. This 385-mile (620 km) route is the second most popular of the caminos.

Take a challenging route through the mountains

CAMINO PRIMITIVO

This, the original route, is a 199-mile (321 km) romp through the stunning mountains of Asturias. The trail begins in the city of Oviedo but after that sticks mostly to rural areas and rewards with superb mountain vistas. It's probably the wildest of the different routes but is also a tough prospect due to all the up and down hiking.

Through the Spanish Pyrenees

LOCATION
GR11, Pyrenees, Spain

DURATION
45 days

DIFFICULTY
Hard

DISTANCE
522 miles (840 km)

MAP
Editorial Alpina GR11 Pyrenean (Trans Pyrenees) 1:50,000 set of 21 maps. No single printed map exists.

START/END
Irun/Cap de Creus

TRAIL MARKING
Red and white waymarks

LEFT Hiking through the Ordesa Gorge toward Monte Perdido on the GR11 trail in the Spanish Pyrenees.

An epic coast-to-coast hike through mountains of mythical beauty.

A mountain range as blessed in beauty as the Pyrenees cannot possibly have been created by dull old geological forces: mountains this gorgeous must have a mythical touch to them. And indeed, the Pyrenees, which straddle the Spanish–French border, do. Long ago, the story goes, the area where the Pyrenees now stand was a flat plain where a powerful king ruled. His daughter, Pyrene, caught the eye of passing Greek demigod Hercules. Pyrene's father disapproved of the relationship (why is not made clear), so when Pyrene fell pregnant, she hid deep in the forest. While there she was attacked by a giant bear. Hercules heard her screaming and came running to her rescue, but he was too late. Hercules buried his love under a giant monument of stones that he made so high that they became a mountain range to match the beauty of Pyrene.

Whether you believe this story or not, as you hike for six weeks along the GR11 trans-Pyrenean route, one thing is certain: the Pyrenees really do live up to the myth of their formation. Although considerably less known internationally than the Alps, the Pyrenees offer such diversity in a small area that, like Hercules, most hikers fall instantly for the charms of Pyrene. In the space of just a few walking hours you can go from flower meadows to beech forests, a sprinkling of jewellike lakes, glaciers, sheep pastures, waterfalls, and canyons to the barren rock of the high peaks.

The Route

This is one of those truly epic trails that has a clearly defined start point (the Atlantic Ocean) and end point (the Mediterranean). Getting from one to the other, along the 497-mile (840 km) trail, promises to be one heck of an adventure. Despite the somewhat daunting statistics, this is a reasonably popular trail, is well marked, and has a good array of accommodations in the form of mountain lodges up high (campers can also eat at these lodges), and hostels and guesthouses in the valleys. Even so, you should be prepared and walk fit. It's said that the GR11 takes forty-five days, but you'd be well advised to set aside two months so as to allow for rest days due to bad weather and so that you can profit from the many, many superb side trips. The best—in fact, only— time you can reliably do this hike is mid-June to early/mid-October.

❶ ORDESA AND MONTE PERDIDO

A huge glacial gash in the surface of the Earth, the mighty Ordesa Canyon is the Pyrenees at its most spectacular. The GR11 runs up the middle of the 7-mile-long (11 km) canyon, which ends at the headwalls of the iconic Monte Perdido ("lost mountain"—a name it well deserves as it plays peekaboo with the clouds for so much of the time) before crossing a Tibetan-like tableland beyond and then falling fast down into the almost equally impressive Pineta Valley. Try to allow for a few rest days here and spend them exploring the high cliffside paths known as *fajas* or the other canyons spiraling out of the flanks of Monte Perdido.

❷ FALL BEECH FORESTS

Throughout much of the Pyrenees—the western half in particular—the lower mountain slopes are comprised of a thick beech forest. Beautifully green in spring and summer, they come into their own in October when whole mountainsides turn a flaming red and orange. Especially good sections of beech forest for the fall light show are to be found around Iraty, the Valle de Tena, and Valle de Bujaruelo.

IRUN

Iraty

Valle de Tena

15 mi.
20 km

3 LAKES, GLORIOUS LAKES

Once you're away from the coastal regions and up in the mountains proper, it would be a rare day indeed that the trail doesn't take you past a lake or three. It's estimated that there are somewhere in the range of 2,500 lakes scattered throughout the mountains. Some are huge, silky smooth expanses of blue in the lower valleys, others are envious green affairs set in wildflower meadows, while still others are iced over and tucked into scree and rock dead ends. Perhaps the richest area for lakes is in and around the Parque Nacional Aigüestortes i Estany de Sant Maurici, where you will fast lose count of all the liquid jewels.

4 WILDLIFE

While wildlife populations are crashing in so many parts of the world, the Pyrenees are a rare exception, with almost all the populations of large mammals and birds increasing over the past couple of decades. You're guaranteed to see marmots, griffon vultures, and chamois (called izard or *sarrio* here), and there's a better than average chance of golden eagles, bearded vultures, ibex, and mouflon. Deer (red and roe) and wild boar are very common, but also shy. And then there's the toothy boys: wolves and brown bears. The wolf population remains very low but is increasing, while the brown bear population is now a fairly healthy seventy and increasing quite fast.

5 BASQUE AND CATALAN CULTURE

You might be walking through Spain, but that doesn't mean that you're only in Spain. The Pyrenees are bookended by the Basques in the west and the Catalans in the east, and both groups of people are very proud of their culture and their homeland. Expect to hear people talking in Basque or Catalan at each end of the Pyrenees. If you're lucky, you'll come across a village festival when Basque or Catalan culture and tradition is really on display.

Valle de Bujaruelo

Monte Perdido

Ordesa Canyon

Parque Nacional Aigüestortes i Estany de Sant Maurici

SPAIN

ANDORRA

FRANCE

CAP DE CREUS

Walk here next

The GR11 isn't the only trek that takes hikers clean across an entire mountain range. Completing the following will also give you a great sense of achievement.

Hike on the greener side
GR10, TRANS-PYRENEES

After you've crossed the Spanish Pyrenees on the GR11, spin right around and hike back again along the French side of the range on the GR10. As only a thin frontier ridge separates the two trails you might expect a lot of similarities, but how wrong you'd be. The French side is notably greener and home to a different range of plants and animals, and the mountains themselves rise up off the plains much more abruptly. It's like a different mountain range altogether.

Tackle tough terrain

GR20

The GR20, which runs across the jagged spine of the French Mediterranean island of Corsica, has a well-earned reputation for being one of the toughest multiday hiking trails in France. It's said that more than half of the people who set out on the trek give up! Hard it might be, but the unusual shaped peaks and rock sculptures, wet meadows, and ancient woodlands mean this is also a very beautiful hike for those who are tough enough to finish it.

Follow a route of historical significance

RUTA DE LA RECONQUISTA, PICOS DE EUROPA

Rising with sudden drama off the Cantabrian coastline, the Picos de Europa are one of the most beautiful mountain ranges in western Europe. A compact range, the Ruta de la Reconquista, which loosely follows the path taken by retreating Muslims during the Christian reconquest of Spain, crosses straight over the most beautiful parts of the range in three tough days.

Tour du Mont Blanc

LOCATION
Alps, France, Italy, Switzerland

DURATION
11 days

DIFFICULTY
Moderate

DISTANCE
106 miles (170 km)

MAP
Tour du Mont Blanc
1:50,000 IGN

START/END
Chamonix

TRAIL MARKING
Red and white waymarks

LEFT The Tour du Mont Blanc, seen during the summer from the French side of the Alps.

Make a triumphant circuit around western Europe's highest mountain.

The world-renowned Tour du Mont Blanc is a 106-mile (170 km), circular hike around the highest mountain in western Europe. Along the way, the lucky hiker will pass through some of the finest mountain scenery in the Alps, and crisscross over the borders of three different countries (France, Italy, and Switzerland). With statistics like this, it's hardly a surprise to learn that the Tour du Mont Blanc is one of the most popular long-distance trails in Europe.

But there's more to this hike than just soul-inspiring visuals. The Tour du Mont Blanc is a trek into the very birth of Alpinism and pleasure hiking. Right up until the late eighteenth century, the high places of the world were generally considered to be the home of evil spirits and dangerous creatures, and nobody in their right mind went anywhere near the summits of the big peaks. But in the summer of 1786 two Frenchmen, Jacques Balmat and Michel-Gabriel Paccard, set out to climb the northern face of Mont Blanc. Their successful summit attempt has often been described as the birth of modern Alpinism and led to a wave of alpine climbing expeditions in the eighteenth and nineteenth centuries. Meanwhile, newspaper stories about the exploits of climbers led to an increase in the number of lesser mortals visiting the Alps to merely hike through the valleys and soak up the views. And so, as you stride the paths that make up the Tour du Mont Blanc, take a moment to reflect on the bravery of men like Balmat and Paccard, without whom modern hiking and climbing might look very different.

The Route

The vast majority of hikers start the Tour du Mont Blanc from Les Houches near the large ski resort and town of Chamonix in France, although there's nothing to stop you from starting from any town anywhere along the route. From Les Houches, the circular trail is normally walked in a counterclockwise direction broken down into eleven stages, with accommodations in the form of staffed mountain refuges or guesthouses at the end of each day. During the course of circumnavigating the Mont Blanc massif, you will stride through alpine corners of three nations (France, Italy, and Switzerland), reaching a height of 8,710 feet (2,665 m) at the Col des Fours in France and again at the Fenêtre d'Arpette in Switzerland. As one of the most popular long-distance trails in Europe, the route marking is impeccable and the trail very clear. But these aren't always just stony mountain trails. At one point you will stride like one of Caesar's legionaries along a two-thousand-year-old paved Roman road!

 **MONT BLANC**

This one is an obvious highlight. Mont Blanc, which at 15,774 feet (4,808 m) is the highest mountain in western Europe, is the very reason you're here at all and staring across the valley at it from Le Grand Balcon is the indisputable visual highlight of the peak. This natural grandstand comes right at the end of the trek and is one of the only places where you get a full sweep view over the massif. What a finish!

② COL DE LA CROIX DU BONHOMME

Every day on the Tour du Mont Blanc has moments of sublime beauty, but descending from the Col de la Croix du Bonhomme (7,900 feet; 2,408 m), with a view over weathered ridges, sheep pastures, and, rearing up behind, the glaciers of Mont Blanc, is one moment you'll remember long after the trekking has come to an end. Savor the moment a little longer by staying the night at the refuge just below the pass.

③ ALL THE REST

While the focus of the hike is on Mont Blanc, this isn't a one-hit wonder trek and you'll soak up views of numerous other mountains, many of which are considerably more graceful than the Blanc bulk. There's Aiguille Vert (15,424 feet; 4,122 m), the Grandes Jorasses (13,806 feet; 4,208 m), and the unforgettable Aiguilles de Chamonix (11,424 feet; 3,482 m), a raft of needle peaks rising up above Chamonix.

④ FOOD, GLORIOUS FOOD

You'll be walking through both Italy and France: of course the food will be good. Hot meals are available in all the mountain refuges; expect simple but supremely tasty (isn't everything after a day on the trail?) mountain food rich in cheese, meat, and potatoes, or perhaps pasta and pizzas in the Italian section of the trail. Also, look out for shepherds selling local cheeses such as Reblochon.

⑤ VILLAGES AND MEADOWS

This is the Alps: the land of Heidi and *The Sound of Music*. So, while the hills may not be actually be alive with the sound of music, you'll certainly get that sense as you skip like Heidi through alpine flower meadows and stroll through villages with wooden balconies covered in deep-red geraniums.

⑥ LUXURY TREKKING

Eleven hard days on the mountain sleeping in refuge dorms or in a tent not really you? Use the services of a trekking company and you can enjoy a shorter five-day highlights version of the Tour du Mont Blanc, which for the most part can be done in luxury with nights spent on the valley floors in comfortable guesthouses with a choice of places to eat. You won't even have to carry your baggage, as all but the gear you might need for the day is transferred by vehicle to the next hotel.

FRANCE

Fenêtre d'Arpette

5 mi.

5 km

SWITZERLAND

CHAMONIX

Le Grand Balcon

③

③

Aiguilles de Chamonix

Grandes Jorasses

① Mont Blanc

ITALY

Col de la Croix du Bonhomme

Col des Fours

②

Walk here next

While the Tour du Mont Blanc crisscrosses three European borders, there are many other nation-hopping hikes in Europe. Pack your passport for these historical multination hikes.

Hike through history along the trench lines

THE WESTERN FRONT WAY

This 621-mile (1,000 km) hiking trail follows the length of the World War I trench lines from Pfetterhouse on the Swiss-French border to Nieuwpoort in Belgium. Although the hiking trail is a new creation, the idea for it actually occurred during World War I when Second Lieutenant Alexander Douglas Gillespie wrote, in a letter from the front line, how he would one day like to see a hiking trail established that would allow people to "learn what war means from the silent witnesses on either side."

Follow a border path

OFFA'S DYKE PATH

Crisscrossing the English-Welsh border, the Offa's Dyke Path is a 177-mile (285 km) path that follows an eighth-century earthen dyke constructed by King Offa to protect his kingdom of Mercia (which would today fall in England) from invasion by the Welsh.

Trek through the Baltic states

BALTIC FOREST WAY

Starting in Lazdijai, on the Polish–Lithuanian border, and running for a staggering 1,330 miles (2,141 km) to Tallinn in Estonia, this epic trail through three Baltic nations focuses on the great conifer forests of the Baltics, but it also includes deep valleys, pretty farming villages, and vast lakes. If you can't manage the full three months required to hike all the route, it can be broken down into handy bite-size portions.

Alta Via I, Italian Dolomites

LOCATION
Dolomites, Italy

DURATION
8–10 days

DIFFICULTY
Moderate

DISTANCE
75 miles (120 km)

MAP
Tabacco, Dolomites Alta Via I, 1:25,000 Map 031, 03 & 025

START/END
Lago di Braies/Belluno

TRAIL MARKING
Red and white waymarks

Mix stirring scenic views and incredible sunsets with a painful human history.

For a long time the Italian Dolomites lived somewhat in the shadow of the Alps (technically the Dolomites are a part of the Alps but most people refer to them separately) as far as walkers were concerned. Now though we've realized our mistake and, thanks to the extraordinary shaped pillars of rock, plunging cliffs, and deep green valleys dotted with lakes, the Dolomites have since become one of Europe's premier hiking regions. Of all the long-distance footpaths across the range the Alta Via I is the hike of choice. It's a ten-day extravaganza that showcases the range at its best.

The Alta Via I isn't just a good-looking trail, though: it's also an educational trail. Hard though it might be to believe, during World War I much of the area through which the Alta Via I passes was a high-altitude battleground between the Italian and Austro-Hungarian forces. It was during this period that the area's famed *via ferratas* and tunnels were installed as a way of enabling troops to move quickly around the terrain. The route will even take you through a couple of open-air museums and down troop tunnels that will give you a deeper look at the dark days of World War I in the Dolomites.

At the end of each day sit in a quiet, meditative state on a high vantage point and watch the sun drop from the sky. As it does so something truly magical happens—the giant fists of rock and cliff in front of you change color from sheet gray to a pulsating orange glow. This is the *enrosadira*, a phenomenon that's symbolic of the Dolomites.

LEFT The five towers (Cinque Torri) on the Alta Via I trail in the Italian Dolomites.

The Route

The 75-mile-long (120 km) Alta Via I takes most people around eight to ten days to walk, though the abundance of mountain lodges means it can be spread over a longer period of time so as to allow shorter walking days if you prefer. With very clear signage, no technical sections, and not overly demanding ascents and descents, it's a walk that can be accomplished by first-time multiday trekkers. But the scenic variety will also keep even the most seasoned hiker smiling. Most people walk it in a north-south direction, starting from the large and surreal turquoise lake, Lago di Braies, and ending, after a drama-filled final descent, in the small valley town of Belluno. If you're reliant on mountain lodges, then it's sensible to book them in advance because demand for beds is heavy in summer. A tent is a good backup plan.

① MOUNT LAGAZUOI

At Mount Lagazuoi, which at 9,302 feet (2,835 m) is also the highest point reached on this trail, you can savor a superb view, sleep in a comfy mountain lodge, and explore the tunnels, trenches, and machine-gun posts that turned this mountain into a virtual fortress. Once you're ready to continue the hike, follow the Alta Via I alternate route to drop down through a World War I–era tunnel for just over two-thirds of a mile. Don't forget a headlamp.

⊢———————⊣ 5 mi.
⊢———————⊣ 5 km

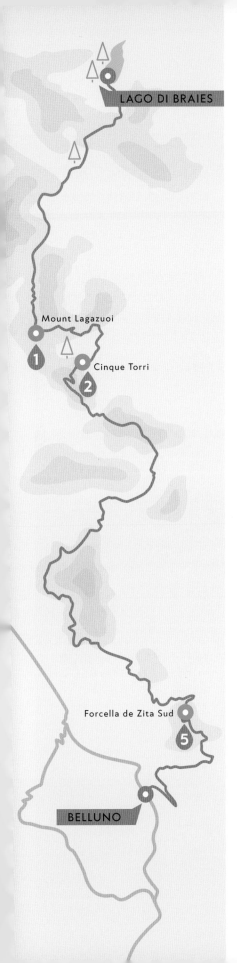

LAGO DI BRAIES

Mount Lagazuoi

1

Cinque Torri

2

Forcella de Zita Sud

5

BELLUNO

4

2 CINQUE TORRI

The Five Towers rather undersells what are giant mounds of rock that seem as if they were created by the mind of Tolkien. They look especially impressive at sunset when they are bathed in orange light. To add to their story is the nearby open-air museum that re-creates life during World War I, when this area was crisscrossed by competing forces.

3 VIA FERRATAS

The Dolomites are famed for *via ferratas*, literally, iron rods and ladders bolted to vertical cliff faces that allow hikers with the necessary equipment (and without vertigo!) to safely access routes that would otherwise be the reserve of climbers only. While there are a couple of minor *via ferratas* actually on the Alta Via I—or rather on variants of the route (no equipment required)—you can easily detour off the main trail to the Ferrata Marmo, which is the real deal and requires special equipment.

4 ENROSADIRA

Enrosadira (Alpenglow) is the term used to describe the phenomenon when the distinctive needlelike peaks that characterize parts of the Dolomites turn a husky pink and blushing red as the setting or rising sun touches them. As long as the weather cooperates, this magical light show can be seen along many points of the Alta Via I.

5 FORCELLA DE ZITA SUD

There are so many fine viewpoints on the Alta Via I that picking the best is always going to cause arguments. But the view from the Forcella de Zita Sud (7,858 feet; 2,395 m), encountered on the final stage of the trek, is truly superb. From this steep pass a panorama of peaks unfolds and you can see the land fall away to the trail's end in the forested valley way below. Savor the moment before your return to normal life.

Walk here next

You've probably guessed from the name that there's more than one Alta Via in the Dolomites. Throughout the larger Alps region there are many other high-altitude hikes and those requiring the use of *via ferratas*.

Swing through the Dolomites with a safety harness

ALTA VIA II

The Alta Via II route is a 100-mile (160 km) swing through the Dolomites that in most respects is actually a better hike than the Alta Via I. So why didn't we focus on this route instead? Well, it's all to do with the *via ferratas*, those iron ladders and bars fixed to cliff faces. On the Alta Via I you're not obliged to use them; on the Alta Via II you are—and you'll need to carry safety harnesses in order to do so.

Tackle a high-altitude alpine trek

WALKER'S HIGH ROUTE

Linking Mont Blanc and the Matterhorn, the two most iconic of Alpine peaks, this incredible, high-altitude, two-week and 125-mile (200 km) slog through the French and Swiss Alps crosses multiple passes and dangles below the giant summits of ten of the ranges' twelve highest peaks. This is a demanding route, but one that rewards with the finest scenery in the Alps.

Trek into the high mountains

ROSENGARTEN TRAVERSE

One of the lesser-known multiday routes through the Dolomites, the Rosengarten traverse crosses the Schlern-Rosengarten Nature Park. It takes most people three to four days to complete this trail, so is ideal for those short of time. The trek takes you deep into the high mountains, and the sights will remain with you for years, but it's not a hike for those without a head for heights as there are a number of *via ferratas* to deal with.

Martuljek Waterfalls and Gorge

LOCATION
Northwest Slovenia

DURATION
2 hours

DIFFICULTY
Easy

DISTANCE
4.7 miles (7.7 km)

MAP
KartoGrafija Triglav,
1:25,000 Map 25

START/END
Gozd Martuljek

TRAIL MARKING
Red and white waymarks

A family-friendly walk up a gorge to a series of beautiful waterfalls.

The best things come in small packages and so even if the small, and very mountainous, central European country of Slovenia didn't have love written into its very name, as a hiker, you'd still almost certainly fall for its charms. Much of the north and west of the country is made up of the Julian Alps, a jagged and vertical land of dense forests that are home to a large population of brown bears, and dotted with castles straight out of a fairy tale. There are also some cave systems here that are home to the olm, a bizarre amphibian that gave rise locally to dragon legends—although if we're honest, you need a bit of imagination to make this connection. There's a huge amount of potential for hikers of all levels here, and compared to many other European mountain ranges, it's all very untapped.

One of the most enjoyable routes, though, is in fact a super-simple, family-friendly walk to the Martuljek Waterfalls. To reach the two different waterfalls encountered on this two-hour stroll you head first up a defile of steeply angled rock through which runs a turquoise and highly energetic river. The first set of falls is a 164-foot-high (50 m) cascade that falls in pencil-thin fashion down natural rock steps. The higher set of falls is even more impressive. Here the water gathers its energy in a deep pool before bursting over the rock lip and falling over 328 feet (100 m) down the mountainside.

LEFT Lower Martuljek Waterfall, Triglav National Park, Slovenia.

The Route

This is one of those pleasurable hiking routes where you don't really need to concentrate too much on keeping on the trail and instead can devote all your energy to admiring the scenery. There are two trails to the Martuljek Waterfall from the parking lot at Gozd Martuljek: one that goes for an hour up the narrow gorge and another that bends around the outside of the gorge walls and takes you through forest. Both unite a short way below the higher of the two sets of waterfalls (the lower set is passed as you walk up the gorge but you can also cut across to these from the forest trail). On the way back you can simply return by the other trail so as to make a neat loop. Do take note, though, that the gorge trail can be impassable after heavy rain.

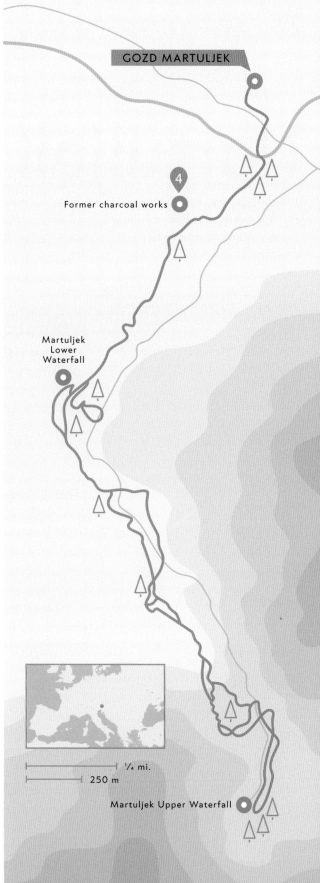

GOZD MARTULJEK

Former charcoal works

Martuljek Lower Waterfall

¼ mi.

250 m

Martuljek Upper Waterfall

1 FUN FOR ALL

When you first start hiking with children it can be easy to be overly ambitious and put them off hiking by pushing them too far, too hard, too fast. But get them on the trail to the Martuljek Waterfalls and you won't have any such problems. The walk is just difficult enough to give the younger members of your group a bit of a challenge, but one that they can easily achieve. And, with plenty to look at on the way up, and the waterfalls as a goal, you might well find that come the end of the day they'll be the ones asking you when they can next go hiking again.

2 SUMMER COOL

Slovenia gets very hot in high summer, so the gorge leading up to the falls, with its spray-infused air and numerous trees, is a lovely place to seek a lungful of cooler air. Bring a picnic and enjoy eating with Mother Nature. We certainly don't suggest you try swimming in the vicinity of the falls, though!

3 THE JULIAN ALPS

You've seen the falls and now you want something a little more challenging. Well, look up and you'll see mountains all around you. The Julian Alps are a phenomenal hiking destination. Many trails are well marked, but other hikers are rare compared to, say, the Alps. Good options include the stunning Seven Lakes Valley, which is a moderate hike along a valley dotted with a handful of lakes, and the more demanding hike to the summit of 6,306 feet (1,922 m) Mount Vogel, with its views down onto Lake Bohinj.

4 CHARCOAL

Shortly after starting the hike to the Martuljek Waterfalls, you will pass the location of a former charcoal making site. The information panels here will give kids a good understanding of how we all used to heat our houses and cook our meals.

5 CAVES AND CASTLES

You won't encounter either caves or castles while walking to the waterfalls, but in the south of Slovenia there are some fairy-tale examples of both, including the extraordinary Predjama Castle, which is actually built inside the mouth of a cave. Speaking of caves, nearby is the incredible Postojna cave system, which is a 15-mile-long (24 km) system of caverns, tunnels, and rock formations. To add to the thrill of a visit, there's also some superb hiking in the cave-riddled mountains around the castle.

Walk here next

Waterfalls make a good goal for many a family-friendly hike, and Europe is full of grand cascades, so grab your umbrella and bask under the spray of these beauties.

Take an easy scenic stroll

KRIMMLER WATERFALLS

Surrounded by pine forest, the Krimmler Waterfalls in Austria's High Tauern National Park are hard to beat for scenic wonder and ease of access. Falling in a series of three steps that in total equate to a 1,247-foot (380 m) drop, these powerful falls can be reached via a very family-friendly 2.5-mile (4 km), easy trail.

Hike to France's highest waterfall
GRANDE CASCADE DE GAVARNIE

In the belly of the huge, vertical walled Cirque de Gavarnie in the central French Pyrenees, a narrow waterfall plummets some 1,385 feet (422 m) to the floor of the cirque. It's the highest waterfall in France and, with its backdrop of giant, glaciated mountain peaks, is one of the most impressive sights in the Pyrenees. A family-friendly, 6-mile (10 km) return hike will take you through woodland and then deep into the cirque for a close-up view of the falls.

Catch cascading colors in the Canary Islands
CASCADA DE LOS COLORES

To see these waterfalls on the island of La Palma in the Canary Islands at their best, it's all a case of timing. Aim to catch them on a sunny spring day, as the waters pour down a small cliff stained yellow, green, and red by the iron-rich waters. The falls are a moderately challenging, 7-mile (11 km), three-hour return hike. When you're done with these, set out to enjoy the rest of the many amazing hiking trails on La Palma.

Peaks of the Balkans

Enjoy a hike that helps make the world a better place.

LOCATION
Kosovo, Albania, and Montenegro

DURATION
10 days

DIFFICULTY
Moderate

DISTANCE
119 miles (192 km)

MAP
Peaks of the Balkans Cross border Hiking Albania-Kosovo-Montenegro 1:60,000

START/END
Theth, Albania

TRAIL MARKING
Red and white waymarks

LEFT A concrete Cold War bunker, a common sight in Albania, near Theth, backed by the Accursed Mountains.

On the Peaks of the Balkans Trail, an epic, feel-good hike through the three Balkan nations of Albania, Kosovo, and Montenegro, the color green is inescapable. Stand on the sheep-trimmed, green grass of a wind-buffeted pass and peer down across a sea of inky green conifers; let your eye linger on a small lake the color of frogs, and admire the rich green meadows watered by soft summer showers. And it's only right that green should be so predominant on this hike, because this is a multiday hike with serious green credentials.

Unusually for a hiking trail, the Peaks of the Balkans Trail didn't grow in an organic manner, with hikers linking together different footpaths to eventually come up with one megatrail. Instead, this was a purpose-built and planned trail born out of a need to foster peace and harmony between neighboring communities and nations in the long-troubled Balkan region. The other reason the trail was created was to allow remote highland communities to generate an income and so halt the process of depopulation of mountain villages. The route was established in 2012 and very quickly afterward started to achieve its aims. Along the entire length of the route there is now a thriving homestay scene for passing trekkers. In fact, so successful has the Peaks of the Balkans Trail been that it's been a winner of the prestigious Tourism for Tomorrow award. In other words, this is green tourism at its best.

The Route

As a circular hike you can start wherever most suits. But the large majority of hikers begin in the lovely stone mountain village of Theth in Albania from where a counterclockwise loop takes in the jagged mountain spires of Albania before moving onto the more rounded peaks of little-known Kosovo and then back through Montenegro to reenter Albania via the 5,600-foot (1,707 m) Pejes Pass. Although most people complete the hike in ten days, there are enough alternate night stops to mean you can spread it out over a longer period.

One of the things that makes the Peaks of the Balkans Trail unusual among European hiking routes is the widespread availability of homestays, which puts cash straight into the hands of locals, and allows the trekker to obtain a closer look at local life and get to enjoy fantastic home-cooked meals.

 THE UNKNOWN

Albania, Kosovo, and Montenegro are the Europe you never knew existed. Wilder and rougher around the edges than the Europe you might be used to, every journey here is an adventure and the mountains of the country are so little known to outsiders that almost every day can feel like a day of discovery.

 COMMUNITY

Unlike many European hiking trails, overnight accommodations aren't normally at dedicated government-run hiking lodges, but rather you will often find yourself settling down for the night in a cozy farmhouse homestay, having eaten a filling traditional meal while your hosts entertain with tales from life in the mountains. You will very quickly start to feel a part of the community of the beautiful stone villages you stay in and get a rare insight into rural Balkan life.

 THETH TO VALBONA

For most people the hike between the Albanian villages of Theth and Valbona will be the first taste of the Peaks of the Balkans Trail, and it's definitely a good start. From Theth the trail climbs hard up through quiet, old-growth forest to arrive at the spectacular rocky outcrop of the Valbona Pass. Staring out from this lofty viewpoint across snow-streaked barren mountain summits, you'll fast understand why these mountains are also known as the Accursed Mountains.

 DETOURS AND SIDE TRAILS

One of the great things about the Peaks of the Balkans Trail is that because it is still so little known even the most minor of detours can lead to great adventure and wonder. The side trip to the so-called Great Valley of Lakes is a prime example of this. Deviate off the main trail between Vusanje (Montenegro) and Theth (Albania) and you will find six surreal greenish-blue alpine lakes strung through meadows at the foot of moody, gray summits. It's one of the scenic highlights of the route.

5 SHEPHERDS, FARMERS, AND TRADITIONS

In this rugged corner of the Balkans, old traditions die hard (fortunately!). While hiking these trails you will come across shepherds and their flocks up on the high summer pastures continuing a lifestyle sadly lost in so much of Europe (a word of caution: steer clear of their often aggressive dogs), and as you enter timeless villages you might find a festival in full swing based on traditions hundreds of years old. It's these little things that make the Balkans such a memorable place to walk.

6 EYE OF THE GRASSHOPPER

Who knew that a grasshopper eye could be so beautiful? Oko Skakavice, which translates as "grasshopper eye," is a beautiful limpid green karstic spring in the Ropojana Valley (on the last day of the hike if you start and end in Theth) that's some 82 feet (25 m) across and an impressive 230 feet (70 m) deep.

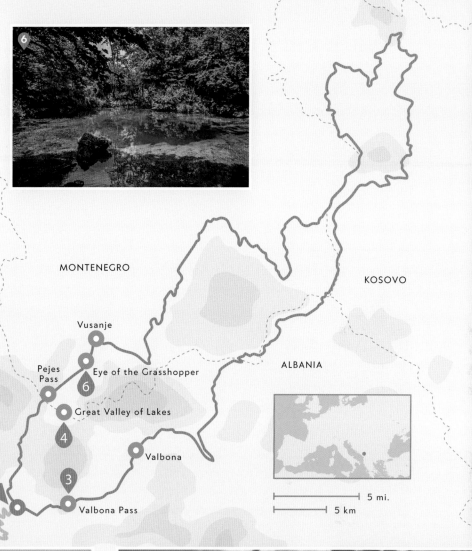

Walk here next

The Peaks of the Balkans Trail is one of Europe's lesser-known multiday hikes, but it's far from being the only route left unfairly in the shadow of bigger and better-known mountains. These hikes will lead you along the trails less trod.

Follow in the footsteps of famous artists
PAINTERS' WAY TRAIL

Germany's 72-mile (116 km) Painters' Way Trail has a stellar reputation among German hikers but is relatively unknown to the international hiking contingent. Yet this trail through gorgeous German countryside and around the foot of the straight-edged Elbe Sandstone peaks has a dreamlike beauty, and you will quickly understand why this landscape has proven so inspirational to painters, photographers, and even Hollywood filmmakers.

Take a gentle stroll in rural Ireland
WICKLOW WAY

Running from Clonegal to Dublin, this 80-mile (128 km) amble through the gentle farming countryside and rolling moorlands of eastern Ireland is a delightful way to discover rural Ireland away from the tourist honeypots. Along the way you will pass an ancient monastery, the largest waterfalls in Ireland, and a lake called Guinness. You will also spend nights in pretty villages where there's always a bar serving something else called Guinness.

Step out on dry stones

RUTA DE PEDRA EN SEC

The Spanish island of Mallorca receives millions of
tourists each year. Most come to roast themselves
on the admittedly very beautiful beaches, but some
come for a different reason. The 87-mile (140 km)
Ruta de Pedra en Sec (Dry Stone Route) is a magnificent
ten-day trail that runs along the sunburned spine of
the dramatic Serra Tramuntana. Well marked and with
accommodations at the end of each stage, this is a
superb way to experience a Mallorca far from the
tourist resort crowds.

Delphi to Kirra

LOCATION
Central Greece

DURATION
4 hours

DIFFICULTY
Easy

DISTANCE
9 miles (14 km)

MAP
Terrain Editions Central Greece 1:200,000 Map 5, Anavasi Mount Parnassos 1:35,000 map 2.1 (note: does not include entire route)

START/END
Delphi/Kirra

TRAIL MARKING
Signposts

Follow in the footsteps of some of the greats of the ancient world.

A long time ago—exactly how long ago, nobody is really sure—according to legend, gods walked the earth and the father of them all was Zeus. One day he released two huge eagles into the skies, one in the east and one in the west. They flew toward each other, and the point at which the two birds met was proclaimed by Zeus to be the center of the world. He named it Delphi, and over time a magnificent city was constructed at the site. At its center was a temple containing an oracle that became famous during classical antiquity. Many of the ancient Greeks coming to Delphi to consult the oracle arrived by boat in the coastal town of Kirra and then hiked for 9 miles (14 km) through olive groves and wildflower meadows to the temple.

Amazingly, some 2,500 years later, parts of that ancient path still survive as do the columns, statues, theaters, and temples of Delphi itself, which is one of the most impressive historic sites in Europe. The walk between Delphi and Kirra retains much of the beauty that must once have left arriving pilgrims spellbound, including the gnarled olive trees, the poppies and anemones in the spring meadows, the glint of sunlight on the translucent Mediterranean down below, and, of course, the majesty of the ruins of Delphi.

LEFT The ancient theater at Delphi, Greece, surrounded by cypress trees.

The Route

As long as you avoid the heat of high summer then this is an easy, family-friendly walk. Most people visit the ruins of Delphi and then walk downhill to Kirra so that they can both profit from the gentle descent and enjoy the coastal views that would otherwise be behind them if they climbed up to Delphi.

The very clearly signed route starts from the edge of the ruins at Delphi and follows the Plestos River valley downhill past ancient olive groves. For the most part the trail sticks to small country roads and footpaths, but about a third of the way down it skirts through the small town of Chrisso before diving into quieter, wilder countryside, passing the pretty Church of Saint George and arriving by the sea at the eastern end of the beach resort of Kirra.

1 DELPHI

The UNESCO World Heritage Site of Delphi is one of the best preserved, most extensive, and certainly most beautiful of all ancient Greek sites. Before starting your hike (or after), take your time to explore this site. The stunning Temple of Apollo, which housed the oracle, is unmissable and sporting fans should make a beeline for the ancient stadium where the precursor of today's Olympic Games was staged. The theater, which still hosts summer performances, is beautifully surrounded by flowers and cypress trees. And then there's the Treasury and the Sanctuary of Athena Pronaia, and a host of other spectacular sites.

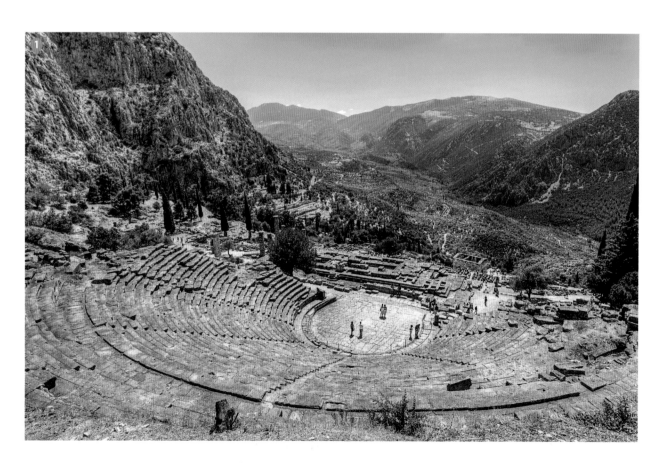

2 OLIVE GROVES AND WILDFLOWERS

Leaving the busloads of Delphi tourists behind, enter a world that would be more recognizable to those who hiked this route two thousand years ago: one of quiet, dusty trails, carpets of spring flowers, and goats and sheep bleating at passersby from the drunken shade of olive groves. Although the ruins are stunning and swimming in the sea a pleasure, this is the truly magical side of the hike.

3 LEGENDS

This part of Greece has a history going back so far it's almost older than legend. The area was said to have once been the stomping ground of the gods of ancient Greece. The Spartans consulted the Oracle of Delphi before going to war against Athens. They were told they would be victorious but that their leader would be killed by a serpent. He was later killed by a man with a serpent image on his shield. In 336 BCE, Alexander the Great hiked the route from Kirra to ask the Oracle if he would soon conquer the known world. The Roman Emperor Nero came here to be told his reign would be cut short by a number seventy-three. He was later killed by a man aged seventy-three. And when a young Roman named Hadrian visited, he had a more positive experience, being told by the oracle that he was destined to become emperor, which indeed he did.

4 COOLING OFF

It's hardly the most beautiful beach in Greece, but on a hot day, as you pant into Kirra at the end of the hike, you probably won't care too much about beach aesthetics and will just leap into the deep blue, cooling waters of the Mediterranean. Afterward, treat yourself to a fish dinner from one of the town's seafood restaurants.

Chrisso

Church of Saint George

DELPHI

KIRRA

1 mi.

1 km

Walk here next

If you like your hiking to come with a history lesson, then follow up the Delphi to Kirra Trail with these fascinating hikes through time. You'll take in stunning scenery along with ancient monuments along the way.

Roam along Roman roads, ancient footpaths, and mule trails

THE LYCIAN WAY

Stretching out across 335 miles (540 km) of southwest Turkey, the Lycian Way crosses the heartland of the Bronze Age Lycian people. Along the way the trail meanders past the ruins and reminders of the Lycians as well as those of other invaders and traders who all left their mark on Turkey. Fortunately, it's not all history: this part of Turkey is home to the country's best beaches, and you'll have plenty of opportunities to drop the backpack and slip on your swimsuit.

Hike through the Holy Land
THE ISRAEL NATIONAL TRAIL

This epic 637-mile (1,000 km) route down the complete length of Israel from the Lebanese border to the Red Sea is truly a walk through biblical history. Along the way you will pass through places such as Mount Tabor, Mount Carmel, and Jerusalem. From Crusader castles to Nabataean towns and Roman cities, there's plenty of nonreligious wonder here, too.

Trek among the ruins of ancient civilizations
JORDAN TRAIL

As you walk down the desert-red defile in the rock and emerge blinking in the bright light at the foot of the rock-hewn Treasury of Petra, you will understand why Petra is considered one of the world's greatest archaeological sites. But there's more to the Jordan Trail than just Petra. This 419-mile (675 km) trail across Jordan takes in small villages, stirring desert scenery, great antiquities, and the coral-fringed Red Sea coast.

Mount Toubkal Circuit

Get acquainted with North Africa's highest mountain on this stunning circuit.

LOCATION
High Atlas Mountains, Morocco

DURATION
4–6 days

DIFFICULTY
Moderate

DISTANCE
37 miles (60 km)

MAP
Mapiberia Toubkal & Marrakech 1:50,000, Map AT07

START/END
Imlil

TRAIL MARKING
None

Rugged up against a bitter wind and feet crunching in the snow, it can be hard to believe that just a short way to the south, past a few declining mountain ridges, below the red haze of sand and heat, are the burned lands of the vast Sahara desert. That's the remarkable thing about hiking Morocco's Mount Toubkal Circuit: the scenery and climate changes radically with every valley, pass, and peak, but at no time is that more apparent than when you stand triumphant atop Mount Toubkal. At 13,671 feet (4,167 m), it's not just the highest mountain in Morocco, but also the highest in North Africa. While getting to the top of Toubkal might have been the original goal of people walking the Mount Toubkal Circuit, most quickly come to the conclusion that the summit is just one of many highlights to this incredible trek.

Known to locals as *Idaren Draren*, or Mountains of Mountains, the Atlas Mountains, of which Toubkal is the high point, are a 620-mile-long (1,000 km) wedge of peaks that is the homeland of the Berber people. Renowned for their hospitality, the Berbers are thought to have lived in the valleys of these mountains for at least ten thousand years, and although Muslim today, they retain customs and beliefs (not least a strong belief in magic and spirits) that are far removed from mainstream Islamic thought. And so it is, that at the end of a long day of hiking, as you sit down in a village house to a home-cooked meal with your hosts, the real reward of this hike becomes apparent.

LEFT Hikers ascend Mount Toubkal, North Africa's highest mountain.

The Route

The Mount Toubkal Circuit starts and ends in the attractive mountain village of Imlil and then dips in and out of valleys, passes a multitude of villages, and crosses three passes including one, the Tizi n'Likemt, that's a breathless 11,860 feet (3,615 m) high. As long as there's no snow, which can linger in sheltered corners and on high passes deep into June, then there's nothing technically difficult about this walk. For the most part, the trail is clear and simple to follow. There are no very long hiking days. Most people do this trek with a local guide, and although that's not strictly necessary, it does open doors to great cultural encounters in villages. Although you are guaranteed nonstop sunshine in July and August, the heat can be draining even at this altitude. Mid- to late June and September are great.

1 CULTURAL IMMERSION

The varied scenery encountered on this trail is superb, but the real highlight for many hikers ends up being not the mountain ridges and views from the passes, but the Berber people themselves. Disarmingly welcoming and natural-born storytellers, they will invite you to sit with them and drink mint tea so sweet it could make a dentist faint in shock. Throughout this trek there are many homestay opportunities that you should grab with enthusiasm. Not only do the homestays provide a cultural interaction, but they also generally serve delicious home-cooked meals: thick, filling tajines in the evening and wonderful breakfasts of dried fruits and bread dipped into honey or olive oil.

② STAND ATOP MOROCCO

There are many worthwhile side trips on the Mount Toubkal Circuit, but it goes without saying that the most popular is the almost compulsory expedition to the summit of Mount Toubkal at 13,671 feet (4,167 m). In summer and early fall the climb is a nontechnical slog up a steep and rather exhausting scree slope. Most people set off around 3 a.m. in order to be standing proud atop the whole of North Africa by sunrise.

③ TOMB OF THE DJINN KING

For the Berber people who inhabit the Atlas Mountains, this dramatic landscape has always inspired belief in magic, ghosts, and *djinn* (invisible spirits that are either inherently bad or good). A short way north of Mount Toubkal is a huge white painted boulder under which is a shrine said to contain the tomb of Sidi Shemharoush, the King of the Djinns. Even today pilgrims come here to make offerings and wash with the spring water that appears out of the ground and is thought to cure certain illnesses.

④ VILLAGE LIFE

While the high mountain slopes are often barren rockscapes devoid of much obvious life, the plunging valleys are a different story altogether. Here small villages of traditional mud and stone houses, which are normally gathered around a whitewashed mosque, seem to grow like a living organism out of the mountain slopes. On the valley floor itself are shockingly bright green fields of crops and orchards with trees heavy with fruit, and everywhere are goats and sheep cared for by shepherds with weathered faces.

⑤ LAC D'IFNI

In this barren and rain-starved region, Lac d'Ifni (Ifni Lake) comes as a shock. A jewel of blue among empty scree slopes, this large U-shaped lake set at 7,546 feet (2,300 m) is the only real lake in the High Atlas Mountains. The trail heads right past the lake.

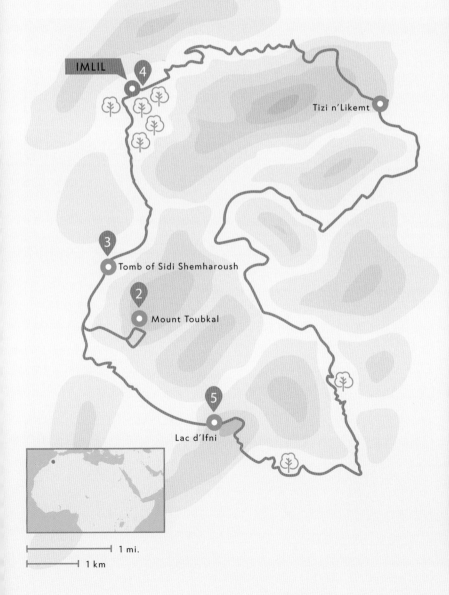

IMLIL

Tizi n'Likemt

Tomb of Sidi Shemharoush

Mount Toubkal

Lac d'Ifni

1 mi.

1 km

Walk here next

If you like your cold mountains to come with a view down onto hot lands, then these trails are a natural follow-up to the Mount Toubkal Circuit.

Experience offbeat hiking

ANTI-ATLAS MOUNTAINS

Standing between the gravel plains and peach-red dunes of the Sahara and the soaring peaks of the main Atlas mountain range, the Anti-Atlas in Morocco is a long wall of weather-beaten rock that reaches a high of 10,840 feet (3,304 m) at Jbel Sirwa. The range is laced with quality hiking trails but remains much less known than the bigger peaks to the north. Lower and hotter than the area around Toubkal, this is a good winter hike destination, though for many routes a guide is required.

Soak up Spain's beauty

ALPUJARRA TRAIL

In the shadow of southern Spain's Sierra Nevada mountain range, the Alpujarra Trail in Andalusia runs for 89 miles (144 km) past villages of cube-shaped, whitewashed houses, a multitude of wildflowers, and plunging valleys covered in terraced fields of crops and orchards full of spring-flowering almond and cherry trees. It's a beautiful walk that combines some of the best mountain scenery in Spain with villages that are every bit the scenic equal.

Saunter through stunning desert landscapes

SINAI TRAIL

Shortly after it was established, the monumental Sinai Trail, which traverses the Sinai Peninsula in Egypt, was voted the best new tourism project in the world by the British Guild of Travel Writers and, in 2017, was described by *Outdoors* magazine as one of the world's best new trails. High claims indeed, but this 342-mile (550 km) route through stunning desert landscapes and past biblical sites truly lives up to the hype.

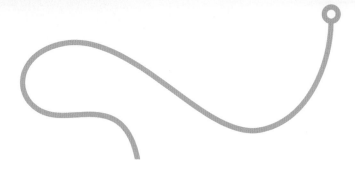

Simien Mountains

LOCATION
Northern Ethiopia

DURATION
3 days

DIFFICULTY
Easy

DISTANCE
Varies

MAP
No single printed map exists

START/END
Debark

TRAIL MARKING
None

Unique wildlife, a one-of-a-kind history, and stunning escarpment views.

In Ethiopia's Simien Mountains there are monkeys with bleeding hearts: you might well scoff at such a thought but it's true. As you'll quickly learn while walking along the sheer edge of a vast highland plateau that soars 2.5 miles (4 km) above sea level, in Ethiopia everything is unexpected. This, after all, is a land of hidden rock-hewn churches, ever-bubbling pools of lava, and biblical trees of frankincense. Its history is one where reality and myth are so entwined it's impossible to know what's real. Does that little chapel in Aksum really contain the biblical Ark of the Covenant? Was the last emperor, Haile Selassie, truly a direct descendent of the Queen of Sheba and King Solomon? Is there any chance that there really are invisible churches in the hills and mountains, and that secret passageways really do lead to the unopened, two-thousand-year-old tombs of godlike rulers? While a hike across northern Ethiopia's dramatic Simien Mountains—which would be more accurately described as a plateau rather than mountains—probably won't give you a firm answer to any of the questions above, it will give you a lifetime of stories worthy of a fairy tale.

LEFT Spectacular views across Ethiopia's Simien Mountains.

The Route

Trekking in the Simien Mountains is always done in the company of a guide and porters, and the exact route you take largely depends on the preferences of your guide. The standard Simien Mountain hike is a three-day trek starting from Debark and heading to a viewpoint just beyond the Chenek campsite, after which you then return to Debark. Normally, you don't start walking directly from Debark, but you'll travel a certain distance by vehicle in order to clear the edge of town and get higher onto the plateau. The walking is generally easy as you undulate along the edge of the high escarpment admiring the needles of rock below and long views north, but the high altitude—most of the time you'll be hovering around 13,120 feet (4,000 m) above sea level, so altitude sickness is possible—makes it harder work than you might expect. There are a multitude of other routes throughout the Simiens including an easy ascent of Ras Dashen (15,157 feet; 4,620m), the highest mountain in Ethiopia, and longer treks of up to ten days that head into truly remote areas.

WILDLIFE

Ethiopia rises up like a sky island above the searing desert lands surrounding it, and this isolation has meant that a lot of unusual creatures, unique to the Ethiopian plateau, have evolved here. Observing some of this wildlife is one of the highlights of trekking through the Simien Mountains. The gelada baboon is one such example: the males of these large primates have a terrifying appearance with large, sharp canines, a lionlike mane, and a splash of bright red across their chests (hence the name, bleeding heart monkey), but in fact they're mellow vegetarians, and you're virtually guaranteed a picnic in the proximity of huge groups of them. Much harder to spot are the super-rare walia ibex, a type of wild goat with sweeping horns, that today occurs only in the Simien Mountains, and the equally rare Ethiopian wolf. The bird life is also tremendous. Scan the thermals rising off the valleys below and you might spot the mighty bearded vulture, which is known for dropping bones onto rocks from a great height!

End o
vehic
sectic

DEBARK

2 ESCARPMENT VIEWS

Calling this a mountain trek perhaps paints the wrong impression. Instead of starting low and working your way ever higher through valleys and over passes, the Simien Mountains are a bit different. Essentially this is one high, tabletop plateau of between 12,140 feet (3,700 m) and 15,160 feet (4,620 m) that was made in an almost unique geological fashion—the only other place in the world with a similar makeup is the Drakensberg range in southern Africa—which means that trekking here involves walking along the edge of this plateau looking at the peaks and gullies below you. It's like spending several days walking around a giant summit!

3 ETHIOPIAN CULTURE

Ethiopian culture has evolved in a manner that's very different to almost anywhere else. The second country in the world to adopt Christianity, around 320 CE, Ethiopia is full of tiny chapels and grand churches. Many of these are hundreds of years old and some are even carved into rock faces or pinned to rock pinnacles high above the ground. Although no churches like this can be seen around the trekking routes of the Simien Mountains, there are a few small settlements up here with examples of Ethiopia's Orthodox churches. And church or not, any trek through the Simien Mountains will introduce you to the subsistence livestock farming prevalent in northern Ethiopia, and because you're walking with Ethiopians, you'll get the rare chance to learn about life in this least known of countries.

4 COMMUNITY HIKING

While some hikers may be aghast at the idea of being forced to hike with a guide and porters, there are a lot of positives to the situation, the most important of which is that by coming here you are putting cash directly into the hands of small, remote communities where people have very few other options for making money. The authorities have worked hard to ensure that the money is fairly spread about, and trekking here has brought much positive development. So, if you like your hiking to come with a big heart, then the Simien Mountains are for you.

Imet Gogo

Geech camp

Chenek camp

Viewpoint

Mount Bwahit

Aynameda camp

Jinbar Waterfall

2 mi.

2 km

Walk here next

Although some trekkers hate the idea of having to hike with a guide, there are a lot of advantages to guided trekking. The following three routes will make you a guided-hike convert.

Ramble through rolling moorlands
BALE MOUNTAINS

Cold and washed by mists and drizzle, the Bale Mountains of southern Ethiopia are the largest area of alpine moorland in Africa. Much of this vast area hovers around 13,120 feet (4,000 m) altitude, and like the Simiens, the mountains here are home to some unique species, including the endangered Ethiopian wolf and giant mole rat, both of which are easily seen while hiking. Scenically, the Bale Mountains are all about rolling moorlands, dark lakes, waterfalls, and big open sky.

Take an ethical hike through superb scenery
TESFA TREKS, LALIBELA

This is socially responsible trekking at its best. Tesfa (tesfatours.com) was set up explicitly to promote village-to-village hiking in Ethiopia. Hikers are hosted by local communities and guided along the trail by them, and over 50 percent of the money charged goes directly into local pockets and development. Tesfa is also using the money to aid Ethiopian wolf conservation. But this isn't just feel-good trekking. These routes take you through superb highland scenery to ancient monasteries and are a great cultural immersion.

Trek through the desert
WADI TIWI TO WADI BANI KHALID

One of the classic treks of the south Arabian nation of Oman is a two-day jaunt virtually from sea level over a 6,560-foot-high (2,000 m) desert escarpment (where most people camp for the night) with astonishing views, before dropping down into a palm tree oasis. A guide is required.

The Loita Hills to the Masai Mara

LOCATION
Southern Kenya

DURATION
4–7 days

DIFFICULTY
Easy

DISTANCE
Varies

MAP
No maps exist

START/END
Nashulai Maasai Conservancy

TRAIL MARKING
None

Stride with the Maasai through the remotest corner of their homeland.

Any old Africa hand will tell you that by far the best way to experience the African bush is on foot. By hiking through these landscapes, where human beings first learned to stand on two legs and walk, you will see, hear, smell, and feel things that no safari tourist in a vehicle would ever experience.

But how can you do this? Well, short half-day bush walks are available on the fringes of many African national parks and reserves, but a multiday trek through a variety of wild landscapes full of animals is something much rarer. However, in the rising hills just to the east of Kenya's Masai Mara National Reserve—home to the world-famous wildebeest migration—it's possible to join expert Maasai guides and set out on an adventure over gentle hills, through thick tropical forest full of unexpected wildlife, and down onto the long grass plains dotted with acacia woodlands that lead to the edge of the Masai Mara. Along the way you will have unforgettable encounters with the wildlife of Kenya, but, more importantly still, as you walk through the most traditional remaining corner of Kenya's Maasai lands, you will get a rare insight into a fast-changing culture. That will make this a trek you will never forget.

LEFT Hiking with Maasai guides through the Loita Hills.

The Route

There are no set trails to or from the edge of the Masai Mara National Reserve and the high Loita Hills, and the tiny number of foreigners (or even other Kenyans) who attempt to walk here means that every time you set out to walk through this region you are embarking on a genuine adventure.

Due to the lack of trails and the abundance of large mammals, a local Maasai guide who knows the route, has local connections, and knows how to deal with the wildlife is essential, and all trips to the area should be organized through an experienced local tour company. Currently only Nashulai Maasai Safaris, which is managed by the award-winning, eco-friendly Nashulai Maasai Conservancy (nashulai.com), offers this trek. Duration can be tailored to the client's needs, with everything from overnight hikes through the dense forests of the Loita Hills to multiday bush camping expeditions between the mountains and the Masai Mara available. Whichever you opt for, the walking itself is fairly gentle over an ever-undulating landscape of constantly changing scenery.

① ADVENTURE

The hills in this southern corner of Kenya are mere molehills compared to those running through the Himalayas. But what hiking in this region offers that almost no other safe, easy to reach, and highly accessible walking area offers is real, unfiltered, unplanned, genuine adventure. The highly trained guides working with a company like Nashulai Maasai Safaris and Conservancy know the lay of the land like the back of their hand, but even so, nobody can predict what creature might be lurking around the next tree. Each hike follows a slightly different route, stops in different places, and allows time for unplanned diversions and distractions. But when it all comes to an end, this is the kind of hike you could write a book about.

② MAASAI CULTURE

For most safari goers, the Maasai are merely exotic models in a photo. But on this trek, far from the safari tourist crowds, the Maasai become friends with whom you are sharing an unforgettable adventure. Accept the many invitations to stop and drink tea, chat with the herder about his flocks, eat *ugali* (cornmeal) in a local café, go to a noisy Sunday church service, and hear the elders recount tales of cattle raiding and lion fighting that seem scarcely believable. On this trek you will really start to get an insight into the rich and deep Maasai culture.

SEKENANI VILLAGE

KENYA
TANZANIA

Higher
Loita Hils

Escarpment
viewpoint

START

10 mi.

10 km

Lake
Natron

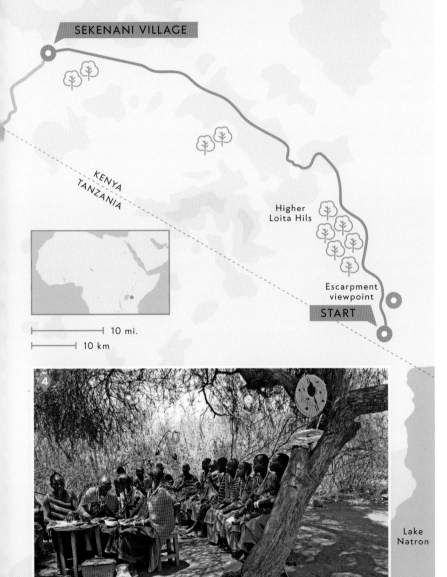

3 WILDLIFE

Walking from the Loita Hills to the edge of the Masai Mara is a trek through the very heart of African safari country. In the hotter, drier lowlands you will walk for hours at a time without a human settlement in view, but you will rarely be alone. Instead of people, great herds of zebras and wildebeest will stomp ahead of you over the grasslands. In thickets of dry acacia woodlands you should tread carefully for fear of disturbing a herd of elephants fifty strong and everywhere baboons, giraffes, and hyenas keep careful tabs on your progress. In the densely forested, junglelike ridges and valleys of the high Loita Hills different wildlife predominates. Beautiful colobus monkeys swing through the canopy, hornbills with a wingbeat that sounds like a helicopter shuttle overhead, and a thousand tiny forest birds reveal their presence through song alone.

4 SUSTAINABILITY

Hiking in and around the Loita Hills and down to the fringe of the Masai Mara National Reserve is responsible tourism at its absolute best. Every hiker pays a daily conservation and community development fee, which is used for worthy conservation and community projects in the area. These can vary from paying to lease the land for wildlife conservation, to female empowerment projects, habitat restoration, school education, and community health to running a wildlife guide training college or funding anti-poaching projects. Essentially with every step you take along the savanna trails, you are making a positive contribution toward protecting this vital ecosystem and the people and animals who live here. That's one heck of a feel-good summit!

Walk here next

Hang out with the local people, meet some of our closest cousins, and enjoy rich green mountain scenery on these East African treks, which combine community and wildlife.

Hike between villages

USAMBARA MOUNTAINS

Northern Tanzania's Usambara Mountains are a shockingly green and fertile ridge of steep-sided hills and mountains plastered with forest, washed through with waterfalls, and dotted with small farming villages. A four-day hike will take you from the small town of Lushoto to Mtae (51 miles; 82.5 km). As well as the wonderful views, this is an ideal area for immersion into the local communities.

Go chimpanzee and gorilla trekking

UGANDA

If there's one hike that every visitor to East Africa really wants to do, then it's the muddy traipse through jungle or high-altitude bamboo forest for a face-to-face encounter with either chimpanzees or mountain gorillas. As a wildlife encounter, these close-up great ape meetings are without equal. The hiking element of it, though, varies. Sometimes you walk no more than a couple of hundred yards, but at other times (when trekking to spot chimpanzees in particular) it can be strenuous.

Experience rural Africa

CONGO NILE TRAIL

Officially the Congo Nile Trail runs for 141 miles (227 km) along the western shores of Rwanda's Lake Kivu. However, due to the paving of dirt tracks and roads, most people only walk the northern half. This definitely isn't a wilderness hike. Almost every yard of Rwanda is intensely farmed, and it's the chance to experience rural life, enjoy the intensely green countryside, and soak up views of Lake Kivu that are the highlights of this trail.

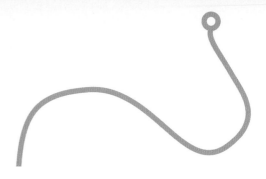

Kilimanjaro

LOCATION
Tanzania

DURATION
5–10 days

DIFFICULTY
Moderate

DISTANCE
48 miles (77 km)

MAP
TerraQuest Maps, Africa the Highest Peaks: Kilimanjaro, 1:50,000

START/END
Various, but Marangu Gate is start/end point of standard route

TRAIL MARKING
None

LEFT Snow and ice on the top of Mount Kilimanjaro, Tanzania.

Admire the view from the summit of the world's highest freestanding mountain.

It's the classic safari image: big-tusked elephants gathered at the foot of Kilimanjaro, its glaciers sparkling in the dawn sun. At 19,340 feet (5,895 m), the ancient volcanic cone of Mount Kilimanjaro is not just the highest mountain in Africa, but the highest freestanding mountain on the planet. After a wildlife safari at the foot of the great peak, the dream for many is to hike to the ice fields that lie across its summit. On the way up hikers will traverse five distinct ecosystems, from the hot Rift Valley lowlands where giraffes meander among acacia trees, through dense tropical forest where monkeys play and birds sing, and then across mist-soaked moorlands full of unusual plants with names such as the everlasting flower and the red hot poker. Traversing the empty rock and scree alpine zone, the hike comes to a finale among the glaciers and ice fields of the summit.

But for all the sense of achievement of finally reaching the top of Africa, there is also a sense of sadness. The mountain's iconic glaciers are dying. A thick coat of ice has existed on the summit for at least ten thousand years, but now, thanks to climate change, the ice is vanishing. According to NASA, between 1912 and 2011, 85 percent of the ice atop Kilimanjaro melted away. Meanwhile, the World Meteorological Organization has predicted that by 2040 all the ice atop Kilimanjaro will have vanished. All this means that summiting Kilimanjaro is like attending a solemn funeral for Africa's last kingdom of ice.

The Route

There are several routes up Kilimanjaro, but the standard one is the Marangu Route, which is the only one to offer hikers' huts at each overnight stop. However, despite the comfort of the huts and the ease of the walking, we don't really recommend this trail because of how busy it is and because it has the least interesting scenery. Most importantly, though, it doesn't allow sufficient time for acclimatization. Instead, opt for the Machame Route, which takes longer, is notably harder, and is camping all the way. But the scenery is considerably better, and the slower ascent allows for a greater chance of success.

No matter which route you take up the mountain, a guide and porters are obligatory. Most people organize these through a Tanzanian tour company, but be careful of budget tours, which tend to cut corners on safety and comfort. And most of all, do not opt for the shortest treks, which leave no time for adequate acclimatization. Not only does this dramatically decrease your chances of getting to the top, but it can also be very dangerous.

1 VIEWS

The view everyone wants is to peer down from the summit onto the plains of East Africa as the sun, rising gold and strong, sends shafts of light bouncing across the last snows of Kilimanjaro. But there are many other amazing views to take in on this unexpectedly diverse trek, including volcanic plugs rising like high-rises out of the scree, plains of dark ash from long-forgotten volcanic eruptions, and forests of weirdly shaped plants swirled by mists. Kilimanjaro is a sky island, and like every island it's a world unto itself.

2 PERSONAL ACHIEVEMENT

You've overcome the physical and mental hardships, withstood the cold, played it safe with the altitude, and ignored the sometimes screaming inner desire to stop. And now here you are, standing on top of the world's highest freestanding mountain. Kilimanjaro might be a nontechnical and highly achievable climb (so long as you pace yourself), but don't let that thought take anything away from what you've just done. This is one for the life experience list!

3 FLORA AND FAUNA

With most routes up Kilimanjaro starting from around 3,280 feet (1,000 m) altitude and the summit being only a little under 19,685 feet (6,000 m), in the space of just a few days you will pass through an extraordinary range of biological and climatic zones. At the base of the mountain the heat can be deadening and the wildlife includes all the safari favorites: elephants, lions, zebras, and giraffes among many others. Gaining altitude, the temperatures cool slightly and rain is more frequent, which creates a montane rain forest of tangled undergrowth and stately trees through which swing colobus monkeys and a wealth of colorful tropical birdlife. You may also see forest buffalo and bushbuck here. Higher still comes the classic moorland landscape full of otherworldly plants including giant heathery bushes, lollipop-like giant lobelia, and eye-catching red hot pokers (look for colorful sunbirds hovering around these), and the endemic and truly surreal giant groundsel, which can reach heights of 19.6 feet (6 m).

4 CAMP LIFE

All ascents of Kilimanjaro are done with guides and porters, and whether you're staying in the cabins on the Marangu Route or camping on one of the other trails, then camp life will play a big part in the Kilimanjaro experience. At its best, highly trained and professional guides and porters will fuss over you while you chat through the day's adventures with a cross section of hikers from all four corners of the globe.

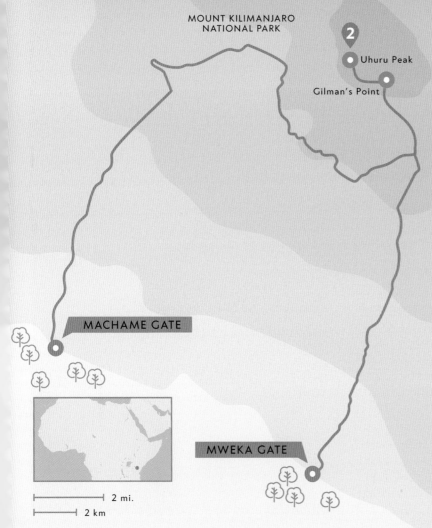

MOUNT KILIMANJARO
NATIONAL PARK

Uhuru Peak

Gilman's Point

MACHAME GATE

MWEKA GATE

2 mi.

2 km

Walk here next

Ice on the equator? Oddly enough, Africa can do that —although, as is the case with Kilimanjaro, climate change means it will likely all be gone within another two decades. Head to these great summits next. A guide is needed for all these mountains.

Hike on ice near the equator
MOUNT KENYA

With the summit being just 10 miles (16 km) shy of the equator, Mount Kenya (17,057 feet; 5,199 m), the second-highest mountain in Africa, is one of only a very few places that can claim to have ice virtually on the equator. Although lower and less arresting to look at than Kilimanjaro, Mount Kenya is, in many ways, the more interesting mountain to climb. It receives only a tiny fraction of the number of climbers, yet it has more scenic interest and variety.

Trek through the jungle

RWENZORI MOUNTAINS

Straddling the border between Uganda and the Democratic Republic of the Congo, the Rwenzori chain, which peaks at 16,762 feet (5,109 m), is another place with ice virtually on the line of the equator. Being a mountain range, there is infinitely more trekking variety here than Kilimanjaro, but the difficulty of the muddy, jungle terrain and incessant, heavy rainfall mean that the trails here are for the experienced only.

Climb Kilimanjaro's little brother

MOUNT MERU

Kilimanjaro's "little brother," Mount Meru (14,967 feet; 4,562 m), sits just 43 miles (70 km) west of Kilimanjaro in Tanzania, and like its big brother, it too is a volcanic cone. Thanks to the lower altitude, it's an easier climb than Kilimanjaro, but it's also considerably less trekked, and there are amazing wildlife-spotting opportunities around the lower to mid-level slopes of the mountain.

Fish River Canyon

LOCATION
Namibia

DURATION
4–5 days

DIFFICULTY
Hard

DISTANCE
53 miles (86 km)

MAP
Slingsby Maps: Fish River Canyon

START/END
Hobas/Ai-Ais Hot Springs

TRAIL MARKING
None

Traverse a giant canyon that's simply a freak of nature.

The statistics are daunting. Namibia's Fish River Canyon, the largest canyon in Africa, is a 100-mile-long (160 km) tear in the Earth's surface that in places is 16.7 miles (27 km) wide and around 1,800 feet (550 m) deep. Incredibly, this monster mark was created by the power of the Fish River, which today is often more a series of drying pools than a river but must once have been a force of nature.

Hiking along the belly of this beast is a tough proposition, but the unique geological character and dreamlike desert canyon landscapes make it a trek to remember. And then there's the thought that you're walking between rock walls that are around a billion years old and are a visual mark of when the supercontinent, Gondwana, was ripped into three to form Africa, South America, and Antarctica.

So, we have the landscape interest, the geological interest, and the challenge, but there's one other string to this hike's bow. This is a wilderness walk in the truest sense of the word. Once down on the canyon floor, all signs of the twenty-first century fade away, and there is nothing but you and nature. This is hiking in its purest form. However, before you lace up your boots, there are a few things you need to know. Due to the intense heat, the trail is only open between May and mid-September (the southern winter). People wishing to hike this trail must make advance reservations through the park authorities, and officially you must be part of a group of at least three people. You will also be asked to provide a medical certificate signed by a doctor.

LEFT The gigantic ravine of Fish River Canyon, Namibia.

The Route

The Fish River Canyon hike is often touted as the toughest hike in Africa. Whether that's true or not is open to debate. Once down on the canyon floor the route finding is easy, and there's very little up and down. But the underfoot terrain is a mix of sand and rock, which gets tiring to walk on. The heat can be intense in the middle of the day, but come the middle of the night it can be bitterly cold. The really hard part for most people, though, is that you must be totally self-sufficient, carrying enough food to see you through the duration of the hike. This makes for a heavy bag, which, when combined with the heat and sand underfoot, makes this a tough trek both physically and mentally.

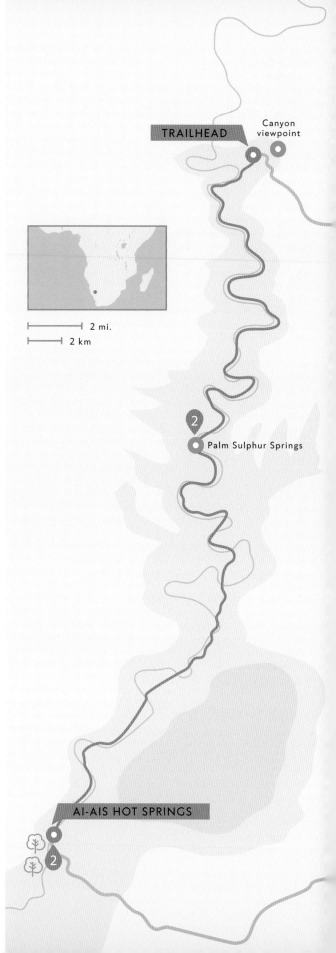

TRAILHEAD

Canyon viewpoint

2 mi.

2 km

Palm Sulphur Springs

AI-AIS HOT SPRINGS

1 GEOLOGICAL MARVELS

The second largest canyon on the planet, Fish River Canyon was once a part of a large mountain range, which was slowly eroded away by oceanic flooding. When the seas had finished causing mayhem, the Fish River itself formed (about 350 million years ago), and slowly, slowly the water carved out the canyon. When hiking it, though, you probably won't need a geology lesson to tell you that however it was formed, the result is mighty impressive.

2 SPRINGS

It's hot, it's sandy, and it's dusty, so thank goodness for the springs (including hot springs) and pools where you can wash away the dust and cool off in the powerful silence of desert Africa. The best-known of these springs, the Ai-Ais Hot Springs, comes right at the very end of the adventure, and its 140°F (60°C) waters are the near-compulsory place to celebrate your achievement. The Palm Sulphur Springs, encountered at the start of day two, is another very popular bathing point. Here, the 122°F (50°C) waters merge with cooler river waters to allow you to shift about to find your heat comfort spot.

3 NIGHT SKIES

There are no huts or hikers' lodges along the route, so you must either bring a tent or sleep out under the open sky. And what a sky it is. With zero light pollution and often crystal-clear visibility, the night skies here offer extraordinary star viewing. So snuggle up in your sleeping bag, lie back, and watch faraway galaxies spin across the black night.

4 WILDLIFE

You're in the desert. You're in a deep canyon. Nothing dares live here. You're all alone—or are you? One of the unexpected joys of the Fish River Canyon is the encounters with the canyon's other life-forms. Here you can find zebras, rock hyrax, klipspringer antelope, cobras, and baboons. Of the avian life, the most obvious are the large black vultures and hovering kestrels, but there are also many special desert birds.

5 SILENCE

Stop walking, sit quietly on a rock, and listen. What do you hear? Probably nothing—no cars, no people, no birds, no wind. Nothing. At times the silence here is as loud as thunder. It's a sound that most of us rarely, if ever, hear in our day-to-day lives. This is a walk that allows deep meditation and can be an almost spiritual experience.

Walk here next

If you enjoy the sensation of walking between giant walls of rock, then don't miss these other spectacular gorge and canyon hikes.

Hike past wildlife

HELL'S GATE

The narrow gorge walls of Hell's Gate in Kenya's Rift Valley were the inspiration behind Pride Rock in the Disney movie *The Lion King*. But you don't need a Disney touch to make this place magical. The gorge itself is short and for most the real highlight of hiking Hell's Gate is the experience of walking past herds of zebras and impalas.

Take a long but easy trail
SAMARIA GORGE

On the sun-blessed Greek island of Crete the Samariá Gorge cuts a 10-mile (16 km) line through olive-speckled hills and down to the bath-warm waters of the Mediterranean. The walk along the length of the gorge, past towering cliffs and cooling pools of water, isn't technically difficult, but it is long (allow at least six hours).

Follow an iconic route
BLANC-MARTEL TRAIL

The toothpaste turquoise Verdon River runs through the Gorges du Verdon, a spectacular 15.5-mile-long (25 km) tear through the landscapes of southern France. There are a number of hiking trails through the gorge—some very challenging—but the best known is the Blanc-Martel Trail, a 10-mile (16 km) one-way route that mixes woodland, gorge, long tunnels (bring a flashlight), fixed metal ladders, and surreal river views to create one of the best-regarded hikes in France.

Table Mountain

LOCATION
Table Mountain, Cape Town, South Africa

DURATION
3 hours

DIFFICULTY
Moderate

DISTANCE
2.2 miles (3.5 km)

MAP
Slingsby Maps, AH01 Table Mountain, 1:20,000

START/END
Lower aerial cableway station

TRAIL MARKING
Yellow and blue waymarks

Take a varied, quiet, and adventurous route up Cape Town's Table Mountain.

It's one of the world's most iconic land formations: a symbol of South Africa and a place that's up there with the Grand Canyon for its instant recognition. We're talking, of course, about Cape Town's sheer-sided, flat-topped Table Mountain. Climbing it (or, at the very least, riding the cable car up it) is high on the wish list of any visitor to the city. The vast majority of Table Mountain ascents are made via the easy Platteklip Gorge Route. But there are other ways to the top, and if you ask a veteran Table Mountain climber which is their favorite line to the summit, most will reply without hesitation: the India Venster Route.

So, what is it that makes the India Venster Trail such a hit? The answer is variety, viewpoints, and just the right amount of challenge. The trail up it is steep—you'll gain around 2,198 feet (670 m) in 2.2 miles (3.5 km)—and at times involves a bit of light scrambling, plus, in places, short sections of fixed chains and ladders; it's not an ideal hike for those who suffer from vertigo. However, once the hard work is done, the fun begins, which in this case is the views. One of the best things about this route is that it traverses three sides of the mountain, which gives an ever-changing panorama over the city, the Cape Peninsula, and the ocean. And this variety of angles and landscapes also provides the opportunity to experience a diverse array of the peak's unique plant life and wildlife.

LEFT Hikers ascend Table Mountain via the India Venster Route.

The Route

While this isn't an especially hard route, there are a few peculiarities that mean some people might find it a toughie. The first thing to note is that there's quite a bit of scrambling. It's not hard but it does get tiring. The next thing you need to know is that it's steep and, in places, exposed. If near-vertical drops make your stomach churn, then go up by a different route. More importantly than the above, though, is that the route finding in certain sections can be difficult—even more so when the mountain's infamous cloud rolls in. For these reasons, the vast majority of hikers hire a guide for at least their first ascent.

This is a one-way-only hike as descending on such a steep trail is not recommended. Once at the top, either descend via the classic Platteklip Gorge Route or take the thrilling cable car back down.

 WILDLIFE

Despite being virtually surrounded by the urban development of one of Africa's most important cities, Table Mountain is home to an unusual and unexpected array of wildlife, though the lions that once tormented the first Dutch settlers here are long gone. The most visible are the rock hyrax (dassie). They might look like guinea pigs, but their closest living relatives are—incredibly—elephants and manatees. Other less commonly seen animals are mongoose, Cape fox, genet, and porcupines, none of which you have much chance of seeing. Come early in the morning, though, and you might spot klipspringer, which is a type of small antelope. At any time you'll get to meet the Himalayan tahr. As the name suggests, these mountain goats aren't native to Table Mountain but were introduced in the early 1900s.

2 CAPE VIEWS

The reward at the end of the route is of course the view down onto Cape Town and the Cape Peninsula and, when the weather plays ball, pretty much anywhere you look. But, that said, some vistas are better than others. Judas Peak (2,487 feet; 758 m) offers unsurpassed views of Hout Bay and the Cape Peninsula. The quiet Silverstream Buttress repays the efforts of getting there with an epic view over the mountain. The strenuous walk to the summit of Corridor Peak leads to a drama-filled panorama from the steep ledge.

3 BOTANICAL BEAUTIES

For shape and setting, Table Mountain is unquestionably stunning. Then there's the views and the wildlife found on top of it, which are both amazing. But what really makes Table Mountain stand out from, well, almost anywhere else, is its botanical wonders. Table Mountain is a veritable Garden of Eden, and the mountain supports one of the highest diversities of flora in the world, much of which is endemic. In fact, the mountain is home to at least 2,200 different plant species. Most of these are what are known as fynbos, a truly ancient plant (which was around when dinosaurs walked the Earth) with a special ability to resist fire. All this means that even if you're not a specialist then a hike up Table Mountain is a hike through one of the world's most important, and beautiful, flower meadows.

4 CABLE CAR

Due to the angle of ascent and descent it's not recommended to walk back down the mountain via the India Venster Route. Instead either go down the classic Platteklip Gorge Route, or whiz down on the gut-wrenching cable car. Yes, we know it's not hiking, but it's hard to deny the thrill of the cable car and the amazing views obtained as you slide back to ground level in just five minutes. Take note, though. If you are planning on walking and taking the cable car down, adverse weather often leads to the cancellation of afternoon cable cars.

India
Venster
Trail

UPPER CABLE CAR STATION

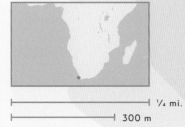

¼ mi.

300 m

Platteklip Gorge Route

Table Mountain   **219**

Walk here next

For vast vistas over low lands, climb these dramatic flat-topped peaks for spectacular views across other corners of Africa.

Hike a varied terrain with panoramic views
GIANT'S CUP TRAIL

The huge Drakensberg mountain range is one of the most rewarding hiking regions of southern Africa. Drakensberg means "Dragons' Mountains," and frankly if you did run into a dragon on these sheer drop-offs and rolling green plateaus, then you probably wouldn't be surprised. There are numerous trails here, but the four-day Giant's Cup Trail gives you a real sense of the Drakensberg and is one of the few hikes in this range with huts at every overnight stop.

Make a quick ascent up a holy mountain

JEBEL BARKAL

Table Mountain isn't Africa's only flat-topped mountain to rise with great drama out of the flat lands surrounding it. At almost the opposite end of the continent is Jebel Barkal, which bursts up out of the dunes of the Sudanese Sahara. Granted, at only 322 feet (98 m) and a fifteen-minute climb, this is hardly Everest. But from the summit you can stare out across a desert horizon, and if you look down, you will see something completely unexpected: a dozen pyramids and a temple to Amun, the ancient Egyptian god.

Stroll along a scenic trail

TSARANORO VALLEY

Butter smooth granite outcrops explode off the floor of the Tsaranoro Valley in central Madagascar. Climbing Mount Chameleon (5,052 feet; 1,540 m) is a good option for a day hike and gives views down onto a kaleidoscopic landscape of small fields, river valleys, forests filled with ring-tailed lemurs, and further rugged ridges. It's also possible to make much longer multiday hikes.

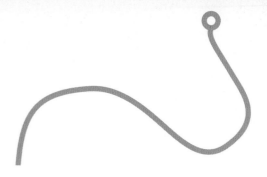

Whale Trail

LOCATION
De Hoop Nature Reserve, South Africa

DURATION
5 days

DIFFICULTY
Moderate

DISTANCE
34 miles (55 km)

MAP
Slingsby Maps Overberg Whale Coast 1:250,000, Map AT07

START/END
Potberg Hut/Koppie Alleen

TRAIL MARKING
None

Search for breeching whales as you walk along this rugged coastline.

On most hiking trails the giants are great shafts of mountains. South Africa's Whale Trail, a five-day extravaganza along a wild and woolly stretch of coastline in the De Hoop Nature Reserve, promises sightings of a different kind of giant: whales. Between late June and early September dramatic sightings of massive breeching southern right whales are almost a given. And we don't just mean a distant view of one or two whales—on the appropriately named Whale Trail it's not at all unusual to see twenty-five whales or more in a day. That's only the whales; huge pods of dolphins are commonly seen leaping and spinning out of the waves all year round. With the salt wind in your hair, sand underfoot, and the ocean's megafauna a glance away, this wilderness walk is one of southern Africa's true greats.

The rugged coastline and the whales are of course the highlight of this hike, but the trail through the ecologically diverse De Hoop Nature Reserve also reveals the Cape Peninsula's unique fynbos flora, an ancient group of plants that occur nowhere else in the world. There are also shipwrecks to see and simple beachcombing to enjoy as you stride the high tide line after one of the frequent storms.

This hike is well organized (you must reserve in advance with the park authorities) with super cozy cabins at the end of each day's walk where tales of the day are told around the *brai* (barbecue) pit.

LEFT Purple succulent flowers in bloom on the Whale Trail coastal hike.

The Route

The Whale Trail is a pretty simple walk with little significant elevation loss and gain and easy route finding (once on the beach you can't exactly go wrong). The hardest day is probably the first. Starting inland, this is the only day with a notable climb—up a 1,968-foot-high (600 m) hill for a superb view—and it's also the longest day with 9.3 miles (15 km) to get under your belt. After that it's a fairly flat beach trail all the way to the end. You'll hike past a mix of stony coves and long sweeping sands and over low, wind-buffeted cliffs.

When you reach the end of the walk at Koppie Alleen, a shuttle bus will return you to your car where the adventure began. The huts (dorm beds only) are very well-equipped, but you'll need to bring all your own food. Fortunately, this is made much easier by the park authorities, who transfer your kit to the next night's hut while you walk with just what you need for the day.

 WHALES

The coastline around the De Hoop Nature Reserve, through which this trail runs, is considered one of the best places in the world for land-based whale watching. These giant creatures, who come here to give birth, come close enough to shore that they are often clearly visible without binoculars. The most common species by far is the southern right whale, but there are also frequent sightings of Bryde's whales, massive humpback whales, and even killer whales. The best time to observe them is from about July to November.

 FLORA

To the untrained eye, the plant life along this coastline might appear fairly inconsequential—just stumpy, low-lying, tough-skinned plants and flowers—but this part of the world has a truly unique flora known as fynbos. The word *fynbos* comes from the Dutch for "fine bush" and refers to the thin, narrow leaves seen on many fynbos plants, an adaption to the region's hard climate that helps to conserve water. Fynbos plants exist nowhere else but the Cape Peninsula, yet this tiny region shows extraordinary diversity, and there are more fynbos species on the Cape Peninsula than native plants in the whole of the United Kingdom! A good time to see many of them in flower is September and October.

3 BEACH TIME

The weather might be notoriously changeable, and the sea is hardly tropical warm, but the beaches this trek takes you past are truly fabulous. Often battered by wind and lashed by waves, they're not beautiful in the classic sense, but they have a raw edge to them that makes you feel exhilarated. While the sea itself can be a little dangerous for swimming due to heavy surf, there are plenty of deep tidal rock pools where you can submerge yourself in the cool waters and then dry out and reheat lying on sun-warmed rocks. While you walk along these beaches, as well as keeping one eye out for offshore whales, keep the other one scanning the flotsam and jetsam for interesting deep-sea treasures washed up along the high tide line.

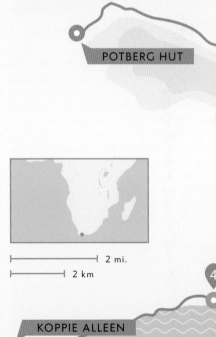

4 THE HUTS

In most parts of the world, hiking huts are basic affairs with little but a row of dorm beds in often drafty and cold huts with a single outdoor tap and not much more. The huts on the Whale Trail don't fall into that category. Yes, it's still all dorm beds, but that's where basic ends. Otherwise expect stylish architecture that blends into the setting, hot showers, warm and comfy communal areas, terraces with a grand ocean view, and impressively equipped cooking and *brai* (barbecue) areas. This is hiking gone seriously upmarket!

POTBERG HUT

2 mi.

2 km

KOPPIE ALLEEN

DE HOOP MARINE PROTECTION AREA

Walk here next

The coastal scenery, the chance to swim, the salt wind, the end of day seafood: it all combines to make one coastal trail never enough. So follow up the Whale Trail with these seaside routes.

Wander along the Eastern Cape
WILD COAST TRAIL

Running along the length of one of the most beautiful corners of coastal South Africa, the Wild Coast Trail is a 43-mile (70 km) amble, up and down rising and falling coastal hills and past small Xhosa villages with homestay opportunities. With several stunning beaches along the route, there's also plenty of opportunities for hikers to get sandy toes. Like the Whale Trail, this hike is also a decent bet for spying whales and dolphins rolling through the offshore swell.

Traverse southwest England on a marathon hike

SOUTH WEST COAST PATH

This mammoth hike, which covers just over 630 undulating miles (1,014 km) of spectacular, rugged coastline in southwest England, links together sweeping sandy beaches, small coves once used by smugglers, indented estuaries, and high cliffs full of seabirds. Along the way are numerous fishing ports, long-since abandoned tin mines, rolling farmland, and busy seaside resorts. It's the longest, and some might say, toughest official long-distance hiking trail in England.

Stroll along for picture-perfect views

CINQUE TERRE COASTAL TRAIL

It's hard to know which is more beautiful on this short, 22-mile (35 km) trail along the Italian Riviera—the coastal cliffs, sea views, and pocket-sized beaches, or the brightly painted villages clinging to those same cliffs and hugging the narrow coastal strip. And then, when the walking is done for the day, settle back in a seaside restaurant to enjoy the pleasures of the Italian kitchen.

Heights of Alay

LEFT A traditional Kyrgyz yurt with Lenin Peak in the background.

Meet nomads trekking through epic high-altitude scenery in the Alay mountains.

Outside, the frosty ground sparkles in the low sun, and it's so cold that the breath of the huddled goats rises as condensation in the early morning air. The sun, just lifting now above the ridge, throws a soft orange glow across the summits of the surrounding mountains, and the shadows in the valley start to retreat. None of this is visible though to the trekkers and their seminomadic Kyrgyz hosts. They're all safely wrapped up in the warmth of the womb-like yurt where they spent the night stretched out asleep on thick rugs next to a large samovar. Awake now, and with fingers wrapped tightly around steaming cups of goat milk tea, a breakfast of cheese, curd, mountain-sourced honey, and pickled cabbage is served before the trekkers heave packs onto their backs, make their farewells, and stride upward to the head of the valley and a 13,120-foot-high (4,000 m) pass.

Could the central Asian country of Kyrgyzstan be the best hiking country you've never heard of? Hike the six-day Heights of Alay Route and you'll almost certainly decide it is. With 3.7- to 4.3-mile-high (6–7 km) glaciated peaks, plunging valleys marked by luminous turquoise lakes, and three high passes (two of which are over 13,120 feet; 4,000 m) to cross, this trail has the scenery to make for a great trek. But the thing that turns it from great to world beating are the seminomadic people you will meet along the way and the chance to eat meals with them and spend several nights sleeping alongside them and their livestock in a yurt. It's a rare insight into a fast-vanishing way of life.

229

The Route

The Heights of Alay is a circular six-day hike (although a shorter four-day version is available) through the Alay mountain range in Kyrgyzstan, a ruggedly mountainous nation in central Asia where the Alay, Pamir, and Tian-Shan mountain ranges collide with one another. With three major passes to cross— two of which are at a lofty 14,110 feet (4,300 m)—and a lot of up and down on rock, scree, and even snow, this is a fairly demanding trek. With little in the way of trail marking, a guide and porters are a very wise idea, easy to arrange through agencies in nearby Osh. The Kyrgyz government has a very progressive view on tourism and actively encourages homestays and deep cultural interactions. This means that on most nights, and again at lunchtimes, you will be hosted by seminomadic sheep and goatherds, eating what they eat and sleeping in cozy yurts (all of the host families have undergone some form of training in what passing trekkers require), and this makes this a cultural as well as a scenic hike.

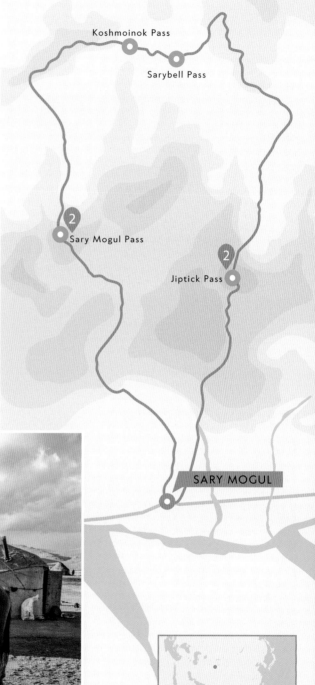

NOMADIC INSIGHTS

When looking back on this trek, most people describe the scenery with a tone of wonder in their voice. But ask them about the single best highlight of it and you can be certain that the answer will be the welcome extended to them by the Kyrgyz nomads. Year after year, generation after generation, they have moved with their livestock from summer to winter grazing grounds, setting up camp in heavy duty and unexpectedly cozy and homey yurts. Today their lifestyle is changing fast as the pressures of schooling and making a living press down on nomadic life. Today, some of the nomadic families encountered along this trail have set up homestays (or, perhaps, yurt stay is a better description) for passing trekkers. It's a good way for the families to make a little extra money on the side and for you, the hiker, to get a rare insight into central Asian nomadic life in the twenty-first century. And yes, that does mean smartphones are as ubiquitous as goats.

 HIGH PASSES

Most of this trek keeps you above 9,840 feet (3,000 m)—good acclimatization is essential—but there are two parts where you're really up among the clouds. The Sary Mogul Pass (14,127 feet; 4,306 m) and the Jiptick Pass (13,730 feet; 4,185 m) are both reached after a hard slog up rock and scree slopes, but the reward is a clean sweep view over a frigid mountain landscape that will take your breath away, if the altitude hasn't done that already. The Sary Mogul Pass in particular is a scenic tour de force with rust-red rock slopes falling hard down to a snow-flecked valley on one side, a string of half-iced lakes on the other, and a shaft of glaciated mountains beyond.

 THREE DRAGONS GORGES AND LENIN PEAK

Here are two wildly different geological landforms: one a small gorge among gorgeous summer flower meadows, the other a 4.3-mile-high (7 km) monster.

The Three Dragons Gorge is a bizarre, small gorge with spiky, red walls that could, with a bit of creative thinking, look like the back of a dragon. Even if you can't see giant fire-breathing reptiles, though, you will appreciate the summertime floral display where the red rock is offset by a mass of yellow flowers. Lenin Peak (23,406 feet; 7,134 m), which frequently fills the distant horizon, is a bulge of snow and ice that sits on the border of Kyrgyzstan and Tajikistan and is the highest mountain visible throughout this trek.

④ COMMUNITY-BASED TOURISM

The Alay mountains, like much of Kyrgyzstan, is a world leader in community tourism initiatives. As well as the yurt homestays, delicious lunches and horse rental can all be organized through the nomads, while elsewhere community-based tourism projects even allow you to meet some of central Asia's last golden eagles, using the eagles to do the hunting rather than hunting of eagles. This network of village and nomad-based accommodations and services means that trekking in Kyrgyzstan is easy, comfortable, cheap, and comes with real local character.

Walk here next

Multiple mountain ranges collide in central Asia, and in between them are equally dramatic deserts and high-altitude grasslands, all offering superb hiking opportunities.

Easy hike, huge mountain
LENIN PEAK BASE CAMP AND TRAVELER'S PASS

This is an ideal add-on to the Heights of Alay trek. The day hike to Lenin Peak base camp and Traveler's Pass carries you up to 13,616 feet (4,150 m) and an epic vantage point of this 23,406-foot-high (7,134 m) mountain. The hike to base camp is easy, then a steep haul will take you up to Traveler's Pass for a clear view of the mountain and glacier extending down the valley off it.

Explore a little-known mountain range

PAMIR LAKES TREK

The Pamir Mountains of Tajikistan are the highest and arguably least-known mountain range in central Asia. There's little in the way of established trekking routes here, and going with a knowledgeable guide is pretty much essential. The Pamir lakes trek is a stunning combination of intricate mountain folds, combined with giant lakes and Tibet-like plateaus. Each trekking agency will have its own variation of the trek.

Hike into Siberian wilds

BLUE LAKE

The Altai Mountains, which straddle the distant borderlands between Russia, Mongolia, and China, are about as remote as it can get. One of the more achievable routes in this Siberian wilderness is the day hike to the spectacular Blue Lake, halfway up the slopes of Mount Aktru (13,268 feet; 4,044m), in the Russian Altai. The trail starts off winding through pristine old-growth conifer forest before running up the edge of a huge glacier and coming to a halt beside the magical and often frozen lake.

Baltoro-Concordia and K2 Base Camp

LOCATION
Pakistan

DURATION
18 days (including 2 days'
acclimatization)

DIFFICULTY
Hard

DISTANCE
111 miles (180 km)

MAP
Leomann Maps, Karakoram
Maps, K2 1:200,000

START/END
Askole

TRAIL MARKING
None

LEFT K2 mountain, the second-highest mountain in the world, seen from Concordia, where the Baltoro and Godwin-Austen Glaciers meet.

Gasp in awe at the sight of the greatest collection of high mountains in the world.

Everest might have the numbers, but K2 (28,251 feet; 8,611 m) is bigger than Everest in every other way. The world's second-highest mountain sits at the heart of the Karakoram range—a convoluted range of massive peaks and statistic-defying glaciers. Within the compact Karakoram is the greatest concentration of 26,250 feet (8,000 m) peaks in the world and the longest glaciers outside of the polar regions. In fact, glaciers are close to the dominant landform here with almost 50 percent of the land covered in ice compared to just 12 percent of the Himalayas.

First climbed in 1954 by an Italian team (the first successful winter ascent was in 2021), K2 fast gained a reputation as a killer. Statistically, for every four people who stand on the summit, one person dies (for Everest, the fatality rate is considerably lower), so it's no wonder that the mountain has gained the nickname the "Savage Mountain."

Fortunately, trekking to Concordia, where the Baltoro and Godwin-Austen Glaciers meet, and then on to K2 base camp, is a lot less risky. Despite its giant size, K2 itself remains discreetly hidden behind lesser peaks for much of the arduous toil over rock and ice, and it's not until you reach the so-called Throne Room of the Mountain Gods that you finally get a clear view of the great peak. And what a view it is. Five huge glaciers and half a dozen mountain monsters all meet at this spot to provide what is almost certainly the world's best mountain vista. It's no wonder then that so many seasoned hikers declare this the single most spectacular trek they ever experienced.

The Route

This trek is no walk in the park. For the majority of the time you will be above 13,120 feet (4,000 m) with a lot of time spent on or around glacial ice, and with no comfortable Nepalese-style trekking lodges, this is a long, hard, and very cold hike for experts only. You must be well equipped and have high mountain trekking experience. On the plus side though, no real technical skills are required and the gentle pace of height gain means that altitude-related health problems are less of an issue here than you might expect. The real problems are the highly changeable and unpredictable weather (you'd be lucky to make it all the way through the trek without at least one day of bad weather) and camping in bitter cold.

A special government permit is required for anyone making this trek, and a professional guide and porters are mandatory. You should allow at least two acclimatization days on the way up, and for weather reasons, it's sensible to allow for a couple of nights up at Concordia, from where you can do a day trip to base camp and even the Gasherbrum I base camp.

① MOUNTAIN PILED UPON MOUNTAIN

In 1835, Godfrey Thomas Vigne, the first-known European to set eyes on the majesty of the central Karakoram, wrote of that first view, "Mountain seemed piled upon mountain, to sustain the most stupendous confusion of mist and glacier, glistening with the dazzling and reciprocated brightness of snow and sunbeam." It's a description that any hiker arriving at Concordia can relate to, because here, in this amphitheater of giants, in one single glance you can take in four of the world's iconic 26,250-foot (8,000 m) peaks, off which stream glaciers that are bigger than some countries. But the mountain views aren't just confined to K2 and the other big boys. There are at least a half dozen mountains above 22,966 feet (7,000 m) here and several 19,685 feet (6,000 m) peaks. And then there are the mountains you passed while hiking up the Braldu Valley, including the Trango Towers, great walls of fingerlike rock rising 3.7 miles (6 km) into the heavens.

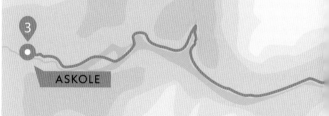

ASKOLE

PAKISTAN

Pakistan is a crossroads and a gateway. Cultures and religions meet here, and the Indian subcontinent and central Asia rub up against each other. The result is a rich history and a people of extraordinary diversity. Indeed, it's long been touted as the "next big thing" in travel, but a combination of unfavorable geopolitics and an undeserved reputation for extreme Islam has meant that the "next big thing" day has never arrived. Yet everyone who hikes to the K2 base camp comes away from the adventure raving about everything else they saw and experienced in Pakistan before and after the trek: the wonderful hospitality, the amazing ruins, and the staggering landscapes. Pakistan is your favorite country in waiting.

KARAKORAM HIGHWAY

In northern Pakistan you don't even need to go to the effort of hiking to be rewarded with astounding mountain vistas. The Karakoram Highway, an engineering marvel, is the highest paved international road in the world. Linking Pakistan with western China, it was carved straight through the mountains and culminates at the 15,397-foot (4,693 m) Khunjerab Pass, which marks the border between the two countries. On the way it heads through stunning mountain scenery and old caravan towns such as Gilgit and Karimabad, capital of the beautiful Hunza Valley. To get to Askole, where the trek to K2 base camp begins and ends, you will travel a good part of the Karakoram Highway.

FOOD

You might think that Pakistani food is essentially the same as north Indian, and in the Punjab region, that's probably a fair assumption. But that's not the case elsewhere in the country. With such a mix of peoples and cultures, a meal in northern Pakistan is a veritable feast of Afghani-style kebabs, with naan breads the size of trash can lids, wonderful dried apricots, grapes, cherries, and apples grown in Hunza's orchards, and thick, rich dals and curries throughout. And, with accomplished chefs accompanying you on the hike, you'll get to enjoy these tasty treats throughout your adventure.

K2

K2 BASE CAMP

Concordia Glacier

Baltoro Glacier

Trango Towers

Trango Towers base camp

Concordia

5 mi.

5 km

Walk here next

Northern Pakistan is a wonderland of giant mountains, delightful summer pastures, vast plateaus, and, on the floors of some of the mountain valleys, surreal desert sand dunes. Add it all up and you have a lifetime of adventurous hiking.

Get ready for K2

FAIRY MEADOWS AND NANGA PARBAT

A short, ideal, and easy warm-up hike for K2 base camp, the romantic in name, romantic in nature Fairy Meadows are green, inviting sheep pastures that offer a stupendous view of Nanga Parbat (26,660 feet; 8,126 m), the westernmost giant of the Himalayan range. A long day hike will take you from Fairy Meadows up to the base camp of this mountain, which has a deadly reputation among climbers.

Trek through ice and snow

SNOW LAKE TREK

On the unlikely chance that the trek to K2 base camp wasn't challenging enough for you, then the Snow Lake trek should sate that desire, because this is a seriously tough hike. At 16,000 feet (4,877 m), this large lake, set between deeply glaciated peaks, perhaps shouldn't even be called a lake at all as it's permanently frozen. This abundance of ice and snow means that trekking here is about as close as you can get to the experience of hiking across Antarctica.

One for the braggers

WAKHAN CORRIDOR

Yes, we know what you're thinking: "Hiking. Afghanistan. I don't think so." But hear us out. The Wakhan Corridor, a thin finger of land that juts deep into Tajikistan and Pakistan and has only a small mouth connecting it to the rest of Afghanistan, sat out most of the horrors that have engulfed Afghanistan. And slowly, slowly a growing band of adventurous hikers are discovering that the corridor offers superb—and safe—hiking, showcasing the best of highland central Asia.

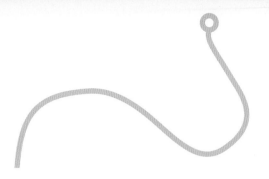

Kailash Kora

LOCATION
Ngari Prefecture, Tibet
Autonomous Region, China

DURATION
3 days

DIFFICULTY
Moderate

DISTANCE
32 miles (52 km)

MAP
Gecko Maps, Kailash, 1:50,000

START/END
Darchen

TRAIL MARKING
None

LEFT Colorful Tibetan prayer flags at the Dölma Pass on the route of the sacred *kora* around Mount Kailash.

Join the pilgrims on a circumambulation of the Precious Jewel of the Snow.

Cold, barren, windblown: the steppe stretches unimpeded for hundreds of miles with few signs of human habitation. But there are people here. A small group of people are advancing forward slowly. They're not walking, not driving, not even riding horses. Instead they're prostrating themselves across the frozen landscape. Stand up, lie down, slide forward. Stand up, lie down, slide forward. Again and again, for hour after hour, day after day, week after week. Finally, their goal is within sight. Mount Kailash rises out of the frozen horizon like a giant crystal, reaching 3.7 miles (6 km) into the heavens. It's the spiritual center of the world, the "Precious Jewel of the Snow."

Situated all alone in the remotest corner of western Tibet, north of the main Himalayan range and far from anywhere, Mount Kailash, which has never been climbed, is sacred to Tibetan Buddhists. Hindus consider the mountain to be the home of Lord Shiva. The Jains say this is where the first Tirthankara attained liberation from the endless cycle of death and rebirth, and, to followers of the ancient Bön religion, Kailash is the center of the world.

Despite its remote setting, a steady stream of pilgrims come here to perform a three-day *kora* (religious pilgrimage) by hiking around the base of the mountain. Joining the pilgrims on this *kora* is an unforgettable experience that mixes challenge, scenery, religious devotion, myth, and legend into a hike that literally has the power to change your outlook on the world.

The Route

The *kora* begins from the small and bitterly cold service town of Darchen after which everyone, hikers included, makes the circuit around the mountain in a clockwise direction as required by Buddhist belief. There are set overnight stops where accommodations are available in basic tented camps (or you can set up your own tent).

All treks in Tibet—indeed all travel in Tibet—must be organized through a recognized Chinese or Tibetan tour company (we strongly recommend using only a Tibetan company) and a guide is compulsory. In addition to this you cannot just board an airplane and travel to Tibet. Special travel permits are required for all visits to Tibet, and further permits are required to head west to Kailash. All of these take time to organize. Be aware also that due to the Chinese occupation, all travel to Tibet can be shut down with little advance notice, depending on the political situation between the Chinese and the Tibetans at the time.

1 PILGRIMS

It's the sheer devotion shown by the pilgrims that is so inspiring. They come from all corners of South Asia and Tibet. Most pilgrims walk the route, stopping to pray at key points. But some—the most determined—prostrate themselves all the way around the mountain and up and over an 18,045 feet (5,500 m) pass in order to gain greater merit. Some even prostrate themselves across the entire, vast Tibetan plateau to get here. And as eye-catching as the mountain is, as rich its mythology and thrilling as the whole adventure is, it's spending time with these pilgrims that is the real highlight of this hike. Join them drinking salty, oily, yak butter tea in the basic tented tearooms that dot the trail. Set up camp alongside them at day's end, talk to them about their journey to Kailash and what the mountain means to them, and celebrate every step of the way with them. It's your fellow pilgrims who bring the Kailash *kora* alive.

 DÖLMA PASS

At a seriously lofty 18,537 feet (5,650 m), the Dölma Pass, the high point of this trek, is dressed in a multitude of bright colors—red, orange, yellow, green, blue, and white—of ten thousand prayer flags fluttering madly in the breeze. Each puff of wind releases and carries the prayers and mantras contained within the flags off and away across Tibet. At the same time, exhausted pilgrims scramble up to the pass, pause to prostrate themselves into the snow, mutter a prayer, and then snap a few quick selfies (after all, everybody wants proof that they made it to this point), before charging down the opposite side of the pass and onto the homestretch.

3 THE MYTH

Kailash is an idea as much as a physical place. Over thousands of years, myth and legend have been piled up on the mountain like winter snow. For Tibetan Buddhists, for whom Kailash is central to their complex cosmology, this is the legendry Mount Meru and the mountain plays a key part in the mythologies of Buddhism, Hinduism, Jainism, and for followers of Bön. But as well as being the home of gods, many other mysteries and legends are entwined around the mountain. These range from the interior of the mountain containing a secret city known as Shambhala, to the mountain being an artificial structure built by a long-forgotten advanced civilization, to it being a representation of a pyramid, or the entrance to the spiritual world. It's even said that seven different types of light can be seeing glowing in the skies above the mountain, that time speeds up in the vicinity of the peak, and that supernatural powers are at work here. One thing that can't be disputed, though, is that four of the major rivers of Asia are born around the slopes of the mountain.

 **THE INNER *KORA***

There's more than one *kora* route around Kailash. The standard one is the outer *kora*, but there's also the secret inner *kora*. Far less trodden than the outer *kora*, and considerably tougher and higher, it allows you to actually approach and touch the holy mountain itself. But there's a catch: you can only do this *kora* once you have completed the outer *kora* thirteen times.

Walk here next

The great highland plateau of Tibet, known as the "Third Pole," offers some fabulous hiking trails. But, as with the Kailash *kora*, a certain amount of red tape must be overcome before you lace up your boots.

From monastery to monastery

GANDEN TO SAMYE TREK

The most popular and easiest to organize trek in Tibet (note that popular doesn't mean busy!) is central Tibet's Ganden to Samye route. Linking two of the oldest and most important monastery complexes in Tibet, this simple four-day hike combines classic Tibetan grasslands, nomad camps, rocky passes, a long gorge descent, and religious interest.

Stroll around a sacred lake

LAKE MANSAROVAR

Within sight of Kailash is the holy Mansarovar Lake, a high-altitude freshwater lake (15,060 feet; 4,590 m). A vast sheet of turquoise-blue in an otherwise sterile environment, this lake is as covered in legend as Kailash and almost as sacred. A four- or five-day *kora* sweeps in a circle right around the lake and is a perfect add-on to the nearby Kailash *kora*.

Circle the holy mount

MOUNT GONGGA SHAN

At 24,823 feet (7,556 m), Mount Gongga Shan, in the former Kham province of eastern Tibet (part of the Chinese province of Sichuan), is the third-highest mountain in the world outside of the Himalayas. It too is considered a holy mountain by Tibetan Buddhists, and a grueling five- to six-day *kora* also works its way around this mighty peak.

Three Passes, Everest

Stand in awe at the foot of the world's highest mountain.

LOCATION
Solukhumbu, Nepal

DURATION
17–19 days

DIFFICULTY
Hard

DISTANCE
92 miles (148 km)

MAP
Nepa Maps, Everest Base Camp, and Gokyo Three Passes, 1:50,000

START/END
Lukla

TRAIL MARKING
Some signs

For trekkers, climbers, and the merely curious, Everest is a beacon that has called out since it was first spotted by a British geological survey team in 1852. As soon as word spread that the world's highest mountain had been discovered, people wanted to climb it. Some of these attempts are the stuff of legend, such as the 1924 attempt by George Mallory and Andrew Irvine. The pair were seen close to the summit when a cloud obscured them from view; they were never seen alive again and the mystery as to whether they became the first to reach the top remains unsolved. Then there were attempts that were comical in their foolhardiness, such as the 1934 attempt by Maurice Wilson. His plan was simple: he would fly a light airplane as close to the summit as he could get, crash it into the mountain, and then stroll the rest of the way to the top. The fact that he had no flying or mountaineering experience was of no concern to him. Needless to say, the mission went fatally wrong.

In the end, it wasn't until 1954 that Tenzing Norgay and Sir Edmund Hillary finally stood on the summit. Since then, there have been thousands of successful summit attempts and many thousands more have hiked the trails surrounding the mountain. The chosen route for most is the straight up and down to Everest base camp, but for a greater challenge, the Three Passes trek is a truly monumental loop through unsurpassed high mountain scenery.

LEFT View from Kala Patthar to Everest and down to base camp.

The Route

The trail starts, like all Everest region trails, from the airstrip at Lukla and then heads straight to the Sherpa "capital," Namche Bazar, for the first of the compulsory acclimatization days (two days would be better). Heading in a counterclockwise direction (going this way around allows for better acclimatization), follow the standard Everest base camp trail to Dingboche. Here you part ways with the Everest base camp trail and continue east to Chukhung and up over the Kongma La Pass (18,159 feet; 5,535 m) to rejoin the main trail up to Everest base camp. Then continue west over the Cho La Pass (17,782 feet; 5,420 m) and down to the gorgeous Gokyo Lakes, before crossing the Renjo La Pass (17,585 feet; 5,360 m) into the wonderful Thame valley, after which it's downhill all the way back to Namche Bazar and Lukla.

Although plenty of experienced hikers do this trek independently, having a guide and porter makes the whole experience considerably safer and more enjoyable, and opens up cultural doors. Plus it puts money in local pockets.

1 KALA PATTHAR

Most people head off on the Everest trails assuming that the highlight will be Everest base camp itself, but that's not normally the case. For the ultimate Everest view, climb the rounded summit of Kala Patthar—18,207 feet (5,550 m), although recent measurements put the summit at 18,517 feet (5,644 m)—where the mighty Everest is revealed in all its glory. But there's more than just the high point of the planet to admire from this prayer-flag-festooned summit. Perhaps even more impressive is the supporting cast of Nuptse (25,791 feet; 7,861 m), Changtse (24,747 feet; 7,543 m), Lhotse (27,940 feet; 8,516 m), and Pumori (23,494 feet; 7,161 m), while filling the valley floor is the giant Khumbu Glacier and a series of glacial lakes.

2 GOKYO LAKES

The Gokyo Lakes are a string of six emerald-green lakes set in the upper reaches of a rocky valley. Seen from the Gokyo Ri viewpoint (17,585 feet; 5,360 m), the lakes (not all of them can be seen from here), which are framed by giant mountains including Everest, are hypnotic in their beauty. Most people spend two or three nights in the lakeside Gokyo village, resting after the long crossing of the Cho La Pass and its glacier. As well as climbing Gokyo Ri, make the daylong hike to the lakes farther up the valley. Few hikers head up here, and there's no sign of human interference. It's the Khumbu region at its wildest.

3 THAME VALLEY

From the Renjo La Pass the trail descends into the Thame valley. By far the most quiet and most traditional of the valleys in the Khumbu region, this is a place far removed from the busy, commercialized base camp trail. Here time moves to the swing of the farming and herding seasons, and the hillsides are dotted with monasteries and stupas. After the exertions of the trail, the small village of Thame, with its stone houses and fields of potatoes, is a wonderful place to relax for a few days, reveling in your achievement and bracing yourself for the return to reality.

CHINA

NEPAL

EVEREST BASE CAMP

Kala Patthar

① ④ EVEREST

② Gorak Shep

Nuptse

Gokyo Lakes · Cho La Pass

Lhotse

Renjo La Pass

Kongma La Pass

Chukhung

③ Thame valley

Dingboche

Namche Bazar

5 mi.

5 km

LUKLA

④ **EVEREST BASE CAMP**

Squatting beside the Khumbu Glacier, the collection of tents that make up the Everest base camp are a natural goal for most hikers, but Everest itself can't be seen from here. Even so, it's interesting to see the complexity of the expedition camps, and in the spring climbing season, the sheer number of climbers whiling away time here waiting for a weather window. Note that due to glacial melt, it's likely that the base camp will be moved back to Gorak Shep (where trekkers already sleep) in the next year or so.

⑤ **THE SHERPAS**

For most hikers a trek through the Everest region is, first and foremost, about the high mountain visuals, and on this front the Three Passes trek exceeds all expectations. But, for many, the human interest turns out to be just as memorable. The Sherpas have lived in the valleys surrounding Everest for around six hundred years (after migrating from eastern Tibet), and their distinctive culture, full of religious festivals and stories of spirits, gurus, and monsters, is fascinating.

Walk here next

It would take a lifetime to tire of hiking Nepal's many mountain trails. After you've wound down from the Three Passes, head up high again on these Nepalese classics.

Tackle Nepal's classic trail

ANNAPURNA CIRCUIT

Long considered one of the world's great treks, the Annapurna Circuit still shines bright. Starting in jungle and farmland, the route makes an enormous two- to three-week loop right around the massive Annapurna range, taking in mountain communities, yak pastures, half-frozen lakes, a dramatic high pass crossing, a finger of dry Tibetan tableland, and long stretches of conifer forest. Facilities are superb the whole way around with comfortable lodges, good food, and fast Wi-Fi.

Try out Nepal's best new trek

MANASLU CIRCUIT

Only recently appearing on trekkers' radars, the Manaslu Circuit is the very definition of a perfect Himalayan hike. Like the Annapurna Circuit, it passes completely around a mountain range, which in this case is Mount Manaslu (26,781 feet; 8,163 m), the world's eighth-highest mountain. In the twelve to fourteen days you will be hiking the circuit, you can expect stirring mountain vistas; a rich cultural mix, which, up high, is strongly flavored with Tibetan Buddhism and, down low, by Hinduism; and all manner of exciting side trips.

Take a family-friendly hike

LANGTANG VALLEY

Directly north of the chaotic Nepalese capital of Kathmandu is the quiet, high alpine valley of Langtang. This short and, for the Himalayas, fairly low-level (maximum altitude 12,664 feet; 3,860 m) hike can be completed in just a week from Kathmandu. But extra days allow for greater exploration of the beautiful upper valley, and to climb some high viewpoints. It's a good family trek.

To the source of the Ganges

Pray with the faithful at the source of the Mother Goddess of the World.

LOCATION
Uttarkhand, North India

DURATION
2–3 days

DIFFICULTY
Moderate

DISTANCE
22 miles (36 km)

MAP
Terra Quest Trekking Maps, Indian Himalaya 1:350,000

START/END
Gangotri

TRAIL MARKING
None

LEFT The River Bhagirathi, the primary source of the River Ganges, flows out from a cave at the bottom of the Gaumukh Glacier.

Flowing across north India, the holy River Ganges sustains and supports tens of millions of Indians. But the Ganges is more than just a mere river. For Hindus across the globe, the Ganges is nothing less than the Mother Goddess of the World and a focus of intense religious devotion. Bathing in its waters can free you of sin, and to die on its banks is to be released from the endless round of reincarnations.

Every year, between April and early November, tens of thousands of Hindu pilgrims make the arduous trek along a Himalayan valley to pray at the source of the river. Known as the Gaumukh (Cow's Mouth), the source of the mighty river is a glacial cave out of which flows the newborn Bhagirathi River, which is the primary source of the Ganges.

If you're a non-Hindu hiker you will very much be in the minority on this mountain trail. But as you climb up toward the glacier your "novelty" status means you will be swept up by other pilgrims and carried along in a big, noisy party to the ice cave. But despite the religious fervor, nobody can avoid noticing the epic Himalayan scenery all around. From the Cow's Mouth itself pause to look around at the massive nearby face of Bhagirathi Parbat (22,493 feet; 6,856 m) and Shivling (21,467 feet; 6,543 m), and you will understand why the Himalayas are considered to be the home of the gods.

The Route

The two-day return hike from the temple town of Gangotri to the source of the river at the Gaumukh Glacier is a technically easy and only moderately rising trail. There's no trail marking, but the path is so clear that there's really no chance of getting lost. However, due to reaching a high altitude (13,199 feet; 4,023 m) in a short period of time, altitude-related health problems are a real concern. Make sure you acclimatize well beforehand at Gangotri (9,980 feet; 3,042 m). Stage one of the hike takes you to Bhojwasa (Bhojbassa: 12,434 feet; 3,790 m) where you should spend the night. There are basic tented camps here. Bring a good four-season sleeping bag and some food. The next day it's another two hours up to the glacier. It's possible to return all the way back to Gangotri on the same day if you're quick.

A limit of only 150 people a day are allowed to set out on the trek, and you must obtain a permit in advance (there's an office in Gangotri). Porters and even ponies are available to carry your gear.

 PILGRIMS

The focus of the trek to the source of the world's holiest river is as much on the people you share the trail with as the mountains themselves. Hindu pilgrims come from across India and the world to partake in this pilgrimage hike. Many are woefully unprepared for the hike, but devotion and determination gets most to the top—eventually. Once at the source of the river offerings are made, prayers are said, and some of the pilgrims even brave frigid temperatures to splash and bathe in the icy river waters, while others fill bottles with holy water to take home to those who couldn't make it. Hiking side by side with these pilgrims, feeling their enthusiasm rub off on you, listening to their stories, and sharing the hardships of the trail with them will be the overriding memory of this trek.

GANGOTRI

2 SADHUS

Most of the pilgrims rush up and down to the source of the river as quickly as they can. But there are some who, having reached this holiest of locations, seem in no hurry to leave again. The glacier, and the high-altitude meadows beyond, are a magnet for holy Hindu ascetics known as sadhus. With long, matted, dreadlocked hair, and often covered in a layer of ash, many of them spend days, weeks, and months in meditation here. One or two even claim to spend the entire winter up by the glacier, naked, unmoving, and totally buried in snow!

3 TAPOVAN MEADOWS

It's normally possible to continue up the valley beyond the Gaumukh Glacier to the beautiful high-altitude pastures and meadows at Tapovan (another two hours) where you can camp near the foot of Mount Shivling. This is much more of a wilderness route than the trail up to the source of the Ganges as only dedicated hikers and a few sadhus and shepherds come up here. The views of the mountains' fluted peaks are spectacular.

4 THE COW'S MOUTH

It's incredible to think that grayish water pouring from the natural cave at the base of the Gaumukh Glacier turns into something as physically and spiritually powerful as the Ganges River. What you've hiked so far to see is, essentially, the life-support system for a huge swath of northern India and Bangladesh (the river flows into Bangladesh, where its name changes to the Padma). It's something to think about as you sit in quiet contemplation admiring the mountain landscape and the birth of a river that, over the eons, has created the great civilizations of northern India.

1 mi.

1 km

Bhojwasa

GAUMUKH 4

Tapovan 3

Walk here next

Not as well known as neighboring Nepal, the Indian Himalayas offer immense variety and some very special treks. Once you've made your offerings to the Ganges, hit these great Indian trails.

Trek through Little Tibet

MARKHA VALLEY

Ladakh, the so-called Little Tibet, in the far northwest of India, is a land of high-altitude desert and steppe enveloped by giant, barren mountains and rich in unfiltered Tibetan Buddhist culture. The region, which is dotted in spectacular, ancient monasteries and huge turquoise lakes, is India's best trekking region with the Markha valley trek being a classic that combines villages, homestays, breathless passes, canyons, and, as an add-on, even the chance to scale an easy 19,685-foot (6,000 m) peak!

Sing the praises of Khangchendzonga

SINGALILA TREK

As you head east along the Himalayas the climate and landscapes get wetter and greener. By the time you get to the tea town of Darjeeling in West Bengal the valleys are a riot of subtropical forests, tea estates, and paddy fields. Lording over all out here is Khangchendzonga (Kanchenjunga: 28,169 feet; 8,586 m), the world's third-highest mountain. The Singalila trek, which starts near Darjeeling, is a five-day classic hike through the region offering stupendous dawn views of the distant mountain.

Hike along the ice river

CHADAR TREK

The Chadar trek from Ladakh to Zanskar, another remote Buddhist valley, down the Zanskar River is not like any trek you've ever done before. It can only be attempted in the depths of the icy cold winter and involves following an ancient, seasonal trade route and actually hiking on the frozen river surface. The six-day trek is demanding and not without risk (a warming climate makes the ice ever thinner).

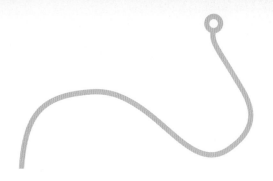

Baliem Valley

LOCATION
Papua, Indonesia

DURATION
3–5 days

DIFFICULTY
Easy

DISTANCE
Varies

MAP
No hiking maps available

START/END
Wamena

TRAIL MARKING
None

Meet former headhunters on the remote jungle trails of the island of New Guinea.

Less than a century ago the interior of the giant island of New Guinea (which is today split between the Indonesian province of Papua and the country of Papua New Guinea) was largely a blank on the maps. People living along the coasts of New Guinea told tales of small groups of hunter-gatherer tribes living in the jungle-coated mountains of the interior. But, by and large, the interior of New Guinea was unexplored and considered mostly uninhabited. So you can imagine the shock the world got when, in 1938, a zoological expedition flew over the interior of the island and discovered a huge highland valley filled with houses and farms: an entire lost civilization that had had no contact with the outside world. The shock increased even further when Western explorers first entered what was to become known as the Baliem Valley and met war-hardened headhunters with cannibalistic tendencies who dressed in little but animal skins, penis gourds, and bone necklaces.

Today, the Baliem Valley has been opened up to the outside world and hikers can meet the Dani people (now, fortunately, non-head-hunting nor cannibalistic) as they hike narrow, muddy jungle trails up and down steep mountain slopes and cross swaying wooden bridges over angry, boiling rivers. In fact, as impressive as the scenery is, it's the chance to meet the Dani people, many of whom still dress in a traditional manner, and stay in their houses and villages that is the most memorable aspect of hiking the Baliem Valley.

LEFT Traditional dome-shaped Dani *honai* houses in the Baliem Valley.

The Route

Treks in and around the Baliem can be as long or as short as you wish. Most of the very few foreigners who come here spend just three or four days on the jungle trails, but by adding in a day or so extra you can get to higher, remoter villages. Although there's no particular set trail with trail marking, you will be trekking along established paths linking settlements. This means that for the shortest trek a guide isn't strictly necessary, but your enjoyment of the hike and understanding of the Dani culture will increase many times over if you do have one.

Once out on the trail expect a lot of mud and a draining humidity. But otherwise, the hiking itself isn't too strenuous. At night you will be hosted in a village either in a purpose-built traditional-style woven bamboo building or in someone's equally traditional home. Food, which seems to consist of almost nothing but boiled sweet potato, will be provided by your hosts.

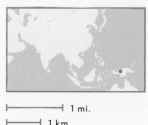

WAMENA

1 mi.

1 km

1 DANI PEOPLE

It only takes a day or so to become so accustomed to stopping to chat with a man whose only item of clothing is a bamboo penis gourd, that you stop taking much notice. And that's the great thing about trekking in the Baliem Valley. Despite the onslaught of church, telephone, education, and the very heavy-handed governance shown by Jakarta, many of the old traditions of the Dani people are refusing to totally die out. It's one of those rare places that seems to be hovering between prehistory and a connected twenty-first century, and for the moment it's unsure which one to focus on. Although this will likely change in the future, for now you should regard the stunning green mountain backdrops as just the background to an incredible human story.

2 WATER, WATER, EVERYWHERE

Whether it's the gentle drip, drip of raindrops falling onto jungle leaves, the burble of dozens of waterfalls, or the terrifying liquid hurricane of a river in full spate, the sound of water is a constant on the Baliem Valley hike. Most of the time the water here is a benefit. It shaped these steep valleys, created such intense greenery, and made for such fertility. But at other times the power and presence of the water here can be overwhelming, with landslides and flash floods being common. And some of the rivers here have to be seen to be believed. Roaring down valley, they must be crossed on swaying wooden bridges with missing and rotten planks, where one slip means game over.

3 HONAI AND SWEET POTATOES

The traditional Dani house is known as a *honai,* and you will see them in every village you encounter on your hike, and most nights will also be spent sleeping in one. These are grass and thatch bamboo buildings built on two levels. The upper part is where the family sleeps, while downstairs is reserved for cooking and entertaining. And what will they be cooking here? The answer is, almost invariably, sweet potatoes—boiled sweet potatoes. To you or me, one sweet potato probably tastes much like another sweet potato, but not to the Dani. They can't get enough of them and will enthusiastically describe the taste differences between each!

4 ADVENTURE

The Baliem Valley is more than enough adventure for most people, but if you need more than New Guinea can provide, head beyond the walls of the valley and you are no longer on a mere hiking vacation. It is now an expedition to who knows where. In remoter corners of New Guinea there are still uncontacted tribal groups, and cannibalism and headhunting are still thought to take place. So, ermm, don't stick your neck out there!

Walk here next

Many of the more rugged corners of Southeast Asia are inhabited by ethnic groups who retain lifestyles and customs very distinct from the mainstream of Southeast Asian life. Discover some of them on the following hiking trails.

Experience hill tribe trekking
LAOS

So-called hill tribe trekking is common to a number of Southeast Asian countries. Wherever you do it, it's an ideal way of mixing beautiful hill country scenery with a cultural immersion among the area's different ethnic groups. While northern Thailand might be the best-known place for hill tribe trekking, we'd recommend heading instead to Laos where the dearth of other foreign hikers makes for a more genuine cultural meeting between hiker and host. There are numerous different routes available.

Trek through tea country

PEKOE TEA TRAIL

Sri Lanka's hill country is an almost unnaturally beautiful area of hard rising peaks and hills laced with rivers and waterfalls that is, for the most part, covered top to toe in neatly clipped tea bushes. The Pekoe Tea Trail is a new three-week-long loop right through the best of the hill country. Put together with the help of the Sri Lankan private tourism sector, the EU, and the United States Agency for International Development (USAID), its goal is to encourage small-scale hiking tourism in rural areas.

Hike into the bowels of the Earth

IJEN CRATER

This is possibly the most bizarre hike in this book. The easy four-hour return hike up to the Ijen crater at the eastern end of Java offers fabulous views across rugged coffee country, but more intriguingly you will get to witness the almost medieval sight of miners descending into the smoking guts of a live, belching, spluttering volcanic crater to extract sulfur. And to make it even more surreal, if you do the trek at night the sulfur glows blue.

Mount Fuji

LOCATION
Fuji-Hakone-Izu National
Park, Japan

DURATION
3 days

DIFFICULTY
Hard

DISTANCE
16 miles (26.5 km)

MAP
www.fujimountainguides.com

START/END
Kitaguchi Hongu Fuji Sengen-Jinja
Shrine/5th Gotemba Station

TRAIL MARKING
Signs

LEFT Hikers ascend the Yoshida Route up
Mount Fuji in August.

Celebrate the sunrise on Japan's highest mountain.

Located on the island of Honshu, less than 75 miles (120 km) from Tokyo, Mount Fuji is a Japanese cultural icon, depicted in countless works of art. As the highest of Japan's three holy mountains, the 12,389 feet (3,776 m) summit has long been held sacred. Witnessing sunrise from the highest point in the Land of the Rising Sun has long been considered a pinnacle achievement for Japanese and tourists alike. But there's a reason for the oft-quoted Japanese saying, "A wise person will climb Mount Fuji once in their lifetime, but only a fool would climb it twice."

Each year, hundreds of thousands of wise people and a few fools climb Mount Fuji, most between July and September, when there is little to no snow on the summit. Climbing is possible from October to June but generally discouraged for all but experienced mountaineers. Mount Fuji is a textbook stratovolcano: a steep-sided, nearly symmetrical volcanic cone. Most of the mountain we see today is the result of major eruptions eleven thousand years ago. Fuji has erupted at least ten times since 781 CE. It last erupted in 1707 and is still considered active.

There are four major routes up the mountain—Kawaguchiko, Subashiri, Gotemba, and Fujinomiya—each starting from numbered stations partway up the mountain that are reachable by car or bus. Additionally, there are four historic routes that start at the base of the mountain: the Shojiko, Yoshida, Suyama, and Murayama Routes. Which route you take will depend on your fitness, experience, and desire for solitude on this busy mountain.

The Route

If you want to aim for the shortest, steepest route up the mountain, head to the Fujinomiya Route, which starts at an elevation of 7,800 feet (2,377 m), leaving 4,589 feet (1,399 m) to be gained in less than 2.5 miles (4 km) to the summit. However, if you're fit and want to retrace one of the historic routes up the mountain, plan on the Yoshida Route, which is one of the oldest paths up Mount Fuji.

The Yoshida Route starts at the Kitaguchi Hongu Fuji Sengen-Jinja Shrine at 2,780 feet (847 m) and is lined with shrines, teahouses, and huts. On the way you'll be following in the footsteps of centuries of countless pilgrims but are unlikely to see many other modern footprints or other people on this seldom-climbed path.

① FROM SHRINE TO TEAHOUSE TO HUT

The historic pilgrim's path up Mount Fuji begins through a wooden gate at the back garden of the Sengen Shrine. From here it's about 2.5 miles (4 km) on the Yoshida Recreational Footpath through a mossy forest to the Naka no Chaya teahouse, where you'll be able to purchase food and refill your water bottles. After another 2.5 miles (4 km) you'll reach the Umagaeshi hut at 4,757 feet (1,450 m) of elevation. This is the entrance to the holy area on Mount Fuji; *Umagaeshi* means "horses return" as this is where people historically had to dismount their horses and continue on foot.

SENGEN SHRINE

4 SUNRISE ON MOUNT FUJI

To catch sunrise on top of Mount Fuji, plan to spend the night at a hut at station 8 or 9, which puts you within striking distance of the summit. You'll need to start hiking around 3 a.m. to reach the summit before first light. The trails are steep but well marked. Hiking at night on Mount Fuji is common practice, but be sure to pack two headlamps and extra batteries.

As the sun peeks over the eastern horizon, join in the chorus of *Banzai! Banzai! Banzai!*, the traditional Japanese greeting for the new day.

5 SUMMIT CRATER

Mount Fuji is a stratovolcano, topped with a summit crater 2,560 feet (780 m) in diameter and nearly 800 feet (244 m) deep. You can't descend into the crater, but you should plan to hike all the way around it, a sacred trek called Ohachimeguri, which takes about an hour. Be sure to tag the true summit of Mount Fuji at the highest point of the crater rim, called Kengamine, the roof of Japan, at 12,389 feet (3,779 m).

6 THE DESCENT

Mount Fuji is often a once-and-done mountain because it's a relentlessly steep hike up crumbly, loose volcanic scree. The descent is much faster, as you can half run, half slide down the loose, ashy slopes. Regardless of which path they take up the mountain, most people descend either the Subashiri or Gotemba Routes because these routes are most conducive to scree skiing down the mountain. As you descend, be careful not to dislodge rocks onto hikers below. Once you reach station 5, you'll be able to take a bus the rest of the way down the mountain.

2 STATIONS 1 TO 5

The route up Mount Fuji is broken up into stations, with most people starting partway up the mountain at station 5 and the summit at station 10. Starting at the Sengen Shrine, you'll hike 7.5 miles (12 km) to reach station 5 on the Yoshida Route at 7,381 feet (2,250 m). Before 1872, women were forbidden from continuing past station 2 at 5,643 feet (1,720 m), as the mountain was sacred and women were traditionally excluded from religious sites.

3 MOUNT FUJI HUTS

To break your hike up into multiple days, make reservations at a hut or two. Camping is not permitted on the mountain. Each of the routes has multiple huts above station 5, with the busier routes having more stations. The Yoshida Route has over a dozen huts between stations 7 and 8. Most huts on Mount Fuji provide very basic sleeping accommodations, food, and drink so you don't have to carry overnight gear up the mountain.

Walk here next

Ask a child to draw a picture of a volcano and they'll probably draw a stratovolcano: a triangular cone with a ring of snow at the top. Stratovolcanoes usually stand high above the surrounding landscape, beckoning hikers and mountaineers to their often snowcapped summits.

See a volcano from all sides

WONDERLAND TRAIL

Climbing 14,411-foot (4,392 m) Mount Rainier, in Washington, USA, is a full-on mountaineering expedition, requiring ice axes, crampons, and a rope team to negotiate the mountain's deadly crevasses and avalanches. But backpackers can admire the volcano from all sides by hiking the Wonderland Trail, a 96-mile (154 km) loop that runs all the way around the volcano.

Hike into a cloud forest

MOUNT LIAMUIGA

This 3,792-foot (1,156 m) stratovolcano towers over the Caribbean island of Saint Kitts, forming the western half of the island, part of the Leeward Islands chain of the Lesser Antilles. Formerly known as Mount Misery, renamed Mount Liamuiga in 1983, the hike up this steep-sided volcano could be miserable if you try to go during the rainy season, when thick mud makes the trail very slippery. But during the dry season between March and October the 3.8-mile (6.1 km) round-trip trek is exquisite, passing through lush, incense-scented rain forest into an ethereal cloud forest. After gaining 2,000 feet (610 m) of elevation, you'll be rewarded with outstanding views over the surrounding Caribbean Sea, dotted by the neighboring islands of Saba, Sint Eustatius, Saint Barthélemy, Saint Martin, Antigua, and Nevis.

Head for the heights

VOLCÁN COTOPAXI

Scale one of the world's tallest stratovolcanoes on this 4.6-mile (7.4 km) out-and-back route to the summit of 19,347-foot (5,897 m) Cotopaxi in Ecuador. You'll likely need a guide unless you're very experienced at glacier travel, but the straightforward route is considered one of the best introductions to true mountaineering. Altitude is often the biggest challenge, so plan to acclimatize slowly and spend at least one night at the José F. Rivas Refuge at 15,748 feet (4,800 m).

Ubirr Trail

LOCATION
Kakadu National Park,
Northern Territory, Australia

DURATION
2 hours

DIFFICULTY
Easy

DISTANCE
1.2 miles (1.9 km)

MAP
Hema Northern Territory
State Map

START/END
Ubirr Road trailhead

TRAIL MARKING
Signs

LEFT Indigenous Australians have been painting the rock walls at Ubirr for many thousands of years as part of their storytelling culture.

Stroll in awe through one of the world's oldest prehistoric art galleries.

On the edge of the Nadab floodplain, in what is now Kakadu National Park (a UNESCO World Heritage Site), sits a cluster of rock outcrops dotted with small natural rock alcoves. People have been finding shade and shelter here for tens of thousands of years, and a few of these people were artists, who were inspired to paint the rock walls. Today the Ubirr Aboriginal rock art gallery is considered to be one of the oldest continuously utilized art galleries. Even without the paintings, this would be a beautiful, family-friendly hike around interesting rock formations. The artwork, however, is simply astonishing.

Using paints sourced from natural pigments like ocher, the paintings were rendered by the Gaagudju people, Indigenous Australians, on their seasonal migrations across the region. They called rock art *kunbim*, and it was an important part of their storytelling culture. Geochemical studies show that the rock faces have been continuously painted and repainted since at least 40,000 BCE, with most of the paintings having been created in the last two thousand years.

Rock art is ancient and extremely fragile. Handrails and boardwalks help keep visitors at a safe distance and reduce the dust kicked up around the paintings. Avoid breathing on the paintings and never touch them. At Ubirr, Indigenous Australian interpreters are often on hand to answer questions and offer interpretations of the artwork. Kakadu National Park is managed by local Indigenous landowners from the Bunitj, Manilagarr, and Mandjurlgunj people, along with Parks Australia.

The Route

The Ubirr Aboriginal art gallery is accessed by an easy 1.2-mile (1.9 km), partially paved wheelchair-accessible trail. The loop winds past three galleries—the main art gallery, Mabuyu, and Rainbow Serpent—that host the densest concentration of paintings. Other smaller panels are scattered throughout the rocks so keep your eyes peeled for less obvious paintings. A steeper optional side trail leads up past two more panels to an overlook of the Nadab floodplain that surrounds the Ubirr rock outcrop. This hike can be done year-round although the road to the site sometimes closes after heavy rains. Check with Parks Australia before your trip.

1 ANCIENT ART

In the Australian Indigenous art tradition, the act of painting is more sacred than the painting itself, so rock wall canvases were continuously recycled, with new paintings being applied directly over old artwork. Most of the still visible paintings on the surface are red, produced with durable iron oxide pigments made from crushed hematite. Orange, yellow, and white pigments tend to fade more quickly and often appear fainter. The panels typically depict creation and ancestor stories, as well as native animals like wallabies, goannas, and barramundi.

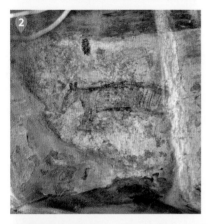

THE MAIN GALLERY

The main gallery at Ubirr is most famous for its "X-ray art," where the skeletons and internal organs of animals and people are depicted within the outlines of the figures. These unique images are from the freshwater period, within the last fifteen hundred years, and are thought to represent the abundance of food and game in the area, as they feature many kinds of plants and animals including fish, mussels, wallabies, and yams. At the northern end of the main gallery is a painting of a thylacine or Tasmanian tiger, an animal that went extinct on mainland Australia around two thousand years ago, a testament to the antiquity of the paintings. There is also a more recent scene that may represent early contact between Indigenous people and white settlers. A man, painted in white, wearing boots and pants, stands with his hands on his hips, in a confrontational pose.

MIMI SPIRITS

If you look high above the main panel, you might see Mimi spirits. These thin, elongated figures represent fairylike beings that live in rock crevasses. According to Indigenous folklore, the Mimi spirits were the first artists to adorn rock walls. They taught people how to paint and are thought of as mischievous but ultimately benevolent spirits. Many of the Mimi figures are painted high on the rock face, with no obvious way for people to reach them.

RAINBOW SERPENT GALLERY

The Rainbow Serpent gallery is the most sacred site at Ubirr. Traditionally, only women were allowed to visit the site, but this rule is not enforced for non-Indigenous visitors. Locals believe that this spot was visited by Garranga'rreli, the Rainbow Serpent, on her journey across Australia. As she crossed the landscape, she sang the rocks, plants, animals, and people into being. Her path, or song line, is still held sacred by Indigenous Australians. The image of the Rainbow Serpent is believed to be a self-portrait, drawn in her human form.

NADAB LOOKOUT

If you don't mind climbing a few stairs, take the side trail up to the Nadab Lookout. On the way up you'll pass by two more galleries, the Crosshatching gallery and Namarrkan Sisters, both with interpretive displays. For a timeless experience, try to save this hike for sunset, where you can watch the sun drop over the landscape as people have been doing from this very spot for eons.

Walk here next

People have been creating art on rock walls and caves for tens of thousands of years. The oldest surviving rock art dates back to forty-five thousand years ago with animals and hunting scenes being the most commonly rendered subjects. Here are a few more places you can visit rock art in Australia and beyond.

A long, hot hike with a grand reward
THE GREAT GALLERY

In the United States, Utah's canyon country is rich in rock art, both carved and painted. One of the best preserved and most striking panels is found in the Horseshoe Canyon area of Canyonlands National Park. Called the Great Gallery, this panel features larger than life-size humanoid figures decorated with intricate geometric designs. The panel is reached by a 10.6-mile (17 km) round-trip hike that starts on the canyon rim and descends into the dry riverbed. The canyon is beautiful, surrounded by sheer sandstone walls and shaded by mature cottonwood trees, but the hike can be a long, hot, sandy slog, so be sure to bring lots of water and plan to visit in the spring or fall, when temperatures are cooler.

Stroll among hundreds of petroglyphs
NGAJARLI TRAIL

The world's densest collection of rock art is protected within Murujuga National Park, on the Burrup Peninsula, in the Pilbara region of Western Australia. More than one million pieces of rock art have been cataloged here, some dating back forty thousand years. Most of the art here is in the form of engravings or petroglyphs, as opposed to the painted pictographs at Ubirr. A 2.6-mile (4.2 km) out-and-back trail through the Deep Gorge showcases hundreds of etchings that depict human figures, as well as animals, some of which are now extinct. The engravings are best viewed in the late afternoon, when the shadows make the shallow engravings stand out against the rock canvas.

Honor the world's oldest art
EL CASTILLO CAVE

Dating rock art paintings isn't easy, but uranium-thorium dating techniques can shed light on when pigments were originally applied to walls. The El Castillo Cave in Spain, discovered in 1903, contains the world's oldest dated rock art, painted at least 40,800 years ago, around when the first anatomically modern humans arrived in Europe. The cave is open for guided tours that last about forty-five minutes and cover about a mile (1.6 km) of ground. The paintings depict animals like horses, bison, aurochs, and mammoths, as well as human and geometric figures, along with hundreds of handprints. A 2013 analysis of the handprints found that the finger length ratio of the prints suggests that most of the hands belonged to women, casting doubt on the assumption that most Paleolithic artists were men.

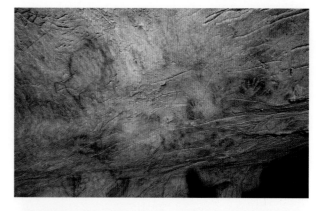

Larapinta Trail

LOCATION
Tjoritja/West MacDonnell
National Park, Northern
Territory, Australia

DURATION
16–20 days

DIFFICULTY
Hard

DISTANCE
138 miles (223 km)

MAP
Larapinta Trail Map Sections 1–10,
Hema Northern Territory Map

START/END
Alice Springs/Mount Sonder

TRAIL MARKING
Signs/posts

LEFT The permanent water hole at
Simpsons Gap reflects the cliffs of the
West MacDonnell mountain range.

Take a multiweek trek across central Australia's caterpillar mountains.

Following the rocky red spine of the West MacDonnell Ranges across central Australia, the Larapinta Trail is one of the country's longest and most spectacular footpaths. The 138-mile (223 km) route between Alice Springs and Mount Sonder was completed in 2000, but people have been traveling in this mountain range for thousands of years. These are the homelands of the Arrernte people, who have numerous sacred sites along what is now the Larapinta Trail, including rock art paintings, ceremonial shelters, and natural features, especially those associated with water sources—a precious commodity in this desert environment.

The West MacDonnell Ranges are a 400-mile-long (644 km) series of parallel-running ridges stretching across central Australia, east and west of Alice Springs. Between the ridges the landscape dips into spectacular notches and gorges; the trail tends to undulate between ridgetops and valleys, where the water sources are generally found. The end of the trail is also the high point, on top of 4,530-foot (1,380 m) Mount Sonder, the fourth-highest peak in the range. Sonder and the surrounding summits are made up of striking red quartzite, a very hard rock that has survived more than 350 million years of erosion.

Seen from the top of Mount Sonder, the West MacDonnell Ranges resemble a family of red caterpillars marching across the landscape. The Arrernte thought so too, as their oral histories of their 47,000-square-mile (121,729 sq km) territory tell of primordial caterpillar-beings forming the range and then giving rise to the Arrernte people.

The Route

The Larapinta Trail begins on the outskirts of Alice Springs, the third-largest town in the Northern Territory, called Mparntwe by the Arrernte. The trail then proceeds almost due west, climbing ridges and descending across gaps and valleys. The path is well marked with posts that track the trail's mileage. Water is available at least once a day, sometimes from natural sources and sometimes from water tanks installed and maintained by West MacDonnell National Park.

 **SIMPSONS GAP**

The first reliable natural water source is found 15 miles (24 km) from Alice Springs, at Simpsons Gap, a sacred place for the Arrernte, who call it Rungutjirpa. Most people break this section up into two days by also stopping at Wallaby Gap, where you'll find campsites and a water tank. Simpsons Gap is a natural watering hole that is an important source for wild animals such as the black-footed rock-wallaby, making this a good spot for wildlife watching. Take care not to camp or linger too close to the water, as your presence will scare away wildlife that need to drink here.

② WATER SOURCES

Central Australia is a very arid environment, with few natural year-round water sources. Planning a Larapinta trek will revolve around available water, and you'll want to double-check availability with the park before leaving on your trek. Most people hike during the cool winter months, as

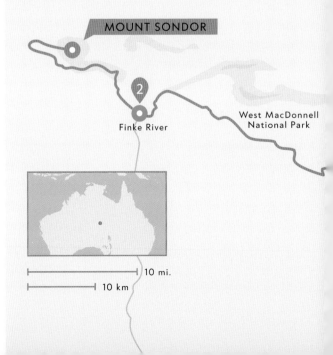

MOUNT SONDOR

② Finke River

West MacDonnell National Park

⊢——⊣ 10 mi.

⊢——⊣ 10 km

summer is far too hot and exposed for trekking. The park maintains many tanks on the route, at all trailheads and a few key locations along the way. Natural water sources can be found at Ellery Creek Big Hole, Serpentine Gorge, the Finke River, and Davenport Creek. All water from both natural and artificial sources should be treated with a filter or tablets before drinking.

③ STANDLEY CHASM

About 40 miles (64 km) from Alice Springs you'll come to Standley Chasm, a narrow canyon that tightens to less than 3 feet (90 cm) across. The Arrernte call this slot Angkerle Atwatye, meaning the "gap of water." Water only flows here occasionally, usually after storms, but the campground has a water tank. This is a popular day hiking destination from a nearby car-accessed trailhead. People aim to be here around noon to catch the sun directly overhead so it illuminates the red canyon walls for photographs.

④ OCHER PITS

Indigenous Australians have used ocher for thousands of years to make pigments for art, adornment, and ceremonies. The soft, vivid ocher from these pits 62 miles (100 km) into the Larapinta Trail is some of the most highly valued ocher on the Australian continent, and the mine is owned by the Western Arrernte people. Geochemists can fingerprint individual ocher sources using the unique chemical signature of each source. Ocher from this pit has been found throughout Australia, traded between neighboring clans. Traditionally, the ocher here was mined by locals and then mixed with emu fat to make pigment.

⑤ GOSSE BLUFF

From some of the high points along the Larapinta Trail, including the grand finale on top of Mount Sonder, you might catch a glimpse of an ancient cataclysm to the southwest. During the Cretaceous period, 142 million years ago, a huge comet slammed into what is now Australia, carving out a crater 14 miles (22.5 km) in diameter. Erosion has erased much of this depression, leaving behind a 3-mile-wide (5 km) ring. The Arrernte people call this place Tnorala, and the site is protected within the Tnorala Conservation Reserve.

TELEGRAPH STATION

Simpsons Gap

Wallaby Gap

③ Standley Chasm

② Serpentine Gorge

Ellery Creek

②

①

①

Alice Springs

Walk here next

Each year, thousands of meteors fall to Earth, but most burn up in the atmosphere, creating shooting stars. A few times in the planet's 4.5-billion-year history, however, meteors large enough to survive entry have collided with the planet's surface, leaving enormous impact craters and even triggering mass extinction events. Today, around 130 of these scars remain on the Earth's surface. Younger craters are often more visible, as they have not yet been eroded into oblivion.

Descend into a salty crater
TSWAING IMPACT CRATER

This salt-filled impact crater in South Africa was formed by a meteor impact 220,000 years ago. Over time the 330-foot-deep (100 m) depression filled with water, which then evaporated, leaving a crust of white salt on the surface. People have been collecting salt from the impact crater for thousands of years. A 4.5-mile-long (7.2 km) trail loops around the crater and descends into its salty interior.

Follow an easy rim route

BARRINGER CRATER

You can't descend into the privately owned Meteor Crater in northeast Arizona, USA, but the easy mile-long (1.6 km) trail along its rim is spectacular. This is considered to be one of the world's youngest and best-preserved meteor craters, as the impact occurred only 50,000 years ago, a short blink in geological time. The informative visitor center and museum are also worth the price of admission.

Walk around a mysterious feature

UPHEAVAL DOME

Depending on whom you ask, this enigmatic landform in Canyonlands National Park, Utah, USA, could be a salt dome or a meteor crater. Get a view from all angles on the 8.6-mile (13.8 km) Syncline Loop that circumnavigates the 6.2-mile (10 km) diameter landform. If that's too much, a 1.3-mile (2 km) out-and-back trail runs up to two overlooks of the landform's oddly concentric rings.

Great Ocean Walk

LEFT The Great Ocean Walk: hikers will
need to take account of the tides.

Take a long walk on the beach along Australia's Shipwreck Coast.

Australia's Great Ocean Road is a scenic drive that runs for 151 miles (243 km) along Victoria's southwest coast, between Torquay and Allansford. A 65-mile (105 km) footpath called the Great Ocean Walk parallels part of the drive, between Apollo Bay and Glenample Homestead, undulating between rocky clifftops and sandy beaches. The trail runs through Great Otway National Park and the Otway Range, a low coastal range famous for its fern-gully forests.

Wildlife is abundant along this trek, both offshore and in the forested hinterlands. Koalas, wallabies, and echidnas, as well as many species of birds and reptiles are commonly seen in the forested areas, while fur seals, little penguins, and southern right and humpback whales are often spotted offshore, particularly between June and September. This trek can be done all year, but the best weather is usually found in the spring and fall months, between late September and late November and early March to mid-May. Winter can be pleasant between storms but avoid the coastline during gales, as the winds and waves can be legendary along this coastline.

The greatest challenge of this hike is the tides; in some locations at high tide, the waves completely cover the beaches and crash against the base of the cliffs. You don't want to get caught on the beaches during high tides, as drowning is a very real danger. You'll need to plan out your daily mileage with the timing of the tides and in some places, you'll need to wait for several hours for the tides to recede before proceeding.

The Route

This is a one-way trail, starting from Apollo Bay and running west to the Twelve Apostles. The hike can be done in shorter sections or as an eight-day thru-hike, making use of the seven designated campsites spaced every 6 to 9 miles (9.5–14.5 km) along the route. Each campsite has between eight and fifteen tent pads, as well as three-sided wind shelters, picnic tables, and toilets. Some also provide water, when natural fresh sources are not available nearby, but you should plan to filter or treat all water on the trek.

① THE SHIPWRECK COAST

The coastline between Cape Otway and Port Fairy is nicknamed the Shipwreck Coast. Over six hundred ships met their end here on the rocks and reefs offshore. More than 240 shipwrecks have been mapped and explored by divers with a few washed up onto the beaches, where their rusting hulls appear and disappear with the tides and the seasons. The hulls of *Marie Gabrielle*, wrecked in 1869, and the *Fiji*, ran aground in 1891, can be seen on Johanna Beach and Wreck Beach respectively. The rest have been lost to the sea, scattered by relentless waves and wind. In 1848, the Cape Otway Lightstation was lit for the first time; it guided ships around the cape until 1994, when it was decommissioned. Today it's the oldest surviving lighthouse in Australia. The lighthouse is open for tours, so check the operating hours if you're craving a bit of history on your hike.

PORT CAMPBELL

The Twelve Apostles

④

Devil's Kitchen campsite

Wreck Beach

Ryan's Den campsite

①

2 DINOSAUR FOSSILS

West of Cape Otway lies Dinosaur Cove. The cliffs here are made up of fossil-rich rocks dating to 106 million years ago, during the early Cretaceous, when dinosaurs roamed what is now Australia. Back then, Australia was newly separated from Antarctica and just beginning its northward journey to its current location. In the 1980s and 1990s several species of dinosaurs were excavated from these cliffs, and the finds helped shed light on the evolutionary history of dinosaurs in Australia and the southern hemisphere.

3 GLOWING WORMS

While the more charismatic animals like koalas and whales get most of the attention along this trek, tiny gnat larvae are also worth watching for along wet stream banks. These larvae are bioluminescent; they produce light-emitting enzymes that give off a bluish glow. The light attracts the larvae's tiny prey to its sticky spiderlike threads. Glow worms are most often seen along the Great Ocean Walk in Angahook-Lorne State Park and Melba Gully Day Visitor Area (in Great Otway National Park).

4 THE TWELVE APOSTLES

One of the most famous viewpoints along the Great Ocean Drive is of the Twelve Apostles, a cluster of limestone sea stacks in Port Campbell National Park. The formations were named after the biblical twelve apostles but the name is a bit misleading, as there were never twelve sea stacks. In modern times, there were eight sea stacks but in July 2015, one of these collapsed into the waves, leaving seven. The stacks are formed from the Port Campbell limestone, dating to the mid to late Miocene, between fifteen and five million years ago. They were once sea cliffs, but wave action has eroded the cliffs into caves and then into arches that collapsed, leaving stacks of rocks as high as 160 feet (49 m).

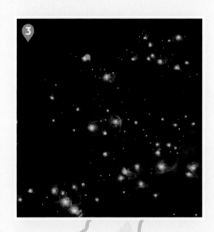

Johanna Beach campsite

Dinosaur Cove

Aire River west campground

APOLLO BAY

Elliot's Ridge campsite

Parker Hill Campsite

Cape Otway Lightstation

5 mi.

5 km

Walk here next

The Australian continent can be thought of as the world's largest island with more than 16,000 miles (25,750 km) of coastline. So it should come as no surprise that Australia has more than its fair share of epic beach hikes. Here are a few more places you can take a long (or short) walk on the beaches down under.

Take an urban hike along the Sydney coast

BONDI BEACH TO COOGEE BEACH

This 3.5-mile (5.6 km) point-to-point trek is an urban hike, as it follows the coastline of Sydney, Australia's largest city. But what it lacks in solitude, it makes up for in scenery and beautiful swimming beaches. To hike this route, park a car at either end and catch a public transport bus to begin your walk back to your car. Along the way you'll pass through several parks and public beaches. Be sure to pack sunscreen and a bathing suit!

Connect two capes

LEEUWIN-NATURALISTE NATIONAL PARK

This coastal walk is bookended by two lighthouses at Cape Naturaliste and Cape Leeuwin, with 76 miles (122 km) of stunning coastal scenery in between. The hike follows the Leeuwin-Naturaliste Ridge, a ridge of limestone that forms the backbone of the national park. Along the way you'll pass by several vineyards, and there are tour companies that offer wine-tasting treks that combine luxury camping with vineyard visits.

Walk on the Great Barrier Reef

THORSBORNE TRAIL

Australia's Great Barrier Reef, just off the east coast of Queensland, is the planet's largest coral reef system, covering more than 133,000 square miles (344,468 sq km) of reefs and islands. Most people explore the Great Barrier Reef by snorkeling or scuba diving, but if you'd rather keep your feet dry, set off on the Thorsborne Trail. This 20-mile (32 km) point-to-point hike crosses Hinchinbrook Island, the largest island in the Great Barrier Reef system. Most people complete the one-way trek in three to four days by taking a ferry shuttle to start in Ramsay Bay and hiking from north to south, ending at George Point.

Dove Lake Circuit

Circle serene Dove Lake at the base of Cradle Mountain.

LOCATION
Cradle Mountain–Lake
St Clair National Park,
Tasmania, Australia

DURATION
2–3 hours

DIFFICULTY
Easy

DISTANCE
4 miles (6 km)

MAP
Hema Tasmania State Map

START/END
Dove Lake trailhead

TRAIL MARKING
Signs

Tasmania's craggy Central Highlands look like a land before time, so much so that when the producers of *Walking With Dinosaurs* and *When Dinosaurs Roamed America* were searching for Mesozoic-looking landscapes, they gave Cradle Mountain–Lake St Clair National Park a starring role in the documentaries.

This pristine landscape is home to many of Australia's famously endemic species. Around half of the park's alpine flora is found nowhere else on Earth. Many of the animals here are unique to Australia, the result of millions of years of evolution on an isolated continent including Tasmanian devils, wombats, short-beaked echidnas, and platypuses. Of these, devils and wombats are marsupials (mammals that carry their young in a pouch) and echidnas and platypuses are monotremes (mammals that lay eggs). Placental mammals that give birth to live young are rare; only dingoes, rodents, and bats are native to Australia. All the other native mammals are either marsupials or monotremes.

People have been thriving in Australia for eons as well. The park sits on the traditional territorial boundary between the Big River and Northern Tasmanian Aboriginal nations. Archaeological evidence of Aboriginal people in the Cradle Mountain area dates back at least ten thousand years, and they were likely there much earlier. These mountains were probably seasonal hunting and gathering grounds, dotted with temporary campsites and huts. Artifacts, campsites, and stone tools have been found around the Pelion Plains and Lake St Clair.

LEFT Hikers on top of Glacier Rock with Cradle Mountain in the background.

The Route

The 4-mile (6.5 km) loop around Dove Lake is one of the best introductions to this incredible park. The trail circles Dove Lake, in the shadow of the impressive spires of Cradle Mountain. Much of the route follows a wooden boardwalk, to minimize erosion around the fragile shoreline. The hike is mostly level and family-friendly. Consider bringing binoculars to help you spot wildlife around the lake.

DOVE LAKE

This high alpine lake sits in a bowl that was scooped out by passing glaciers during the last ice age. The lake is strikingly blue. Tea tree leaves and button grass fibers leach into the water, creating an oiled-mirror effect on the surface that perfectly reflects the sky. As you circle the lake, keep your camera handy to capture a picture-postcard-worthy shot of the sky-blue lake reflecting the jagged peaks of snowcapped Cradle Mountain.

THE BALLROOM FOREST

Like much of Tasmania, this area sees a lot of rain in the summer and snow in the winter, totaling over 100 inches (2,540 mm) of precipitation each year. The consistently wet weather gives rise to incredibly green moss-spangled temperate rain forests populated with myrtle beech trees. This type of forest is increasingly rare in Australia, due to brush fires that sweep across the continent most summers. Many plant species in Australia, such as eucalyptus trees, have evolved to cope with and even thrive after fires, but myrtle beech tree forests tend not to recover after fires, with other species moving in to take their place.

③ GLACIER ROCK

On the east side of Dove Lake, the trail passes by Glacier Rock. If you look closely, you'll see that this enormous boulder is etched with striations from a passing glacier. As the mass of ice scraped past the rock, it left behind parallel-running lines on the face of the rock. The boulder is made up of quartzite, an incredibly hard metamorphic rock, a testament to the erosive power of moving ice. This same ice also scooped out the bowl of Dove Lake as it retreated downslope from the crown of Cradle Mountain.

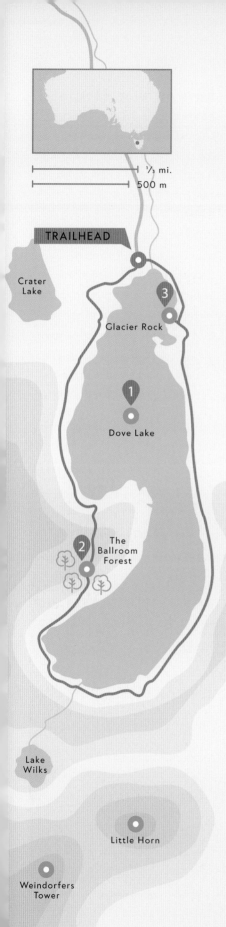

TRAILHEAD

Crater Lake

Glacier Rock

1

Dove Lake

2 The Ballroom Forest

Lake Wilks

Little Horn

Weindorfers Tower

⅓ mi.
500 m

4 CRADLE MOUNTAIN

Dove Lake sits at the base of Cradle Mountain, the centerpiece of the northern section of the national park. Cradle Mountain is the sixth-highest mountain in Tasmania, with four named summits: Cradle Mountain, topping out at 5,069 feet (1,545 m), Smithies Peak (5,010 feet; 1,527 m), Weindorfers Tower (4,787 feet; 1,459 m), and Little Horn (4,446 feet; 1,355 m). Named for its resemblance to a gold-mining cradle, the mountain's jagged spines are formed from dolerite, an igneous rock that intruded underground millions of years ago and was brought to the surface by erosion and then carved by glaciers during the last ice age.

Walk here next

Dove Lake is a great place to start exploring Cradle Mountain–Lake St Clair National Park, but there are several other world-class hikes in the area, if you have the time and energy to hike a few more miles through this prehistoric landscape.

A grueling fair weather scramble

CRADLE MOUNTAIN SUMMIT

For a bird's-eye view of Dove Lake, head to the top of Cradle Mountain. The 8-mile (13 km) out-and-back trail to the summit gains about 2,000 feet (610 m) of elevation, on an occasionally steep and exposed trail. Don't attempt this trek in anything but bluebird weather; high winds, wet weather, and freezing temperatures pose a very real threat to unprepared hikers. But if you find yourself in the park on a rare clear, sunny day, the spectacular views are worth the effort.

An easier hike for spectacular views of the park

MARIONS LOOKOUT

If you'd like to see Dove Lake from above but don't have the gumption to head for the summit of Cradle Mountain, aim for Marions Lookout instead. This moderate 5.7-mile (9 km) loop, best hiked counter-clockwise, visits Dove Lake, as well as several other alpine lakes in the shadow of Cradle Mountain. Instead of a harrowing scramble to the mountain's summit, this well-constructed trail tops out at Marions Lookout, a vantage point at 4,013 feet (1,223 m) that also provides epic views of the park.

Follow an ancient Aboriginal footpath

OVERLAND TRACK

Hit all the highlights of Cradle Mountain–Lake St Clair National Park on the Overland Track, a 50-mile (80 km) north to south route that links Cradle Mountain with Lake St Clair, Australia's deepest lake. The trail follows an ancient Aboriginal footpath that runs along the boundary between the Big River and Northern Tasmanian Aboriginal nations. Hikers are required to stay in a series of six huts along the route, with tent camping allowed on platforms outside of the huts. Most people complete the trek in five or six days, except for the runners of the annual Cradle Mountain Run, who complete the grand traverse in under eight hours.

Three Capes Track

Hike to the ends of the Earth on the ragged edge of Tasmania.

Curiously, there are only two capes along Australia's famous Three Capes Track: Cape Pillar and Cape Hauy. To hike the third, you'll need to tack on an 8.7-mile (14 km) out-and-back day hike to the tip of Cape Raoul, west of Port Arthur, best done as a warm-up before tackling the other two capes on your four-day hut-to-hut trip. But even if you skip the day hike and only visit the two capes, you won't feel short-changed on this gorgeous multiday hike along the Tasmanian coast. Between the colorful stands of eucalyptus trees and stunning views of the Tasman Sea along the narrow, clifftop peninsulas, there are many reasons that this is one of Australia's most popular treks.

Devils and Tigers

The island of Tasmania, located 150 miles (241 km) south of the mainland, was separated from Australia by rising sea levels around 11,700 years ago. The Bass Strait has presented a formidable barrier to animal and plant migration for at least that long, resulting in a unique assemblage of flora and fauna on the island. The most famous endemic residents of Tasmania are the Tasmanian devil, a small carnivorous marsupial, and the Tasmanian tiger, or thylacine, which was declared extinct by the Tasmanian government in 1986. The last thylacine was shot in the wild in 1938, but rumors and unconfirmed sightings of the doglike tiger-striped marsupial persist to the present day.

LOCATION
Tasman National Park, Tasmania, Australia

DURATION
4 days

DIFFICULTY
Moderate

DISTANCE
28.5 miles (46 km)

MAP
Hema Tasmania State Map

START/END
Port Arthur/Fortescue Bay

TRAIL MARKING
Signs

LEFT View of Tasman Island and lighthouse from the sheer cliffs of the Blade, Cape Pillar.

The Route

The Three Capes Track begins at Port Arthur, once a penal colony, now a historic site, where you'll catch a boat across the bay of Port Arthur to Denmans Cove. From there you'll trek for four days, stopping each night at modern huts, so you don't need to carry a tent or cooking equipment. The four-day walk visits Cape Pillar, Cape Hauy, Mount Fortescue, Arthurs Peak, and the Ellarwey Valley, and ends at Fortescue Bay.

 PORT ARTHUR

Port Arthur is a beautiful place with a notorious past. Located 60 miles (97 km) southeast of the state capital Hobart, Port Arthur operated as a large penal colony from the 1830s until 1877. Touted as an inescapable prison, the peninsula on which Port Arthur sits is a natural fortress, surrounded by water. The only connection to the Tasmanian mainland is via a 100-foot-wide (30 m) isthmus called Eaglehawk Neck. Today the penal colony is preserved as the Port Arthur Historic Site.

 CAPE PILLAR

The southeasternmost point of the island of Tasmania is a long, narrow strip of land that juts out into the Tasman Sea. This cape is named for its distinctive pillars of Jurassic-era dolerite, a type of volcanic rock that forms the tallest sea cliffs in Australia, soaring 980 feet (299 m) high above the waves. As you approach the needlelike end of the cape, the towering columns of dolerite narrow to a dramatic, crumbling knife-edge called the Blade. Offshore sits the oval-shaped cliff-bound Tasman Island, home of the Tasman Island Lighthouse, truly the ends of the Earth.

 OVERNIGHT HUTS

On the Three Capes Track you can choose to carry a tent and camp in designated campsites or book beds in the three backcountry huts—Surveyors Cove, Munro, and Retakunna Creek—along the way. Each hut has running water, gas top stoves, sleeping cots, and toilets, as well as modern amenities like USB charging stations, yoga mats, and memory foam mattresses. The huts sleep four to eight people so tenting will likely be a quieter option.

 CAPE HAUY

The second cape of the Three Capes Track isn't as dramatically narrow as Cape Pillar, but the views of the rocky coastline and the sea beyond on both sides of the cape are just as spectacular. You'll descend a series of steps toward the end of the cape, which is also lined by towering dolerite columns that plunge straight down into the sea. Be careful of the cliff edges as it's often windy here. You might consider carrying binoculars on your trek as this is an epic spot to watch for humpback whales, seals, seabirds, and the endangered Tasmanian wedge-tailed eagle.

 MOUNT FORTESCUE

The high point of this hike comes on day three, with a climb up 1,608-foot (490 m) Mount Fortescue. The trail up the mountain runs through mossy, fern-filled eucalyptus forest. Keep an eye out for the elusive Tasmanian short-beaked echidna, a spiny-backed insect-eating mammal that lays eggs. From the summit, through thick vegetation, you'll be able to see Cape Pillar, Cape Hauy, Fortescue Bay, and the rest of the trek.

DENMANS COVE

Cape
Hauy

Port
Arthur

FORTESCUE

Surveyors Cove
hut

Mount Fortescue

Retakunna Creek
hut

TASMAN SEA

Munro
hut

Cape
Pillar

The
Chasm

The
Blade

2 mi.

2 km

Tasman
Island

Walk here next

These scenic cape treks combine rugged terrain with dramatic, steep cliffs, native bush, and spectacular coastal views of crystal clear waters.

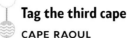

Tag the third cape

CAPE RAOUL

The third cape of the Three Capes Track, Cape Raoul, is located west of Port Arthur, whereas the rest of the Three Capes Track is on the east side of the bay. This hike to the southernmost tip of the Tasman Peninsula is best done as a day hike before you undertake the four-day Three Capes Track. The 8.7-mile (14 km) out-and-back trail is well-maintained by the park but requires 4,400 feet (1,341 m) of elevation gain, mainly on the tip of the peninsula, which is paved with many stairs to negotiate the rugged clifftop route, and on the way back to Port Arthur. Like Cape Pillar and Cape Hauy, Cape Raoul is lined with dramatic dolerite columns that have been eroded to a point by the crashing waves of the Tasman Sea.

A challenging hike through dramatic coastal scenery

CAPE BRETT TRACK

Can't get enough of cape treks? Set out for this 18.8-mile (30.2 km) round-trip adventure to the top of the long, narrow Cape Brett, near the tip of New Zealand's North Island. At the very end you'll find the Cape Brett hut, with stellar views of the Cape Brett Lighthouse and the aptly named Bay of Islands. Pack a swimsuit and beach towel for the hour-long side trip to Deep Water Cove, where you'll find a picturesque sandy beach.

Milford Track

LOCATION
Fiordland National Park,
New Zealand

DURATION
4 days

DIFFICULTY
Moderate

DISTANCE
33 miles (53 km)

MAP
Hema New Zealand South
Island Map

START/END
Glade Wharf/Sandfly Point

TRAIL MARKING
Signs

LEFT Hikers pass the tarn pond atop
McKinnon Pass on the Milford Track.

Hike New Zealand's most famous Great Walk to its most famous fjord.

Long before this area of the South Island of New Zealand was set aside as a national reserve in 1904, it was explored and revered by the Māori people. Many of Fiordland National Park's famous trails are built atop ancient Māori footpaths. The Milford Track, arguably the most famous of New Zealand's ten Great Walks, follows a 33-mile (53 km) route linking U-shaped glacier-carved valleys along the southwest coast.

This trek begins and ends with a boat ride across two different lakes. It begins on the South Island's largest lake and passes New Zealand's tallest waterfall before the grand finale at Milford Sound, one of Fiordland National Park's many fiords.

Fiordland is named for the fourteen narrow inlets carved into the coastline by glaciers. During the last ice age, rivers of ice spilled from the 8,000-foot (2,438 m) summits of the Darran Mountains down to the coast, gouging deep grooves in the landscape, some reaching as far as 25 miles (40 km) inland. These deeply incised fjords, paired with the rugged alpine landscape of the New Zealand Southern Alps, combine to make Fiordland an incredibly scenic but highly inaccessible park.

In contrast with the craggy cliffs, this is a lush, green landscape. Prodigious year-round precipitation is brought by the prevailing westerly winds from the Tasman Sea into the mountains, producing considerable rainfall in the summer months and snow in the winter. All that rain gives rise to temperate rain forests rich in biodiversity, as well as incredible waterfalls—some of the highest in the world.

The Route

To get to the start of the Milford Track you'll need to catch a ferry from Te Anau Downs boat harbor to the north shore of Lake Te Anau, a one-and-a-half-hour journey. Some people spend their first night here at Glade House before hitting the trail north. The trek takes four days, stopping at a hut each night before ending at Sandfly Point on the south shore of Milford Sound. From there you'll board another boat for the last leg of the journey back to Lake Te Anau.

 MCKINNON PASS

The biggest physical test of the trek comes on day three with the hike up McKinnon Pass. Māori call this pass Omanui, meaning the "great escape," as it's a bit of a hidden route up and over the mountains between the Clinton River valley and the Arthur River valley. The trail zigzags up through dense rain forest before emerging into the alpine zone between Mount Hart and Mount Balloon, gaining more than 2,400 feet (731 m) of elevation. On clear days, you'll be rewarded with a 360-degree view of the surrounding landscape, but these days are rare; visibility at the the pass is often restricted by clouds and rain. But even wet weather is beautiful here, as fog adds an air of mystery to the landscape. If you find yourself wet and shivering at the top of the pass, warm up in Pass Hut, a day lodge at the summit. The current hut is the fifth built at the pass, with three of the previous four having been blown off the summit by high winds.

TASMAN SEA

Stirling Falls ④

MILFORD
SOUND

SANDFLY POINT

④ Lady
Bowen
Falls

③

Lake Ada

② Quinton Lodge

Sutherland Falls ⓢ
McKinnon Pass

Lake
Quill ①

5 mi.
5 km

GLADE HOUSE ④

② SUTHERLAND FALLS

After the steep descent from McKinnon Pass into the Arthur River valley, you'll reach Quintin Lodge, your third and last hut of the trip. After dropping your gear, be sure to take the ninety-minute round-trip side mission to Sutherland Falls, the fifth- (or seventh, depending on how you measure) highest cascade in the world. These impressive falls drop in three tiers from Lake Quill, cascading for more than 1,900 feet (579 m) down precipitous cliffs. If the falls look familiar, it may be because they appear in the 2012 fantasy film *The Hobbit*. If you're curious about the source of the falls, Lake Quill can be visited on the side trail from the top of McKinnon Pass.

③ LAKE ADA

On the last day of the trek, you'll hike along the western shore of long, skinny Lake Ada. Around nine hundred years ago, a massive landslide dammed the Arthur River, creating Lake Ada. Landslides are common in New Zealand, due to the steep terrain and plentiful rainfall that lubricates steep slopes. Slides can also be triggered by earthquakes; the North and South Islands of New Zealand sit atop the seam between two major colliding tectonic plates, the Pacific and Australian plates.

④ MILFORD SOUND/PIOPIOTAHI

Milford Sound, also known by its Māori name, Piopiotahi, is a fitting end to this spectacular trek. This fjord is hemmed in by sheer rock faces that rise nearly 4,000 feet (1,219 m) on either side of the narrow opening to the Tasman Sea. Two 500-foot-high (152 m) waterfalls run down the cliffs surrounding the sound: Lady Bowen Falls and Stirling Falls. If you're lucky enough to be here on a rainy day—chances are high as this is one of the rainiest places on Earth—you'll be treated to many more temporary waterfalls spilling down the cliffs.

Walk here next

In some countries, they're called fiords and in others, fjords, but no matter how you spell it the landform is the same: a long, narrow arm of seawater that stretches inland when the ocean invades a glacier-carved valley. The term fjord comes from a Viking phrase meaning "ferry crossing" as the seafarers often used fjords to travel throughout Scandinavia.

Overlook Norway's deepest fjord

VIDASETHOVDEN

Norway has the highest concentration of fjords in the world, with over 1,700 named fjords along its 3,500-mile (5,633 km) coastline. The 5.6-mile (9 km) round-trip hike up to Vidasethovden leads to an overlook of one of the deepest fjords in the world. Reaching more than 120 miles (193 km) inland, the Sognefjord is Norway's longest and deepest fjord, plumbing depths of 4,300 feet (1,311 m) below sea level.

Get your feet wet

GLYMUR FALLS

Iceland has over a hundred fjords, most clustered in the Eastfjords and Westfjords on opposite sides of the island. Hvalfjörður Fjord in the Westfjords is home to Iceland's second-tallest waterfall. Fed by the Botnsá River, Glymur falls 650 feet (198 m), spilling down moss-covered volcanic rocks. The hike to the falls is a 4.7-mile (7.5 km) loop, best hiked counterclockwise. Be prepared for two cold river crossings with water shoes and hiking poles for balance.

Tongariro Alpine Crossing

LEFT Hikers on the Tongariro Crossing,
with Ngāuruhoe in the background.

Follow in Frodo's footsteps in the shadow of Mount Doom.

New Zealand is a land of superlatives, so when a hike is touted as the best day hike in the country and one of the best day hikes in the world, it's sure to be an incredible experience. Tongariro National Park, New Zealand's first national park, established in 1887, features scenery so fantastic that it was featured in the *Lord of the Rings* movie trilogy, with the volcanic cone of Ngāuruhoe standing in for Middle Earth's Mount Doom.

The 12-mile (19 km) Tongariro Alpine Crossing traverses a vast, alpine landscape of recent lava flows, active fumaroles, electric blue crater lakes, and sulfurous hot springs. The landscape is dominated by the park's three largest volcanoes: 9,177-foot (2,797 m) Ruapehu, 7,516-foot (2,291 m) Ngāuruhoe, and 6,490-foot (1,978 m) Tongariro. Be sure to check current conditions before setting out on a hike, as these volcanoes are still active and eruptions may occur at any time.

The twelve volcanic vents of Tongariro National Park sit at the southern end of a 1,550-mile (2,494 km) line of volcanoes that stretches across New Zealand, marking where the Australian tectonic plate is subducting under the Pacific plate. This process of subduction triggers melting along the slab interface, creating buoyant magma that rises to the surface. The Tongariro volcanic complex is at least two million years old, with the older, northernmost volcanoes Pīhanga and the Kakaramea-Tihia Massif last erupting over twenty thousand years ago.

The Route

You'll need to catch a shuttle for this point-to-point hike. Plan to leave your car at the end of the hike at Ketetahi Hot Springs parking lot and take a free park shuttle to the higher elevation western end at Mangatepopo. From Mangatepopo, the Tongariro Alpine Crossing trail passes between 7,516-foot (2,291 m) Ngāuruhoe, and 6,490-foot (1,978 m) Tongariro before turning north to pass over the summit of Red Crater, a 6,129-foot (1,868 m) volcano that's the high point of the hike. The trail then descends past the Emerald Lakes and the larger Blue Lake before ending back at your car at Ketetahi Hot Springs.

1 VOLCANIC VISTAS

For the entire length of the crossing, you'll be hiking on solidified lava flows, loose tephra—smaller rock particles ejected from the volcanic vent—and lava bombs, larger rocks thrown by a volcano during an eruption. The landscape is amazingly colorful with many hues of red iron and yellow sulfur standing out against the dark rock. In several areas, active fumaroles roil at the surface, spewing steam and sulfur dioxide.

2 MOST RECENT ERUPTIONS

In August and November 2012, the Te Maari craters on Mount Tongariro erupted, showering the route with a layer of ash and volcanic rocks. Nobody was hurt, but the Ketetahi Hut was damaged by volcanic bombs, and the trail was closed for several days after both eruptions. Ngāuruhoe has erupted more than sixty times in the last 150 years, with the most recent events occurring in 1973 and 1975.

Ketetahi
Hot Springs

Blue
Lake

Mount
Tongariro

Emerald
Lakes

MANGATEPOPO

3 EMERALD LAKES

The contrast between the stark volcanic landscape and the luminous Emerald and Blue Lakes is one of the things that makes this walk so spectacular. The otherworldly color of the pools is due to sunlight reflecting off volcanic minerals dissolved in the water. These lakes sit inside craters from past eruptions that have filled with rainwater and snowmelt. In a few places, orange tendrils on the edge of the lake indicate colonization by thermophilic microorganisms. The hike also features several scalding hot springs, including Ketetahi Hot Springs. None of the hot springs are safe for soaking, and the mineral-laden water is not safe for drinking. Plan on bringing all the water you'll need for your hike.

4 MOUNT DOOM

Tempting as it might be to try to re-create some of the *Lord of the Rings*' dramatic scenes on Mount Doom, the local Māori tribe campaigned to have Ngāuruhoe closed to outsiders after the movie, to protect the mountain from erosion. But don't be too disappointed; the volcano's steep slopes are covered in loose, volcanic ash, and the hike to the summit is a slog. If you really want to tag a high point along this route, Tongariro is a far better climb to a spectacular view. Just be aware that it adds considerable mileage and elevation gain onto an already long day.

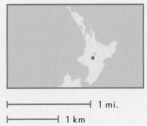

⊢——————⊣ 1 mi.
⊢————⊣ 1 km

Walk here next

If you can't get enough of the raw volcanic beauty of Tongariro National Park, consider setting out on a 31-mile (50 km) loop that circumnavigates Mount Ngāuruhoe on the Tongariro Northern Circuit, one of New Zealand's ten Great Walks. The North Island has another spectacular volcanic hike, to Mount Taranaki.

Explore the volcanic heart of Tongariro
TONGARIRO NORTHERN CIRCUIT

Most people take three or four days to tackle the Tongariro Northern Circuit loop in either direction, beginning and ending at Whakapapa Village. Hikers stay in three huts along the way—Mangatepopo, Oturere, and Waihohonu—each with bunks, gas stoves, and running water. The trek passes through a uniquely stark but colorful volcanic landscape, including the ashy aftermaths of recent eruptions.

Scale a snowcapped summit

MOUNT TARANAKI

Touted as New Zealand's most climbed mountain, Mount Taranaki is located in Egmont National Park, on the west side of the North Island. According to Māori mythology, Taranaki once resided next to Tongariro, but a fiery fight between the volcanoes resulted in Taranaki fleeing westward to its current location; Tongariro's frequent eruptions are said to be a warning to Taranaki not to return. The 7.6-mile (12.2 km) round-trip hike to the volcano's symmetrical summit gains 4,600 feet (1,402 m) of elevation and is best tackled from December to April, when you won't have to contend with as much snow on the 8,262-foot-high (2,518 m) summit.

Index

Picture credits

The publisher would like to thank the following for permission to reproduce copyright material:

T = top, B = bottom, L = left, C = centre, R = right

p5, 9, 10 Stuart Butler; 12 Pavlina Hajzlova/Shutterstock; 14T EB Adventure Photography/Shutterstock; 14B All Canada Photos/Alamy Stock Photo, 15T Linus Strandholm/Shutterstock; 15B Erica Ellefsen/Alamy Stock Photo; 16 TMI/Alamy Stock Photo; 17T Mary Caperton Morton/The Blonde Coyote; 17B PhotoSky/Shutterstock; 18 All Canada Photos/Alamy Stock Photo; 20T Zhukova Valentyna/Shutterstock; 20B PhotoSpirit/Alamy Stock Photo; 21L, 21R Leigh McAdam; 22 HYPE-A-VERSION/Shutterstock; 23T Polifoto/Alamy Stock Photo; 23B BeautifulBlossoms/Shutterstock; 24 David Fleetham/Alamy Stock Photo; 26T Mary Caperton Morton/The Blonde Coyote; 26–27B Jeffrey T. Kreulen/Shutterstock; 27T, 27C Mary Caperton Morton/The Blonde Coyote; 28 Raphael Rivest/Shutterstock; 29T Warren Ishii/500px/Getty Images; 29B Marisa Estivill/Shutterstock; 30 Pmmrd/Shutterstock; 32T Kodie Gerritsen/Shutterstock; 32CT Pmmrd/Shutterstock; 32CB Tyler Meester/Shutterstock; 32B Kelly vanDellen/Shutterstock; 34T Jimmy W/Shutterstock; 34B dave stamboulis/Alamy Stock Photo; 35T Andrew Gittis/Shutterstock; 35B Jan Jerman/Alamy Stock Photo; 36 Mar Kue/Alamy Stock Photo; 38, 39LT, 39RT, 39RB Mary Caperton Morton/The Blonde Coyote; 39LB Billy McDonald/Shutterstock; 40 Mary Caperton Morton/The Blonde Coyote; 41T reisegraf.ch/Shutterstock; 41B Philip Game/Alamy Stock Photo; 42 Craig Sterken/Shutterstock; 44 John McCormick/Shutterstock; 45T Nagel Photography/Shutterstock; 45C Craig Sterken/Shutterstock; 45B Doug Lemke/Shutterstock; 46 topseller/Shutterstock; 47T Tilpunov Mikhail/Shutterstock; 47B Marisha_SL/Shutterstock; 48 Raymond Klass/Alamy Stock Photo; 50T Monika Salvan/Shutterstock; 50B Mr. Klein/Shutterstock; 51T Mihai_Andritoiu/Shutterstock; 51B Mike Ver Sprill/Shutterstock; 52 MarynaG/Shutterstock; 53T traumlichtfabrik/Getty Images; 53B Sergi Reboredo/Alamy Stock Photo; 54 Jon Bilous/Shutterstock; 56T Mary Caperton Morton Morton/The Blonde Coyote; 56B Photo Spirit/Shutterstock; 57T Bram Reusen/Shutterstock; 57B PhotosbyAndy/Shutterstock; 58T Jerry Monkman/Aurora Photos/Getty Images; 58B Vladimir Grablev/Shutterstock; 59 Gaertner/Alamy Stock Photo; 60 Kelly vanDellen/Shutterstock; 62T Betty Shelton/Shutterstock; 62BL Harry Collins Photography/Shutterstock; 62BR BlueBarronPhoto/Shutterstock; 63 Kelly vanDellen/Shutterstock; 64 Cory Seamer/Shutterstock; 65T mauritius images GmbH/Alamy Stock Photo; 65B Robin Runck/Shutterstock; 66 Ronny Wolf/Shutterstock; 68 Cavan Images/Alamy Stock Photo; 69T Evgeniyqw/Shutterstock; 69B Douglas Peebles Photography/Alamy Stock Photo; 70T cb_travel/Shutterstock; 70B Mary Caperton Morton/The Blonde Coyote; 71T Minden Pictures/Alamy Stock Photo; 71B Lisa Banfield/Shutterstock; 72 EyeEm/Alamy Stock Photo; 74 Phil Reid/Shutterstock; 74–75 Suzuki Kaku/Alamy Stock Photo; 75T Esdelval/Shutterstock; 76T Lua Carlos Martins/Shutterstock; 76B Pramen/Shutterstock;

77T Mary Caperton Morton/The Blonde Coyote; 77B LouieLea/Shutterstock; 78 PRILL/Shutterstock; 80T Eman Kazemi/Alamy Stock Photo; 80C Panther Media GmbH/Alamy Stock Photo; 80B Joerg Steber/Shutterstock; 81T Wirestock, Inc./Alamy Stock Photo; 81B Renato Granieri/Alamy Stock Photo; 82 Mary Caperton Morton/The Blonde Coyote; 83T Anna ART/Shutterstock; 83B DeltaOFF/Shutterstock; 84 Herbert Eisengruber/Shutterstock; 86T Anthony Haigh/Alamy Stock Photo; 86C Oomka/Shutterstock; 86B Mary Caperton Morton/The Blonde Coyote; 87T Maiquel Jantsch/Getty Images; 87B Jan Nedbal/Shutterstock; 88 NiarKrad/Shutterstock; 89T Tobias Uhlig/Alamy Stock Photo; 89B Erick Manga/Shutterstock; 90 dave stamboulis/Alamy Stock Photo; 92T Raquel Mogado/Alamy Stock Photo; 92C Ecuadorpostales/Shutterstock; 92B Jef Wodniack/Shutterstock; 93 Cory Smith/Shutterstock; 94 Africa Media Online/Alamy Stock Photo; 95T Mary Caperton Morton/The Blonde Coyote; 95B allouphoto/Shutterstock; 96 Pulsar Imagens/Alamy Stock Photo; 98T, 98B CARLOS SANTOS RODAPEBR/Shutterstock; 100T Matheus Guerreiro/Shutterstock; 100B imageBROKER/Alamy Stock Photo; 101 Cacio Murilo/Shutterstock; 102 Geoff Marshall/Alamy Stock Photo; 104T Efrain Padro/Alamy Stock Photo; 104C Mainmap/Shutterstock; 104B abriendomundo/Shutterstock; 105 Hemis/Alamy Banque D'Images; 106 Fernando Tatay/Shutterstock; 107T BRUNO LACERDA/Shutterstock; 107B imageBROKER/Alamy Stock Photo; 108 gary yim/Shutterstock; 110T Bradley Smith/Alamy Stock Photo; 110B Pakawat Thongcharoen/Shutterstock; 111 Mekdet/Getty Images; 112 Slepitssskaya/Shutterstock; 113T Mary Caperton Morton/The Blonde Coyote; 113B Bob Pool/Shutterstock; 114 Steve Barze/Shutterstock; 116T Mark Green/Shutterstock; 116C Steve Barze/Shutterstock; 116B fallarto/Shutterstock; 117T Ondrej Bucek/Shutterstock; 117B FreezeFrames/Shutterstock; 118 Mary Caperton Morton/The Blonde Coyote; 119T K_Boonnitrod/Shutterstock; 119B pratan ounpitipong/Shutterstock; 120 Pedro Carrilho/Shutterstock; 122T matt griggs/Alamy Stock Photo; 122C Design Pics Inc/Alamy Stock Photo; 122B Mikko Karjalainen/Alamy Stock Photo; 123 Panpilas L/Shutterstock; 124 Tomas Zavadil/Shutterstock; 125T Ilona Bradacova/Shutterstock; 125B Alena Vishina/Shutterstock; 126 Nature's Charm/Shutterstock; 128 David C Tomlinson/Getty Images; 129T Loop Images Ltd/Alamy Stock Photo; 129C Atmosphere1/Shutterstock; 129B Apostolis Giontzis/Shutterstock; 130 Alice-D/Shutterstock; 131 Benny Marty/Shutterstock; 132 Richard Bowden/Shutterstock; 134T Stephen Talas/Shutterstock; 134B rightclickstudios/Shutterstock; 135T Pete Stuart/Shutterstock; 135B travellight/Shutterstock; 136 SolStock/Getty Images; 137T L F File/Shutterstock; 137B Michal Szymanski/Shutterstock; 138 aasllani/Shutterstock; 140T INTERFOTO/Alamy Stock Photo; 140C PositiveTravelArt/Shutterstock; 140B Ondrej Zeleznik/Shutterstock; 141 Arne Jw Kolstø/EyeEm/Getty Images; 142 Galyna Andrushko/Shutterstock; 143T Po S/Shutterstock; 143B Suratwadee Rattanajarupak/Shutterstock; 144 minimum/Getty Images; 146T Stuart Butler; 146B Richard Semik/Shutterstock; 147T Natursports/Shutterstock; 147B Tony Carbajo/

Shutterstock; **148** StockPhotoAstur/Shutterstock; **149T** Shcherbyna Nataliia/Shutterstock; **149B** alfotokunst/Shutterstock; **150** Stuart Butler; **152T** Stuart Butler; **152B, 153L** Stuart Butler; **153R** ElenaDM/Shutterstock; **154** Stuart Butler; **155T** OUESTUSA/ Shutterstock; **155B** Sebastian Wasek/Alamy Stock Photo; **156** ELEPHOTOS/Shutterstock; **158T** Petteri Kari/Shutterstock; **158C** Image Professionals GmbH/Alamy Stock Photo; **158–159** imageBROKER/Alamy Stock Photo; **160T** mognev/Shutterstock; **160B** Nature Picture Library/Alamy Stock Photo; **161** Olga_Ionina/Shutterstock; **162** Igor Tichonow/Shutterstock; **164T** imagoDens/Shutterstock; **164B** Silvia Valde/Shutterstock; **165** Marek Kania/Shutterstock; **166** makasana photo/Shutterstock; **167T** robertharding/Alamy Stock Photo; **167B** mauritius images GmbH/Alamy Stock Photo; **168** Nature Picture Library/Alamy Stock Photo; **170** Ana Hudobivnik, Družinski izleti; **171BL** Marisa Estivill/Shutterstock; **171T** Haidamac/Shutterstock; **171BR** Gunter Nuyts/Shutterstock; **172** Icrms/Shutterstock; **173T** Milan Sommer/Shutterstock; **173B** Henner Damke/Shutterstock; **174** Tomas Laburda/Shutterstock; **176** iwciagr/Shutterstock; **177T** Hamdija Feratovic/Shutterstock; **177BL** iwciagr/Shutterstock; **177BR** Lenar Musin/Shutterstock; **178T** Klaus Jung/Shutterstock; **178B** AllaStasy/Shutterstock; **179** tolobalaguer.com/Shutterstock; **180** Sergii Figurnyi/Shutterstock; **182** Anastasios71/Shutterstock; **183T** andronosh/Alamy Stock Photo; **183B** CC BY-SA 3.0/Schuppi; **184** Galyna Andrushko/Shutterstock; **185T** Warlock_97/Shutterstock; **185B** iwciagr/Shutterstock; **186** Carlos Neto/Shutterstock; **188T** Ryzhkov Oleksandr/Shutterstock; **188C** brimo/Alamy Stock Photo; **188B** Lukas Bischoff Photograph/Shutterstock; **189** Saad Gouzou/Shutterstock; **190** Hemis/Alamy Stock Photo; **191T** Japhotos/Alamy Stock Photo; **191B** A.Pushkin/Shutterstock; **192** Artush/Shutterstock; **194** Henk Bogaard/Shutterstock; **195L** evenfh/Shutterstock; **195R** Artush/Shutterstock; **196** Olivier Bourguet/Alamy Stock Photo; **197T** WitR/Shutterstock; **197B** Anita SKV/Shutterstock; **198** Stuart Butler; **200** Piu_Piu/Shutterstock; **201T** Lennjo/Shutterstock; **201B** Rosemarie Stennull/Alamy Stock Photo; **202** Gideon Ikigai/Shutterstock; **203T** GUDKOV ANDREY/Shutterstock; **203B** by Marc Guitard/Getty Images; **204** JMx Images/Shutterstock; **206T** Steve Lagreca/Shutterstock; **206B** Juergen_Wallstabe/Shutterstock; **207** chrisontour84/Shutterstock; **208** Martin Mwaura/Alamy Stock Photo; **209T** Morgan Trimble/Alamy Stock Photo; **209B** LP Production/Shutterstock; **210** Vincent van Oosten/Shutterstock; **212** Yury Zap/Shutterstock; **213TL** Cavan Images/Getty Images; **213TR** Janelle Lugge/Shutterstock; **213B** imageBROKER/Alamy Stock Photo; **214** Lucas Vallecillos/Alamy Stock Photo; **215T** YRABOTA/Shutterstock; **215B** marako85/Shutterstock; **216** PrincessTamTam/Stockimo/Alamy Stock Photo; **218T** Marcel Alsemgeest/Shutterstock; **218C** jbdodane/Alamy Stock Photo; **218B** Eric Nathan/Alamy Stock Photo; **219T** PeopleImages.com - Yuri A/Shutterstock; **219B** John Martin Media/Shutterstock; **220** Quentin Oosthuizen/Shutterstock; **212T** hecke61/Shutterstock; **212B** Ffaure/Shutterstock; **222** Shem Compion/Getty Images; **225T** Sergey Uryadnikov/Shutterstock; **225B** A. Emson/Shutterstock; **226** Robert Wedderburn/Shutterstock; **227T** Jason Jones Travel Photography/Getty Images; **227B** JeniFoto/Shutterstock; **228** New Production pictures/Shutterstock; **230** The Road Provides/Shutterstock; **231** EVGEIIA/Shutterstock; **232** DaryaU/Shutterstock; **233T** Galyna Andrushko/Shutterstock; **233B** Stanislav71/Shutterstock; **234** Thrithot/Shutterstock; **236** Daniela Collins/Shutterstock; **237L** Pawika Tongtavee/Shutterstock; **237R** J Marshall - Tribaleye Images/Alamy Stock Photo; **238** num_skyman/Shutterstock;

239T Feng Wei Photography/Getty Images; **239B** Babaorum/Shutterstock; **240** Almazoff/Shutterstock; **242** Alexander Verevkin/Shutterstock; **243** Almazoff/Shutterstock; **244** Pav-Pro Photography Ltd/Shutterstock; **245T** Lihana/Shutterstock; **245B** clkraus/Shutterstock; **246** Daniel Prudek/Shutterstock; **248, 249L** Stuart Butler; **249R** Vixit/Shutterstock; **250** Yongyut Kumsri/Shutterstock; **251T** Baisa/Shutterstock; **251B** Tetyana Dotsenko/Shutterstock; **252** Dinodia Photos/Alamy Stock Photo; **254** Aroon Thaewchatturat/Alamy Stock Photo; **255TL** Stuart Butler; **255TR** Mikael Utterström/Alamy Stock Photo; **255B** CC BY 2.0/Barry Silver; **256** Marisa Estivill/Shutterstock; **257T** Shridhar's/Shutterstock; **257B** Siriwatthana Chankawee/Shutterstock; **258** Pvince73/Shutterstock; **260** Stuart Butler; **261L** Michele Burgess/Alamy Stock Photo; **261R** Stuart Butler; **262** Robert Wyatt/Alamy Stock Photo; **263T** Rawpixel.com/Shutterstock; **263B** hilmanfajar/Shutterstock; **264** Nong4/Shutterstock; **266T** Ikunl/Shutterstock; **266B** Various images/Shutterstock; **267** Nonchanon/Shutterstock; **268** Nat Chittamai/Shutterstock; **269T** Bogdan Dyiakonovych/Shutterstock; **269B** Mary Caperton Morton/The Blonde Coyote; **270** Kirsty Nadine/Shutterstock; **272T** katacarix/Shutterstock; **272B** Ray Wilson/Alamy Stock Photo; **273T** rweisswald/Shutterstock; **273C** agefotostock/Alamy Stock Photo; **273B** Jason Roberts/Alamy Stock Photo; **274** montgomerygilchrist/Shutterstock; **275T** Suzanne Long/Alamy Stock Photo; **275C** CC BY 3.0 ES/Gabinete de Prensa del Gobierno de Cantabria; **275B** Angelo Gandolfi/Nature Picture Library; **276** Benny Marty/Shutterstock; **278T** Stephanie Jackson - Australian wildlife collection/Alamy Stock Photo; **278B** Henry During/Shutterstock; **279L** Photodigitaal.nl/Shutterstock; **279TR** puyalroyo/Shutterstock; **279BR** Auscape International Pty Ltd/Alamy Stock Photo; **280** Ajbadenhorst/Shutterstock; **281T** turtix/Shutterstock; **281B** Mary Caperton Morton/The Blonde Coyote; **282** John Le/Shutterstock; **285T** Gerckens-Photo-Hamburg/Shutterstock; **284B** Ingo Oeland/Alamy Stock Photo; **285L** Aqmal Hadi/Stockimo/Alamy Stock Photo; **285R** Darryl Leach/Shutterstock; **286** Wozzie/Shutterstock; **287T** domonabike/Alamy Stock Photo; **287B** Andrew Bain/Alamy Stock Photo; **288** David Moore/Australia/Alamy Stock Photo; **290** Andrew Bain/Alamy Stock Photo; **291T** Adwo/Shutterstock; **291B** Olga Kashubin/Shutterstock; **292** Andrew Bain/Alamy Stock Photo; **293T** Greg Brave/Shutterstock; **293B** Andrew Bain/Alamy Stock Photo; **294** Chasing Light - Photography by James Stone james-stone.com/Getty Images; **297TL** Adwo/Shutterstock; **297TR** Rowena English/Shutterstock; **297C** Ray Wilson/Alamy Stock Photo; **297B** Ryan Hoi/Shutterstock; **298** Desintegrator/Alamy Stock Photo; **299** Joshua Windsor/Alamy Stock Photo; **300** Timothy Mulholland/Alamy Stock Photo; **302–303T** Jiri Foltyn/Shutterstock; **302B** frans lemmens/Alamy Stock Photo; **303** Galyna Andrushko/Shutterstock; **304** Stefan Wille/Shutterstock; **305** robertharding/Alamy Stock Photo; **306** ColsTravel/Alamy Stock Photo; **308–309T** Filip Fuxa/Shutterstock; **308B** Martin M303/Shutterstock; **309B** ChameleonsEye/Shutterstock; **310** imageBROKER/Alamy Stock Photo; **311** imagoDens/Alamy Stock Photo

About the authors

Stuart Butler has written numerous hiking guidebooks covering destinations as diverse as the Himalayas, England, Sri Lanka, the Ethiopian highlands, the Balkans, Scandinavia, and the Pyrenees among others. Stuart also writes travel guidebooks for Lonely Planet, Rough Guide, and Bradt and is a regular contributor to many international newspapers and magazines for whom he writes about hiking, wildlife, and conservation issues. Stuart is also an award-winning photographer. He lives in France at the foot of the Pyrenees mountains. *stuartbutlerjournalist.com*

Mary Caperton Morton is a science and travel writer based in southwest Montana. She is the author of *The World's Best National Parks in 500 Walks* (Thunder Bay Press) and *Aerial Geology* (Timber Press), and has written for EARTH and EOS magazines. Mary documents her travels in her popular hiking blog Travels with the Blonde Coyote. When she's not writing, Mary can be found climbing mountains, hiking, skiing, and taking photographs.